Meaning in tl

*Meaning in the Media* addresses the issue of how we should respond to competing claims about meaning made in situations such as bitter public controversies 'and expensive legal disputes. Alan Durant draws attention to the pervasiveness and significance of such meaning-related disputes in the media, investigating how their 'meaning' dimension is best described and explained. He analyses deception, distortion, bias, false advertising, offensiveness and other kinds of communicative behaviour that trigger interpretive disputes, and shows that we can understand both meaning and media better if we focus in new ways on moments in discourse when the apparently continuous flow of understanding and agreement breaks down. This lively and contemporary volume will be invaluable to students and teachers of linguistics, media studies, journalism and law.

ALAN DURANT is Professor of Communication at Middlesex University Business School, London. His previous publications include *How to Write Essays and Dissertations: a guide for English Literature students, Second Edition* (2005) and *Ways of Reading, Third Edition* (2007). He was also co-editor of *The Linguistics of Writing: arguments between language and literature* (1987).

# Meaning in the Media

*Discourse, Controversy and Debate*

Alan Durant

CAMBRIDGE
UNIVERSITY PRESS

CAMBRIDGE UNIVERSITY PRESS
Cambridge, New York, Melbourne, Madrid, Cape Town, Singapore,
São Paulo, Delhi, Dubai, Tokyo

Cambridge University Press
The Edinburgh Building, Cambridge CB2 8RU, UK

Published in the United States of America by Cambridge University Press, New York

www.cambridge.org
Information on this title: www.cambridge.org/9780521199582

First published 2010

Printed in the United Kingdom at the University Press, Cambridge

*A catalogue record for this publication is available from the British Library*

ISBN 978-0-521-19958-2 Hardback
ISBN 978-0-521-13640-2 Paperback

Cambridge University Press has no responsibility for the persistence or
accuracy of URLs for external or third-party internet websites referred to in
this publication, and does not guarantee that any content on such websites is,
or will remain, accurate or appropriate.

For Aliya and Maya

# Contents

x        Contents

# Acknowledgements

This book has been some time in the making. In one sense, that is always true. There are few books that do not have origins much earlier than is evident on the page. What follows is an engagement with the unresolved nature of meaning I have been involved in from at least as far back as my efforts to teach myself semantics during a university English degree. Like many people of my generation in Britain, I also grew up with many unquestioned assumptions about freedom of expression, only to be troubled later by how formulaic debates about meaning in the media then become.

I have benefited from support and advice, at different stages of this project, from a number of people and organisations. I am grateful to Bhikhu Parekh for an invitation to participate in a series of Commission for Racial Equality (CRE) seminars about *The Satanic Verses* held in London at the time of the controversy. I was fortunate later to observe the practice of English defamation law during a mini-pupillage at a London libel chambers, 1 Brick Court, with Patrick Moloney QC. I am also grateful to a number of universities which offered related teaching opportunities, including USP, São Paulo, where I taught a postgraduate course with Laura Izarra. Thanks are due to the Japan Society for the Promotion of Science (JSPS) for a visiting fellowship at Tokyo University. More recently, I would like to thank Jennifer Davis, Lionel Bently, Jane Ginsburg and others associated with the Centre for Intellectual Property and Information Law (CIPIL) at Cambridge University for teaching me some law during interdisciplinary collaborations on trade marks and copyright.

A number of colleagues and friends have commented on different parts and stages of the manuscript. I would like to thank them for their encouragement: Ron Carter, Jennifer Davis, Bill Downes, Graeme Dinwoodie, Philip Durkin, Chris Hutton, Colin MacCabe, Ian Mackenzie, Pia Pichler, Ifan Shepherd, Roger Shuy, Nick Wadham-Smith and Guido de Zordi. As is inevitable with a book whose aim is to look in several different directions at once, it has not always been possible to respond adequately to the advice I received.

At Cambridge University Press, I would like to thank Helen Barton for her support to work at the intersection between linguistics, media and law, and Frances Brown for detailed work on the manuscript. Finally, thanks to Anna Kyprianou, Dean of Middlesex University Business School, for granting time during a difficult period to complete a book which nevertheless remains in terms of its content a first approximation.

# Introduction

They shouldn't be allowed to get away with saying that. It's misleading, obscene, defamatory, inflammatory, blasphemous, malicious, intrusive, disrespectful or deceitful. Or alternatively, reflecting a number of newer categories of alleged communicative disorder, something might be considered to be 'edited in a misleading or dishonest way' (of a broadcast documentary). Or it could be 'glorifying' (of a statement referring to a terrorist incident or campaign). Most days some dispute about media discourse forces its way into public consciousness on one or other of these grounds. Disputes along such lines have become an almost continuous, reflexive dimension of meaning in the media. Allegations rarely go undefended. You've misunderstood, there was a legitimate public interest, it can be shown to be true, this was reasonable comment in the circumstances, no offence was intended.

Contestation of media communication is part of everyday modern life. In many cases quarrels blow over as quickly as they blew up, made irrelevant by subsequent events. But this is not always what happens.

Sometimes interpretive disputes drag on as major public controversies. As well as having their own momentum, they become defining reference points in public thinking about what communication is, almost as much as public thinking about the subject matter communicated. This was the case with Salman Rushdie's novel *The Satanic Verses*, which ignited worldwide controversy following the book's publication in September 1988 and the fatwa imposed by Ayatollah Khomeini of Iran five months later. Nearly two decades later, the controversy was rekindled, albeit in a less incendiary way, by the award of a knighthood to the author in 2007. Something analogous, if based on a different kind of grievance and spread across different political groups, surrounded the British government's 'dodgy dossier' about Iraq of September 2002 (and again in February 2003). The dossier claimed that Saddam Hussein had imminently threatening WMDs (Weapons of Mass Destruction), a claim controversially referred to in a live radio broadcast by BBC journalist Andrew Gilligan as having been 'sexed up' beyond the available evidence. In the United States, major public controversy surrounded President Clinton's assertion under oath during the Monica Lewinsky scandal of the late 1990s, that 'I did not have sexual relations with that woman, Miss Lewinsky.' Partly because of President Clinton's apparently reluctant substitution of 'sexual' for the words 'not appropriate' in earlier statements (and before 'not appropriate', the still earlier 'improper'), this notorious assertion attracted relentless scrutiny from cross-examiners during the Grand Jury hearings of 1998. It also prompted nationwide discussion about precisely what constitutes 'sexual relations'.

Away from these internationally discussed cases – but equally painful to those immediately concerned – disputes often find expression in only minor, unreported legal actions. Or they may be resolved following complaint to an extrajudicial media regulatory body. In other, still less newsworthy cases, disputes over published utterances or media discourse are calmed down or brought to a close without intercession from any formal body or procedure. They burn out, in a to-and-fro of media commentary and conversation among media audiences. Such disputes can still create anger, humiliation and embarrassment. They may also turn on mendacity and distortion. But the drama of powerful forces and feelings they enact takes place in the shadows, by comparison with the international spotlight of fatwas or possible impeachment proceedings.

All three kinds of contestation of what disputed stretches of media discourse mean are important in their own way. In this book I discuss cases of each: public dispute and controversy; legal and regulatory complaint; and 'never formally contested' interpretive disagreement. What encourages me to consider the three categories together, despite the obvious difference of public impact between them, is a common problem of interpretation they share: what counts as evidence for or against the meanings in contention?

## 0.1    Meaning troublespots

In the pages that follow I hope to throw light on public arguments over meaning, and on practical challenges that must be faced in resolving them. Under a common heading I will consider different scales of public dispute together, as well as different fields or domains in which disputes arise: the various topics people argue about and kinds of harm that such quarrels inflict. The resulting field is large, and unified only by the processes and structures of the struggles over meaning it contains. I give this combined field of areas and types of interpretive contestation an informal, collective name: 'meaning troublespots'. This is not a clear-cut analytic category. But my class of 'troublespots' should illuminate why contestation of meaning in the media is relevant not only to people actively engaged in interpretive disputes, or to students of meaning (whether in linguistics, law or cognate fields), but to anyone concerned with problems of modern communication and citizenship.

What form should investigation of such meaning troublespots take? It is possible simply to narrate the well-known controversies. Rather than doing this, I propose to investigate three slightly more abstract questions.

- Why are competing interpretations put forward so often about media discourse?
- How are alternative interpretations in contention questioned and evaluated?
- What obstacles stand in the way of arbitration or settlement?

I illustrate my discussion of these questions with numerous short (and sometimes longer) examples. I also anticipate that readers will test my arguments against the almost daily controversies aired in the media and judgments reported on legal and regulator websites.[1]

My focus in what follows may sound similar to other work in 'language and law'. But the field of 'language and law' consists of a number of different kinds of study and it is important to see their different approaches. Sometimes investigations are concerned with language in the machinery of law (e.g. with the form of writs and injunctions, legal warnings, technical terms and courtroom jargon). On other occasions, discussion focuses on legal interpretation: how judges and lawyers tackle problems of meaning in their own legal terminology, for example in deciding between 'original' and 'contextual' meanings in construction of statutes. Other work again – this is the field that this book seeks to contribute to – is concerned with language as the *content* of legal inquiry. Sometimes, non-technical, 'ordinary' public discourse becomes an object of contestation (e.g. in libel, false advertising, obscenity, misrepresentation and other fields of media law). The different approaches to 'language and law' are

---

[1] A continuous stream of examples of interpretive disputes and controversies can be found in the multimedia environment of news and comment, as well as on media regulator websites (e.g. in UK, www.asa.org.uk, www.ofcom.org.uk, etc.). Legal case reports provide a source for legal actions (via sites like Westlaw, as well as in print). Many critical accounts can be found of the language used in news and political reporting, such as Nick Davies, *Flat Earth News* (London: Chatto and Windus, 2008). There is also the established genre of exposés of government deception, such as Peter Oborne's *The Rise of Political Lying* (London: Free Press, 2005) or Nicholas Jones's blow-by-blow accounts of New Labour lying, including *The Control Freaks: How New Labour Gets Its Own Way* (London: Politico's Publishing, 2002). Examples of contested social keywords can be found in Steven Poole, *Unspeak*[TM] (Little, Brown, 2006 and at www.unspeak.net). A thought-provoking and sometimes moving account of modern British controversies is Tim Slessor, *Ministries of Deception: Cover-ups in Whitehall* (London: Aurum Press, 2002). Vividly polemical but less probing is Sheldon Rampton and John Stauber, *Weapons of Mass Deception: The Uses of Propaganda in Bush's War on Iraq* (London: Robinson, 2003). The linguist George Lakoff's influential *Don't Think of an Elephant: Know Your Values and Frame the Debate* (White River Junction, Vt.: Chelsea Green Publishers, 2004) investigates techniques of 'reframing', often by systematic use of alternative metaphors, within contemporary political and commercial discourse (see also the related website, www.rockridgeinstitute.org). Other useful sources include Spinwatch (www.spinwatch.org.uk) and MediaWise (www.mediawise.org.uk, formerly Presswise, www.presswise.org, as well as links from those sites).

not just different in detail or nuance.[2] When it comes to meaning, they differ fundamentally as regards where authority for decisions is looked for.

Adjudicating meaning at what I will call meaning troublespots requires a particular approach to meaning. To see why this is so, compare the task of deciding between incompatible meanings that people put forward for something they have just read, heard or watched with what you need to do in order to grasp what is meant by a conversation you overhear or in order to understand some difficult piece of technical terminology you encounter (such as a legal term, or some other expression of professional or scientific terminology).

If you want to grasp what is going on in a conversation, you focus on the continuously developing 'insider' understanding being constructed by the conversational participants. That process is intuitive, but it can be made more precise by bringing to bear linguistic techniques such as those of conversation analysis. Faced with a specialised or technical term, on the other hand, although you might learn something useful by listening in, you must go elsewhere for explanation: terms of art are defined by specialised knowledge agreed for a particular field, even if some degree of ordinary meaning is still infused into them. You learn the meaning of such specialised or technical terms by hearing from experts or by looking them up in reference works, including dictionaries.

Adjudicating meaning for stretches of discourse that have become a focus of controversy or legal contestation calls for something different. It is necessary to look beyond how the discourse is understood by its 'insiders' (that is, either by its producer(s) or by people who allege harmful effects). But for an appeal to meaning beyond the participants to have social legitimacy, that appeal must strive for some standard other than expertise in a specialised field – precisely because what is sought is some kind of 'ordinary' meaning that everyone is supposed to get. Linguistics *as a whole* is occasionally pushed aside in this process. But mostly it is not even thought of. The aim in trying to establish the

---

[2] The literature on language and law is vast. But there are some useful starting points. For a mainly linguistic perspective, see John Gibbons (ed.), *Language and the Law* (London: Longman, 1994) or John Gibbons and M. Teresa Turell (eds.), *Dimensions of Forensic Linguistics* (Amsterdam: Benjamins, 2008). See also, Judith Levi and Anne Graffam Walker (eds.), *Language in the Judicial Process* (New York: Springer, 1990) and Lawrence Solan, *The Language of Judges* (Chicago: University of Chicago Press, 1993). For legal discussion of interpretive questions, see H. L. A. Hart, *The Concept of Law* (Oxford: Oxford University Press, 1961); a compelling record of Hart's efforts to bring together law and philosophy of language is given in Nicola Lacey's biography, *A Life of H. L. A. Hart: The Nightmare and the Noble Dream* (Oxford: Oxford University Press, 2004). Other useful sources include A. R. White, *Misleading Cases* (Oxford: Clarendon, 1991) and Brian Bix, *Law, Language and Legal Determinacy* (Oxford: Clarendon, 1993). A recent guide to debates about linguistic meaning and interpretation in relation to legal language, which covers many of the key topics discussed below, is Chris Hutton, *Language, Meaning and the Law* (Edinburgh: Edinburgh University Press, 2009).

meaning of a contested utterance or text is not to prove that meaning using scientific or expert techniques, but to assess what the utterance or text conveyed to language users who encountered it in everyday circumstances, without drawing on any special skill or knowledge. To establish meaning in these cases, appeal is made to intuitions thought to be shared by a population at large: to a kind of community competence in interpreting a culture's symbolic codes. My main claim in this book, put simply, is that there are problems in expecting media law to function as a 'meaning umpire' like this.

Is a claim of this order of generality worthy of investigation? I suggest that examining problems of meaning breakdown is illuminating both about meaning and about media, especially in societies with a lot of cultural diversity or which are undergoing rapid social change.

## 0.2    Approaches to meaning

In the course of my discussion I will draw, inevitably selectively, on frameworks for discussing meaning developed in linguistics, philosophy and psychology. I will also compare approaches in these fields with the sometimes strikingly different but equally closely argued accounts of meaning put forward in media law and regulation.

By bringing these different approaches to meaning into dialogue with one another, I hope to push discussion in two main directions. Firstly, rather than treating media communication as being like an ordinary conversation that has simply been amplified and made public, or alternatively as a matter of isolated textual 'objects' set free from their communicators or addressees, I propose to explore meaning problems in media discourse as being specific to the communicative capabilities, use and circumstances of different media. Secondly, rather than talking about meaning on the basis of apparently successful instances of communication, I want to show how new insights can be prompted by moments when the spontaneous flow of meaning in the media is interrupted.

My focus on moments when meaning breaks down differentiates this study from most existing work on verbal meaning in the media. I hope nevertheless that my work will complement rather than compete with existing approaches. Just as there are different ways of thinking about 'language and law', there are different ways of bringing linguistics to bear on interpreting media texts. I should indicate briefly what the differences are, and how this book relates to them.

One possible line in thinking about interpretive disputes is to start from the idea that disputes often centre on a particular crux expression (a problematic word or phrase). That crux expression is not a legal concept, like 'recklessness' of intention or alleged 'blasphemy' of content. It is an expression used prominently or repeatedly within the utterance itself. 'Sexual relations', as said by President

Clinton, is an example. Another example would be whether an expression like 'economical with the truth' has a specific meaning of its own or merely offers convenient cover in accusing someone of lying. If the crux of a dispute involves concentration of meaning into such a contested expression, then it may be helpful to clarify matters with detailed analysis of the troublesome word or phrase. Such an approach would accordingly have investigation of word meaning at its core and would engage closely with available (e.g. philological, lexicographical, corpus linguistic) tools for investigating word meanings.[3]

But 'meaning' might be more diffused across an utterance or text than this kind of concentration in a troublesome crux word. If so, it may be preferable to start from the idea that when a text is disputed, the whole text rather than only some part of it should be examined. What is of interest then is the text's overall terms of interaction with an audience. If we start from this point, then we will expect not close analysis of isolated 'key' expressions that are interpreted differently by the parties to the dispute, but investigation of the overall texture of the discourse: its structure of turn-taking, if the text is conversational in character; how the topics it deals with are linked to one another, and by whom; how impartiality or fairness is established within it, if those qualities are claimed; and what implied relationship between communicator and addressee is created by the way that the text addresses its audience. All of these are topics in the fields of discourse analysis and conversation analysis.[4]

[3] For an explanation of 'dictionary' approaches to word meaning, see Howard Jackson, *Lexicography: An Introduction* (London: Routledge, 2002). The fullest account of any given word of English is likely to be found in the OED: the *Oxford English Dictionary* (www.oed.com), first published, in parts, as *A New English Dictionary on Historical Principles*, ed. J. A. H. Murray, H. Bradley, W. A. Craigie and C. T. Onions (Oxford: Oxford University Press, 1884-1928). For a detailed account of what each OED entry contains and how to read it, see Donna Lee Berg, *A Guide to the Oxford English Dictionary* (Oxford: Oxford University Press, 1993). For discussion of lexicography within corpus linguistics, see Douglas Biber, Susan Conrad and Randi Reppen, *Corpus Linguistics: Investigating Language Structure and Use* (Cambridge: Cambridge University Press, 1998); and on reading electronic concordance lines in particular, see John Sinclair, *Reading Concordances: An Introduction* (London: Pearson, 2003). An especially detailed account of corpus approaches to word meaning is Michael Stubbs, *Words and Phrases: Corpus Studies of Lexical Semantics* (Oxford: Blackwell, 2002).

[4] There are many introductions to discourse analysis; the most usefully detailed remains Gillian Brown and George Yule, *Discourse Analysis* (Cambridge: Cambridge University Press, 1983). The same is true of conversation analysis; for an advanced guide, see Ian Hutchby and Robin Wooffitt, *Conversation Analysis* (Cambridge: Polity, 2008). Numerous studies have applied discourse analytic frameworks to media discourse. Examples investigating media interviews include Allan Bell and Theo van Leeuwen, *The Media Interview: Confession, Contest, Conversation* (Sydney: New South Wales University Press, 1994) and Steven Clayman and John Heritage, *The News Interview* (Cambridge: Cambridge University Press, 2002). On news discourse, see Martin Montgomery, *The Discourse of Broadcast News: A Linguistic Approach* (London: Routledge, 2007), and on argumentative radio talk, see Ian Hutchby, *Confrontation Talk: Arguments, Asymmetries and Power on Talk Radio* (Hillsdale, NJ: Lawrence Erlbaum, 1996). A valuable collection of work in a 'discourse' paradigm is David Graddol and Oliver Boyd-Barrett (eds.), *Media Texts: Authors and Readers* (Clevedon: Multilingual Matters / Open

An approach influenced by discourse analysis appears especially well suited to interpretive conflict over whether someone is bullied or patronised in a TV or radio interview, or left out of a discussion agenda (for instance if women contributors are said to be marginalised during a studio discussion). Analyses of discourse structure also have a part to play in institutional discourse of various kinds: courtroom discourse, doctor–patient interaction, and public meetings (such as meetings forming part of a political campaign, or annual shareholder meetings).[5] Since evidence from such situations is often presented in recorded or otherwise mediated form, there can often be a 'media' dimension to controversies that arise. In mainstream mass media such as radio and television, controversies amenable to such analysis take many forms, including disputes over aggressive interviewing, the handling or mismanagement of discussion programme formats, biased vox pops, and the alleged offensiveness of 'shock jocks'.

Is either of the two general approaches I have described here more suitable than the other in investigating meaning troublespots? This depends on what kind of trouble is involved, and the kinds of dispute I explore in this book invite comment based on both.

Troublesome keywords are always used in a given context. So lexical analysis (whether undertaken by consulting intuitions, conducting surveys, looking up words in a dictionary, or searching an electronic corpus) is unlikely to be sufficient. To understand what is meant in a given instance, 'dictionary meaning' must be set in the context of how particular statements unfold in a given broadcast, advert or other text; and what tone something is said in. Crux words, as the name suggests, are crucial, but the limbs of the cross also matter. Crux words are not only used in a context, either; they are used differently in different contexts. This is what gives them their 'crux' significance, and makes them controversial.

What if instead our effort to decide between conflicting interpretations begins routinely with aspects of discourse structure? In this case, while we range more freely across different aspects of context the conceptual aspects of meaning conveyed by nuance, connotation, allusions and echoes of other styles of

University, 1993). Also useful are chapters in Paddy Scannell (ed.), *Broadcast Talk* (London: Sage, 1991). A recent treatment of what makes media discourse specific is Mary Talbot, *Media Discourse: Representation and Interaction* (Edinburgh: Edinburgh University Press, 2007). Innovative use of corpus linguistic techniques in analysing media discourse can be found in Anne O'Keeffe, *Investigating Media Discourse* (London: Routledge, 2006).

[5] For examples of work on discourse in these settings, see Norman Fairclough, *Critical Discourse Analysis: The Critical Study of Language* (London: Longman, 1995); Paul Drew and John Heritage, *Talk at Work: Interaction in Institutional Settings* (Cambridge: Cambridge University Press, 1992); William Labov and D. Fanshel, *Therapeutic Discourse* (New York: Academic Press, 1977); and Ruth Wodak, *Disorders of Discourse* (London: Longman, 1996). For a useful reader of research in this field (that includes extracts from other works referred to in this chapter), see Adam Jaworski and Nikolas Coupland (eds.), *The Discourse Reader* (London: Routledge, 1999).

discourse may be pushed too far into the background. The sting of many kinds of verbal dispute (for instance in libel, in indirect comparative advertising, or in cases of alleged offensiveness) is often felt most in the peculiar power of a single, loaded or poisonous expression. We should therefore look to specific inferences invited by and drawn from such expressions, alongside directly stated meanings and recurrent patterns of style or interaction, if we are to grasp what is being said: what speech act we think is being performed; what indirect meanings speakers give to the words they choose; and what presuppositions and expectations they rely on in building up their overall meaning.

If linguistics is to help in analysing interpretive disputes, then what is likely to be needed is attention to overall discourse structure with extra spotlights directed towards word-meaning and utterance-meaning. At the same time, we must not overstate the contribution of linguistic analysis of *any* kind in helping with interpretive conflicts. It is true that forensic linguistics has achieved notable successes (arguably more in the fields of phonetics and syntax than in relation to meaning, for reasons I consider later).[6] At the same time it is easy to underestimate scepticism about the value of linguistics – and especially about semantics – felt by judges, barristers, juries and many members of the wider public. In legal and regulatory disputes about meaning, as well as in controversies adjudicated by the court of public opinion, solutions are only rarely brought about by linguistic proof or deference to linguistic expertise.

My own interest in meaning troublespots is partly linguistic and partly social. I am concerned with linguistic accounts of meaning and also with other frameworks for describing and analysing meaning, including legal approaches. In interpretive controversies, no single account of meaning – from any source or background – goes unquestioned, whether based on legal, linguistic or religious grounds. Meaning is actively contested precisely because people bring conflicting experiences, assumptions and interests to bear. Opposing statements of meaning are made, justifications of alternative viewpoints are advanced, and the meanings claimed remain in contention until a court or regulatory judgment is reached, or some other form of settlement is agreed, or until an oblique way is found of getting round the impasse.

---

[6] For wide-ranging coverage of the field of forensic linguistics, see John Gibbons (ed.), *Forensic Linguistics: An Introduction to Language in the Justice System* (London: Wiley Blackwell, 2003); and Janet Cotterill (ed.), *Language in the Legal Process* (Basingstoke: Palgrave, 2002). A clear introduction is Malcolm Coulthard and Alison Johnson, *An Introduction to Forensic Linguistics: Language in Evidence* (London: Routledge, 2007). For accounts of US cases from the point of view of an expert witness, see Roger Shuy, *Fighting over Words: Language and Civil Law Cases* (Oxford: Oxford University Press, 2008), as well as his earlier *Language Crimes: The Use and Abuse of Language Evidence in the Courtroom* (Oxford: Blackwell, 1993). The main journal of research in this field is the *International Journal of Speech, Language and the Law* (known from 1994 until 2003 as *Forensic Linguistics*).

*Meaning in the Media* is about struggles over discourse meaning as viewed from different perspectives. Each perspective typically offers a confident view (as linguistics itself often does) of what the meaning of a contested utterance or text is. My concern in this book is not to vindicate a series of particular meanings put forward using linguistic analysis, as an expert witness might if called upon. My aim is to show how competing views of meaning within a dispute or controversy engage with one another. On those occasions when arbitration of an interpretive conflict is achieved, it is usually brought about by some specific combination of argument, evidence of different kinds, and the social authority or straightforward executive power of the adjudicator. My aim is to illustrate different perspectives on the 'meaning' aspect of media disputes, and to explore common ground and scope for dialogue between them.

Throughout this book, I do of course draw on general work in linguistics in describing interpretive controversies. I have tried as far as possible, however, to keep the text uncluttered and only to go into detail regarding any particular author's work where it is essential to the argument (as with Austin's work on performatives and illocutionary force discussed in Chapter 11). Readers familiar with linguistics will recognise names and theories implied by my exposition as well as stated in it, and will be able to elaborate on and refine my account as appropriate. To assist the reader who is not familiar with work in linguistics, on the other hand, I draw attention to essential concepts and positions in footnotes. I do not, it should be noted, claim to be putting forward a coherent theoretical account of meaning in disputes, or offering a critical review of existing approaches. I am describing a largely uncharted field: the different grounds appealed to, and assumptions relied on, in public disputes about meaning. To this end, I have tried to identify and outline concepts and problems rather than to build up a general system of analysis.

Readers more engaged with linguistic accounts of meaning than my own aims allow for will look for a clearer statement of the main traditions of work I have drawn on. Such readers are encouraged to follow up the references provided throughout the book. But it is worth saying at the outset that my arguments are underpinned by reference to three main, intersecting traditions. The early stages of my argument (especially my discussion of disagreement in Chapter 1) draw especially on insights in discourse analysis, conversation analysis and sociolinguistics. My initial account of spoken interaction and mediated communication events, for example, reflects accounts of verbal interaction that run from Dell Hymes and Erving Goffman into current sociolinguistics, critical discourse analysis, and studies of mediated discourse.[7] Other sections of the book build on a sometimes neglected tradition of

---

[7] See works referred to in note 4 above, as well as the references contained in them.

semantics beginning with General Semantics of the 1930s and 1940s (including work by writers such as Korzybski, Hayakawa and Chase), through attempts made to measure meaning in behaviourist semantics (e.g. in the work of Osgood and his collaborators), through Raymond Williams's cultural analyses of meaning, into what is now a dispersed field of linguistic approaches to meaning in the media, squeezed into the margins of mainstream media and cultural studies.[8] This 'semantic' tradition comes to the fore in my discussion in Chapter 4. Thirdly, I have drawn on concepts in linguistic pragmatics, especially in Chapter 5 (and prominently again in Chapter 11), especially the role played in utterance interpretation by inference.[9] In introducing pragmatic approaches I suggest that the ideas of Austin, Grice and Searle, as well as more recent approaches such as Sperber and Wilson's Relevance Theory, offer potential grasp of meaning in the media that can elude ethnographic research such as that associated with media audience studies (exemplified for instance by the work of Morley).[10]

Given the broad aims I have stated, it would be impossible to do justice to theoretical arguments related to the interaction between these different theoretical approaches. The brief orientation offered here, however, together with footnotes throughout the text, should allow readers to see the potential of linguistic frameworks to engage with questions about meaning that arise not only in academic circles but also in professional legal and media circles.

---

[8] Particularly notable among works of General Semantics are Stuart Chase, *The Tyranny of Words* (New York: Harvest Books, 1938) and S. I. Hayakawa, *Language in Thought and Action* (New York: Harvest Books, 1939). Charles Osgood, G. Suci, and P. Tannenbaum's *The Measurement of Meaning* (Chicago: University of Illinois Press, 1957) is an outstanding exception to the now usually negative view of approaches to meaning of its period. Raymond Williams's investigation of meaning runs through virtually all his writing, but is most clearly expressed in the 'Preface' and entries of *Keywords: A Vocabulary of Culture and Society*, 2nd edition (London: Fontana, 1983). Writing in this 'semantic' tradition connects in interesting ways with the thinking about meaning of C. K. Ogden and I. A. Richards (for example in *The Meaning of Meaning*, 10th edition (London: Routledge and Kegan Paul, 1972).

[9] A clear introduction to pragmatics, elaborating (and extensively illustrating) concepts from Austin, Searle and others, is Jenny Thomas, *Meaning in Interaction: An Introduction to Pragmatics* (London: Longman, 1995). More theoretical exposition can be found in Stephen Levinson, *Pragmatics* (Cambridge: Cambridge University Press, 1983). Dan Sperber and Deirdre Wilson's Relevance Theory is presented in *Relevance: Communication and Cognition*, 2nd edition (Oxford: Blackwell, 1995). A helpful textbook introduction to relevance is Diane Blakemore, *Understanding Utterances: An Introduction to Pragmatics* (Oxford: Blackwell, 1992). Connections between pragmatics in linguistics and in other fields are explored in Louise Cummings, *Pragmatics: An Interdisciplinary Perspective* (Edinburgh: Edinburgh University Press, 2005).

[10] Ethnographic research on meaning was inspired particularly by Clifford Geertz's *The Interpretation of Cultures* (New York: Basic Books, 1973). This approach became especially popular as a means of investigating media meaning in the movement in media studies known as 'New Audience Studies'. For a collection of essays charting his own development from audience studies of *Nationwide* to more open-ended ethnography, see David Morley, *Television, Audiences and Cultural Studies* (London: Routledge, 1992).

## 0.3    Historical context for a media dispute culture

Arguing in general terms over what public discourse means, when communication breaks down or is challenged, is hardly new. Nor are the practices of lying, deceiving, misleading, vilifying, or falsely advertising things for sale that give rise to interpretive disputes. Such practices have a long and complicated history. There is reason to believe, however, that developments over the last century and a half represent a new historical phase. The ways in which, and extent to which, we now experience public discourse depend substantially on features of our modern communication environment. Developments in printing and then electronic communication technologies from the nineteenth century onwards (from steam printing and the telegraph, through radio and television, to mobile phones and the Internet) have radically extended the scale of social circulation of discourse between different social groups, including with unprecedented international reach.[11]

These changes are not only a matter of exposure to mass-communicated messages. They also create changing networks of person-to-person and group-to-group interaction. Expectations about communication have been transformed, including in the socially defining fields of buying and selling goods and services, gaining access to public information, participating in political life, and entertainment. In the modern media environment more people are able to communicate more, about more topics, largely as a result of broadcasting of different kinds, mobile telephony and the Internet. The volume of publicly expressed opinion is as a result much greater than in any previous period; and, in consequence, the priority given to discourse as an aspect of civil life, by comparison with other concerns, tends to be greater. These factors begin to explain why so much attention is now given to – and why more concern is expressed about – communication and language controversies. Arguments over meaning are also affected by demography. Many different niche producers and segmented audiences participate in contemporary media communication, reflecting the increasingly multicultural composition of societies during a major period of globalisation. This changing social make-up of audiences presents a considerable challenge to thinking about meaning and values as something shared and presumable across a whole society. Yet without such presumption of shared meanings and values, the appeal to common, shared understandings I outlined above, as how media law and regulation set about adjudicating contested meaning, may be seriously jeopardised.

Perhaps most defining for modern *disputes* about meaning, as regards changes brought about by modern communications technologies, is the capability of modern media to store communication in recorded, fixed form. The availability

---

[11] The main developments are traced in Asa Briggs and Peter Burke, *A Social History of the Media: From Gutenberg to the Internet*, 2nd edition (Cambridge: Polity, 2005). See also Brian Winston, *Media Technology and Society: A History From the Telegraph to the Internet* (London: Routledge, 1998).

of stored discourse can present major challenges as regards privacy. But publication of discourse of so many new kinds, in a range of new media, has another consequence. It allows huge amounts of earlier communication, including a great deal of originally spoken communication, to be kept available as a historical record, stored in media ranging from local hard drives to national archives and databases, and accessible by Internet.

The six centuries that have passed since the invention of printing, as well as the history of manuscript discourse before that, have given time for social adjustment to the idea of a written, social record. But the equivalent situation has only recently been established with speech. Whereas speech is conventionally an 'event', taking place only at one precise place and time, writing transforms spoken discourse into texts in a cumulative social archive. Recent forms of electronic media 'speech' can be usefully thought of, therefore, as in this respect extended kinds of writing. Such a reifying transformation, or fixation, of speech has important social effects. In recorded form, speech is consolidated as intellectual property. Spoken discourse is linked, as a tradable object or commodity, to brand value and personal reputation as well as to more direct sales and licensing. In its permanent, recorded form, spoken discourse also becomes more widely and publicly valued, influential and important. Its details, lapses, calculated vagueness and shock effects are all argued over more intensively.

In this book, I maintain that the combined technological, legal and cultural transformation signalled by developments in modern media calls for a related shift in how we conceive the social circulation of meaning.

Perhaps the most important implication of the shift I am describing can be seen more clearly if we recall the protracted historical transition in most societies from oral communication into simultaneously available forms of orality and literacy. That major social upheaval, typically lasting over several centuries, produced increased heterodoxy of ideas and contestation of established opinion. Modern media, in making the momentary experience of spoken interaction available for sustained interpretive scrutiny, invite similarly intensified contestation of discourse that often starts out as spontaneous, informal interaction. Recording and storage of speech alter our expectation of accountability in relation to spoken behaviour in the same direction as use of CCTV and DNA evidence (and more trivially use of video technology in sport) alter our ideas of evidence and accountability in other fields. Seen in a larger historical context, the social changes that frame the more specialised topics I discuss below are part of a deeper historical process in which relations between dispersed social opinion and centralised cultural authority are being reinterpreted.[12]

---

[12]  An overview of contrasts between oral and literate societies is Jack Goody, *The Interface between the Written and the Oral* (Cambridge: Cambridge University Press, 1987). Comprehensive accounts of the role of literacy in contemporary societies include Kenneth Levine, *The Social*

## 0.4     Outline of main arguments

*Meaning in the Media* consists of twelve chapters. I move from an initial outline of media disputes, through discussion of processes involved in communicating and ascribing meaning, to a series of three more recognised fields of media law and regulation. In the chapters dealing with particular fields of contested meaning in law, I bring the approaches I outline in earlier chapters together in more extended discussion of social problems in particular areas of the circulation of meaning.

In Part I, 'Communication failure and interpretive conflict' (consisting of Chapters 1–3), I look at how meaning disputes arise, what causes them, and how questions about meaning are formulated. Part II, 'Making sense of "meaning"', consists of Chapters 4–6. In these chapters, I consider what meaning is for the purpose of dealing with conflicts over interpretation, and how different dimensions of meaning can be distinguished. Part III, 'Verbal disputes and approaches to resolving them' (Chapters 7 and 8) addresses questions of how disputes over meaning are handled, *as disputes*: what roles are played by the parties; how the parties engage with one another; and what standards are appealed to in arriving at adjudications. Part IV, 'Analysing disputes in different fields of law and regulation' (Chapters 9–11) presents more extended studies of particular areas: firstly, of a specific legal cause of action, defamation; secondly, of an area of communicative practice governed by a mix of laws and self-regulatory procedures, advertising; and thirdly, of a more diffuse array of actionable harms commonly referred to as offensiveness. In each of these chapters, I describe the main legal procedures and issues that bear on meaning. I also illustrate my discussion with accounts of complaints to regulators and legal actions. Finally, in Part V, 'Conclusion' (Chapter 12), I explore the relation between disputes over interpretation and wider social questions of representation and misrepresentation. I consider the social climate in which media meanings are contested, and close by asking how much trust or suspicion we should feel towards contemporary media communicators.

*Context of Literacy* (London: Routledge, 1986) and David Barton, *Literacy: An Introduction to the Ecology of the Written Language* (Oxford: Blackwell, 1994). Discussion of social consequences associated with changes in available media can be found in Elizabeth Eisenstein, *The Printing Press as an Agent of Social Change: Communications and Cultural Transformations in Early Modern Europe*, 2 vols. (Cambridge: Cambridge University Press, 1979); Michael Clanchy, *From Memory to Written Record* (Oxford: Blackwell, 1993); and Irving Fang, *A History of Mass Communication: Six Information Revolutions* (Burlington, Mass.: Elsevier Science, 1997). Walter Ong's concept of 'secondary orality' (or a resurgence of spoken media forms, alongside writing and print) is outlined in *Orality and Literacy: The Technologizing of the Word* (London: Routledge, 1982). Particularly celebrated among attempts to grasp implications of recent technological changes, and to forecast our future media environment, are Marshall McLuhan, *Understanding Media: The Extensions of Man* (London: Ark, 1964) and Manuel Castells, *The Rise of the Network Society* (Oxford: Blackwell, 2000).

## 0.5    Why meanings matter

How do I expect investigating meaning troublespots in the ways I am describing to move discussion of meaning in the media forward? Closer attention to how meaning circulates and is contested can contribute, I believe, to two strands of academic and wider social debate.

Firstly, I urge a shift in efforts to understand meaning if we wish to *engage with* contested utterances and texts as well as engaging in theory construction about them. We already have accounts of the discourse devices by means of which meaning effects are created, including semantic and pragmatic approaches. To be applicable in social situations, however, approaches to meaning are also needed, I suggest, that are pragmatic in a social as well as a linguistic sense. Such treatments of meaning must give weight simultaneously to both the communicative and broader social (including commercial and political) interests and intent of the protagonists. Work on such lines is inevitably interdisciplinary. This book supports such work where it has started and I hope encourages further combined study of language, law and social policy.

Secondly, I hope to make some meaning-related points about legal adjudication. I suggest that the meaning of a contested utterance or text meets a standard of 'correctness' only to the extent that some kind of practical judgment is needed to meet a socially determined policy goal. This point is likely to seem commonsense to some people but heresy to others. Legal and regulatory bodies are obliged, I argue, to balance benefits that follow from precise characterisation of meaning (e.g. by means of surveys and other research studies) against costs incurred in establishing such meanings. Courtrooms and tribunals are different from seminar rooms. Recognising limitations of interpretive procedures that reach decisions without close analysis, on the other hand, may help direct attention towards the challenges that media law and regulation face in a digital communication environment. This book encourages readers outside the professional field of law to engage with questions about regulation of communication in a rapidly changing communication and information sphere.

Without a compass provided by disciplinary background (of the kind available in linguistics or law), public discussion of meaning is often polarised between descriptive and normative approaches. It veers backwards and forwards between an apparently democratic impulse to accept any perception of what something means, without passing value judgment on it, and an almost opposite concern – also democratic, in trying to uphold truth-seeking integrity in a marketplace of ideas – to work out what the 'correct' meaning of something actually is, when conflicts arise. Reconciling these two positions in the terms in which they mostly present themselves appears impossible. Yet fuller engagement between them is essential. What something means to the person who interprets it is whatever they say it means; for most people, this is an article of faith in our entitlement to 'making meaning'. Yet the personal nature of this kind of 'meaningfulness' places a major obstacle in the way of arbitration in disputes where people find themselves at loggerheads, each claiming an interpretation (in which they express complete conviction) that is incompatible with the opposing party's.

Whatever progress is made on this issue, however, for the parties engaged in an interpretive dispute meaning is mostly not something to stop and think about. Communication as a whole is just another kind of action – one more instrument in the toolbox for getting things done. Interpretive conflicts are typically a subplot in some larger conflict over commercial or political interests, or in a struggle about moral or religious values, or in a confrontation triggered by personal feelings such as ambition, anger or desire for revenge. Evidence of facts, about events and actions, is accordingly at the core of most disputes. What makes the *interpretive* dimension of disputes also worth examining is that people usually defend their interpretations as vigorously, and sometimes as violently, as they fight over the situations or interests that the utterances and texts are about.

Because interpretive disputes can act in this way as a short fuse to a dangerous powder-keg, meaning troublespots in my wider definition have a larger political significance. They play a defining role in the jostling of meanings and values through which societies establish what they expect and what they will tolerate as communicative behaviour, and how communicative behaviour fits into other kinds of social action.

It may seem as if there is no need to worry about this larger climate of communication. Aren't standards already in place, prescribed by media law and settled by social convention? I argue that the established social order of communication is sometimes too easily taken for granted. Even in areas where conventions seem settled (e.g. the convention in favour of telling the truth rather than lying), public standards of behaviour are constantly tested against changing expectations and variable standards of practice. And in online environments, new rules frequently apply. Traditionally private concerns can become instantly global and public, sometimes in overblown expressions of praise, blame, anger and abuse; and the identities of communicators are often refracted through avatars and the various personae that go with alternative screen names. In commercial settings – especially during difficult periods of intensified competition – communicative behaviour can seem uprooted from any underpinning framework of cooperation and pushed towards pursuit of competitive advantage. How we adjust our expectations about meaning, as well as our communicative behaviour, to these tensions will have a substantial impact on societies of the future.

*Part I*

# Communication failure and interpretive conflict

# 1 From personal disagreement to meaning troublespot

## 1.1 Introduction

Chapters 1–3 (Part I: 'Communication failure and interpretive conflict') look at how meaning disputes arise, what causes them, and how questions about meaning are formulated. In this first chapter, I suggest that controversies over media meaning, and complaint procedures in media law and regulation, involve different kinds of speech event from spontaneous disagreement in conversation. Processes for understanding and adjudicating such contestation of meaning, I claim, should reflect these differences of speech event structure and the roles in them of the various speech event participants.

## 1.2 Interpretive disagreement

As they leave the cinema one evening, Anita and Bobby fall into conversation about a film they have just seen, a film which portrayed life in an English country village. Bobby finds it difficult to agree with Anita's view that the film exploits people's sentimentality about animals and misrepresents what goes on in the countryside. His opinion is that the film, which he enjoyed, appeals to public sympathy towards animals rather than exploiting it. He can't really understand Anita's overall response either. Why does she think the film gives a distorted picture of how traditional villagers and urban newcomers interact? It seems to him that the film gives a basically accurate account of how things are. In any event, if the film expresses a viewpoint, perhaps it is treating its subject light-heartedly rather than cynically. As the conversation develops, Anita and Bobby discover (as people commonly do in conversations about something they've just heard, read or watched) that despite shared experience and background the different strands in their interpretations become difficult to disentangle. Questions arise partly over what the film seems to say, partly in shadings of the meaning of words they use to talk about it, and partly because of different ideas they already hold, in this case about the countryside. Distinctions between the sources of misunderstanding or disagreement are not clear-cut.

But there may be some pointers. Where the differences between Anita and Bobby reflect their general views about the countryside, you might expect a similar pattern of disagreement to be repeated if they discuss a different account of the countryside (not a film, but a newspaper article or description of a country walk that one of them has taken). Where a point at issue arises as a result of interpreting differently what the film seems to convey, they would be likely to refer in one way or another to filmic devices (its dialogue, music, costumes or choice of locations), or to use words indicating how intentions are expressed, like 'implies', 'shows', or 'intention' itself. And where their disagreement arises from words they have chosen as vehicles for their opinions, then you might expect corresponding divergence in conversations about topics quite different from that of the present film. If Anita and Bobby are to achieve greater mutual understanding about the film they have just seen, or simply to iron out immediate differences between them, they must find a way of talking that doesn't give up in the face of divergent opinion but tries to take account of different dimensions of their misunderstanding. In doing so, they must of course at the same time avoid being diverted from their evening's entertainment into reflexive commentary that it is easy to ridicule.

Now imagine a twist in the situation. Suppose Anita works for an organisation engaged in countryside lobbying or activism. While watching the film, she has noticed a series of details that seem modelled on the organisation she works for. Those apparently inaccurate details are critical in ways she considers untrue and probably damaging if people see the connection and believe what the film seems to suggest. Her disagreement is no longer with Bobby. Now it is with what must be thought of as something like the film's 'speaker' (with unavoidable difficulties that then arise as regards who the 'speaker' of a film is). This slightly altered situation no longer permits the kind of potentially clarifying dialogue just outlined. Who, for example, should Anita 'speak to' in order to air her point of view and weigh up whatever the film maker has to say on the subject? The film's scriptwriter? Its distributors? Its producer? Or its lawyers? More importantly, how will strands of disagreement such as those outlined above be disentangled in these new circumstances? Could Anita, in such dialogue, ever be on an equal footing with the film's 'speaker', in a situation where she is one among a very large number of potential (but not individually intended) addressees, watching in different places and even in different years? What expectation can Anita have of a meaningful response if she gets in touch to complain? And what framework for discussion, and what kind of language, is available for working through elements of disagreement towards some kind of resolution?

Extend the situation a little further. When Anita goes in to work the following morning, she discovers that some of her colleagues feel the same way she does about the film. After discussion a decision is made to consult formally on a possible complaint – they are not sure who to – in order to seek some kind of remedy for being misrepresented. The issue now arises what the precise grounds of such a complaint should be and how those grounds are to be formally stated. If courts become involved, costs will be incurred (of legal advice, and on preparation). Defence statements and counter-claims must be expected, incurring further costs over which secondary arguments will develop. Issues of possible damages, in view of the seriousness of the threat to its producers if the film were to be withdrawn, may be at stake if Anita's organisation loses. Whatever process of interpretive discussion ensues will involve arbitration at a distance, by correspondence or involving intermediaries. At worst, the dispute may grow into the legal equivalent of a fight to the death. Anita may begin to wish they had never gone to see the film in the first place.

## 1.3    Informal disagreement and more public 'media' disputes

The differences between these scenarios – personal disagreement in conversation; sense of grievance at what some public, media text says; and formal complaint or litigation – may seem matters of institutional procedure rather than of meaning. But the three related situations illustrate importantly different interpretive settings that affect how we view 'meaning'.

The cross-purposes and disagreement that arose between Anita and Bobby on their way home from the cinema can sometimes be sorted out there and then. Utterances can be clarified if the listener shows some sign of puzzlement or disagreement, and they can be repaired where an opinion was poorly or rashly put. An informal metalanguage (or set of words designed to comment on expressions being used) may be introduced as a way of managing specific misunderstandings. Just as often, though, such disagreement is simply abandoned. It blows over rather than being resolved to anyone's satisfaction. This commonly happens when the topic does not seem to either party worth pursuing. But it is also a result of how conversation works. Topics come and go, styles and levels of talking about any given topic shift, and new themes and conversational opportunities present themselves. Unfinished matters and unresolved issues get left behind.

Interpretive disagreements show conversation to be not only 'dialogue' but also what has been called, in one sense of that complex term, 'dialogic'.[1] It involves an unfolding cooperation that depends on interaction between contributions made by each person, as well as on continuous monitoring of understanding as it develops. It is largely because of this 'dialogic' character of face-to-face talk that correction and negotiation of meaning are possible as a

---

[1] On Bakhtin's use of the term 'dialogic', see Tzvetan Todorov, *Mikhail Bakhtin: The Dialogical Principle* (Minneapolis: University of Minnesota Press, 1984). For a comprehensive study of Bakhtin's ideas and social context, see Michael Gardiner (ed.), *Mikhail Bakhtin*, 4 vols. (London: Sage, 2002).

way of building on the grounding provided by shared information in order to achieve some degree of common perspective. Problems of reference assignment ('who do you mean?'), disagreement over denotation ('I wouldn't call that a ...'), and other kinds of confusion and cross-purposes surface, and can be addressed in relatively brief time-loops. We are so used to coordinating action in language that our collaborative construction of knowledge and understanding, and our continuous repair strategies, are automatic to the point of going mostly unnoticed. As the linguistic field of conversation analysis has shown,[2] in important respects conversation can only be explained as a joint effort, supported by questioning and expressions of disagreement, reiteration, paraphrase, and explication of terms where necessary. Even where meanings of particular words or whole utterances are in question, interaction and feedback are available. They are the means by which participants in the conversation negotiate ideas and half-formed impressions, as well as how they shape the interpersonal relationship between them.

It is different, though, with the modified, second and third scenarios introduced above. Anita's grievance is against what the film says rather than what Bobby says about the film. The repair toolkit for dialogue is no longer available. If you watch a film or television programme and wish to query its terms or point of view, or if you see yourself referred to in a public notice or publication, you cannot negotiate meaning in the 'dialogic' way outlined. This is not just because the social relationships involved are different, and more remote. Media communication events are structured differently from person-to-person conversation.[3] As a result they present greater difficulty when misunderstanding, disagreement over meaning, or a sense of being offended arises. And where divergent interpretations go beyond resolution in the flow of communication, an escalation of the scale and ramifications of conflict follows. Grievance, in this area, incubates at a distance.

In the circumstances of the 'media complaint' scenarios I have outlined, someone's sense of being misled, offended or otherwise harmed must be addressed, if at all, through more formal channels of reply and protest. The varying degree of publicness of media texts increases their potential for offence. It also complicates how to establish the competing interpretations from which arbitration must start. In these different and more formal scenarios, relations

---

[2]  See Hutchby and Wooffitt *Conversation Analysis*. For investigation of conversational 'grounding', see Herb Clark, *Using Language* (Cambridge: Cambridge University Press, 1996). Also Neil Mercer, *Words and Minds: How We Use Language To Think Together* (London: Routledge, 2000). For theoretical discussion in relation to other areas of linguistics, see Levinson, *Pragmatics*.

[3]  See O'Keeffe, *Investigating Media Discourse*; also, Alan Durant and Marina Lambrou, *Language and Media* (London: Routledge, 2009). A detailed account of the 'mediation' of discourse is Ron Scollon, *Mediated Discourse and Social Interaction* (London: Routledge, 1999).

between participants are those of a more complex kind of speech event than face-to-face conversation:

- There is a different *mode of address*. In the first scenario, Anita addresses Bobby, who is the original speaker of the opinions she is responding to, and he replies by directly addressing her. In the 'complaint' scenarios, Anita's disagreement is with a collective or corporate author of the film. She addresses unknown others involved in its making or exhibition. She is no longer replying to a specific speaker about what that speaker has said, but addressing her view to multiple, unknown readers or hearers.
- The *channel* of the 'dialogue' has changed, from spoken to written (at least in early stages – back to spoken if taken all the way to court).
- Relatedly, the *register* has changed (both in written letters and in courtroom speech), from informal conversational to formal and possibly technically legal or quasi-legal.
- The *dialogic structure* has changed. Whereas Anita might expect an almost instant response from Bobby, there is no longer the same degree of reciprocity. Through intermediaries such as lawyers, Anita will hope for a reply after some lapse of time from representatives of an organisation she almost certainly hasn't met. The representatives who reply will have a different relation to what is said or shown in the film than either that of the 'speaker of the film' or anyone going to see it in a cinema. In this way, the complaint 'conversation' introduces an extra, third-party dimension. It becomes essentially a discussion of what different people state about an original communication whose 'speaker' – a general term now encompassing a collective intention involved in text production – has been largely replaced.
- There is less *common ground*, or mutual knowledge and shared assumptions, to be drawn on. In conversation, Anita and Bobby have an immediate sense of what they share in terms of background and experience; what beliefs and expectations they probably have in common; and points at which they already know they disagree. In the complaint scenarios, opinions and arguments will have to be spelt out, as if from first principles. The parties need to establish precisely what they disagree about, before anyone can even try to reach agreement.
- The *participant structure* is different. When Anita and Bobby disagree, it's personal. Any bystanders who happen to be around may become involved, taking sides or just feeling embarrassed. But when organisations disagree, there are more communicative bystanders. Some of those bystanders will be interested stakeholders. Others may be working on aspects of the same project or on related cases, aware of and likely to be affected, if only indirectly, by what is going on. The relation between the protagonists in the dispute and what they each say is also different (what the linguistic

ethnographer Erving Goffman has called the 'footing'[4] on which acts of speaking take place). Anita talking spontaneously to Bobby in conversation differs significantly from the more calculated stance of a lawyer or press officer speaking as corporate mouthpiece on behalf of a film maker. In this respect, the dispute has become a far more complex, public conversation, with multiple participants in different relations to the core interaction. 'Authorised' participants comment on, and may even formally advise on, the direction of the exchange and strategies to be adopted; other bystanders and overhearers may influence it simply by their presence, even without any active involvement, raising the stakes for both sides and giving interpretation of the film an extra spectator interest.

- In terms of social structure, Anita and Bobby had roughly equivalent power and status in their conversation (allowing for gender and relationship variables). But when Anita's organisation complains about the film there will be a more explicit set of *power relations* in play. Power asymmetry will be reflected not only in what the respective parties can spend (e.g. on their lawyers) but in other kinds of capital as well (e.g. how far they are used to dealing with disputes of this kind, or how reliable or authoritative they can present themselves as being in a public setting). In extreme cases, the relationship will be David and Goliath: a relatively disempowered complainant challenging a large and powerful corporation. In other cases, the relationship may be that of complaining bully and victim.[5]

Collectively, the differences listed here show why it is necessary to recognise different *sorts* of disagreement taking place in different kinds of communicative event. Media discourse, and discourse about media discourse, can appear to be simply an amplified continuation of face-to-face communication. But media discourse is in key respects different from conversation. In the three scenarios described above – each concerned with debating the same film's meaning – there

---

[4] On discourse participants, see Erving Goffman, 'Footing', in *Forms of Talk* (Oxford: Oxford University Press, 1981), pp. 124–59. For application to media discourse of Goffman's differentiation of notions of speaker and hearer into layered production and participation roles, see Allan Bell, *The Language of News Media* (Oxford: Blackwell, 1991), pp. 84–103. On media language as styles of quasi-interaction, see O'Keeffe, *Investigating Media Discourse*. For theoretical discussion of 'participation', see Stephen Levinson, 'Putting linguistics on a proper footing: explorations in Goffman's concepts of participation', in Paul Drew and Anthony Wootton (eds.), *Erving Goffman: Exploring the Interaction Order* (Cambridge: Polity, 1988), pp. 161–227.

[5] One case often viewed in such terms is usually referred to as 'McLibel', and led to the longest-ever English libel action. The case spanned fifteen years, from an initial writ against two activists (for distributing leaflets campaigning against McDonald's) through to the Court of Appeal and a decision from the European Commission of Human Rights on whether the defendants' right to freedom of expression had been interfered with under ECHR Article 10. Several TV documentaries and a commercial DVD narrate the story and have made the case a cause célèbre. A detailed account, with links to relevant legal documents and media coverage, can be found at www.mcspotlight.org/case/trial.

are differences in respect of a majority of the eleven salient components of communicative events distilled from linguistic research sources by the communication ethnographer Muriel Saville-Troike.[6] The components (in Saville-Troike's terms) of genre, topic, and purpose or function – even overall message content – are broadly the same in the three cases. But the setting, key, participants, message form, act sequence, rules for interaction and norms of interpretation all differ notably between the face-to-face scenario of Anita and Bobby's conversation and the distance-negotiation between Anita's organisation and the film makers or their representatives.

## 1.4    Communication and the nature of disagreement

Differences between communicative events such as the ones I have described reflect communicative formats at a deeper level. Historically, those formats (face-to-face, phone conversation, letters, cinema, e-mails, etc.) vary with changing communication technologies. They also reproduce (and over time reshape) social relations, varying slightly from occasion to occasion, and so contributing to social change. The structures I have identified in relation to the film above affect both the film's meaning and also the available ways of contesting it.

In this context, it is ironic that part of the celebrated power of modern media discourse is its apparent closeness to 'ordinary, everyday language': how it transmits and reproduces textures and patterns of personal speech and dialogue. While media discourse may appear in this way to *be the same as* everyday discourse, however, that sameness is 'mediated' (or as some writers prefer, 'mediatised')[7] in ways that significantly affect how much and also in what manner discourse meaning can be queried or challenged.

The history of communication media is not only a history of successive technologies and institutions. It is also one of changing social relations governing interaction between people. If we are to get a precise sense of the *object* of media disputes over meaning – the contested media discourse – then we need to disentangle often hybrid forms and genres in our contemporary mix of technical resources and media institutions. A great deal of simplification enters into

---

[6] Muriel Saville-Troike, *The Ethnography of Communication: An Introduction*, 2nd edition (Oxford: Blackwell, 1989), pp. 138–9. The concept of communicative events is often traced back to Dell Hymes, *Foundations in Sociolinguistics: An Ethnographic Approach* (Philadelphia: University of Pennsylvania Press, 1977).

[7] Preference for 'mediatised' is discussed in Norman Fairclough, *Media Discourse* (London: Longman, 1995) and a useful checklist of questions about discourse functioning is outlined in his conclusion, 'Critical media literacy', pp. 201–5. More specific concepts including 'distanciation', 'mediated visibility', 'non-reciprocal intimacy at a distance' and 'contextualised appropriation' allow John Thompson to develop a historically grounded account of media discourse in *The Media and Modernity: A Social Theory of the Media* (Oxford: Blackwell, 1995).

discussion if we model interpretive dispute on a default setting of two people talking to each other face-to-face (like Anita and Bobby on the way home from the cinema). Yet it is equally simplistic to see dispute as a matter of an isolated textual object (the film itself) simply exhibited, published or posted in the public domain in such a way as to make available around it a cluster of positions from which reactions are stated, without acknowledging either intention, different anticipated interpretations, or complicating social facts about reception.[8] To make progress in understanding contested media meanings, attention must be given to *processes* involved in media communication as well as to assumed properties of the *object* of contestation.

## 1.5     The concept of 'meaning troublespots'

The distinctions I have made so far may seem commonsense. We communicate all the time and mostly have firm intuitions about communicative intent. We easily understand, for instance, how and when we can answer back and when we can't. We also have rich intuitions as regards who is getting at what when they say something, what tone they are adopting, in what adopted role or persona, and for roughly what purpose. It is true that we can spell these things out more carefully. But intuitively we are mostly quite good at Harold Lasswell's 'who, what, when, where, why' questions about communication.[9] As regards media discourse in particular, skills of instant recognition seem especially pronounced among young people, who grow up surrounded by the latest mix of media technologies, forms and styles.

Recognising what is going on is one thing. But things are less straightforward where interpretations have to be verbalised and defended against disagreement, particularly in formal contexts such as tribunals or legal proceedings. Developing an ability to talk about meaning is an important aspect of engaging actively with a changing media environment, and is an important aspect of 'media literacy'.

Difficulties in formulating and explaining competing interpretations of a discourse that is contested are significant enough to make it useful to group

---

[8] For description of the face-to-face 'canonical speech situation', see John Lyons *Semantics*, 2 vols. (Cambridge: Cambridge University Press, 1977), pp. 637–8. For extension of this model to take account of cognitive dimensions of communication, see Sperber and Wilson, *Relevance*, pp. 1–64. On models of mass communication (dyadic, centre–periphery, with or without intermediary opinion formers, etc.), see Denis McQuail and Sven Windahl, *Communication Models: For the Study of Mass Communication* (London: Pearson, 1993).

[9] Harold Lasswell, 'The structure and function of communication in society', in L. Bryson (ed.), *The Communication of Ideas* (Urbana: University of Illinois Press, 1948), pp. 117–30. For the historical context of Lasswell's ideas in communication theory, see Armand and Michèle Mattelart, *Theories of Communication: A Short Introduction* (London: Sage, 1998), esp. pp. 19–41.

disputes together for closer consideration: a class of what I will call 'meaning troublespots'. 'Meaning troublespot' is an informal rather than technical notion. It is based on an analogy between the personal, social and financial cost to protagonists involved in disputes over meaning and the serious damage and injury associated with physical accidents and political conflicts.

Disputes over meaning take many forms, and are embedded in more general traits of conflict processes (such as incompatibility of objectives, struggles over an identical resource, and incompatible goals or activities). Only some of the features that characterise conflicts, however, make them 'meaning troublespots' in my sense. That is why, in Chapter 2, I will distinguish a number of different sorts of communicative trouble more precisely, to focus attention on the aspects I am interested in. Disputes occur, for instance, in different media (newspaper, TV, radio, Internet page or blog); they also occur in different genres (in news, documentary, fiction, magazine features). The controversies they precipitate are handled by different regulatory procedures (in the courtroom, by extrajudicial media regulators, in discussion by TV commentators, and in newspaper columns). Yet none of these classes of difference is relevant to whether a situation constitutes a meaning troublespot in my sense: the category I am proposing includes examples of each. Disputes also differ as regards the scale or amount of discourse involved. They vary from controversies focused in a precise crux (say a single word or phrase), through contested episodes within longer stories, or about a single fictional character (e.g. where a description is alleged to be defamatory of a living person), to problems surrounding a whole text (e.g. where adverts or whole campaigns of interconnected adverts are considered deceptive, or novels or films are claimed to be obscene or blasphemous). Again, all of these I include in my meaning troublespot category.

What makes a meaning troublespot distinctive and worth investigating, for me, is *how* the meanings to be contested are put forward and argued over, as well as how some outcome to contestation – some kind of effective calming or closure – is achieved. In each instance of what I will call a meaning troublespot, what is involved is a structure of events that is not necessarily fixed but (as the sociologist John Thompson has shown for political scandal[10]) which unfolds unevenly over time, with distinct contours and dynamics.

Here is a rough outline of typical processes involved at a 'meaning troublespot':

- An utterance (or representation) is made public by being published, broadcast or exhibited, involving (a) words (or images, or both), in (b) some specific social setting and (c) against a backdrop of expectations, attitudes

---

[10] John B. Thompson, *Political Scandal: Power and Visibility in the Media Age* (Cambridge: Polity, 2000).

and beliefs that shape how the communicator anticipates the message will be understood.

- Various readers, hearers or members of an audience who encounter the utterance or text attribute a meaning to it; on the basis of that meaning, they derive some particular significance or effect that they associate with what has been said, written or shown.
- One or more people claim, given their particular way of interpreting the piece of discourse, to have experienced an effect which they believe to be harmful (they may feel they were lied to, misled or misrepresented, or they may feel in some way let down or offended).
- To seek some relief from, or remedy against, the perceived harmful effect, the party who feels injured sets in motion some form of public complaint, protest or litigation.
- The producer of the utterance or text denies that it means what the injured party *says* it means, and puts forward an alternative, competing account.
- A relevant adjudicating body (or the wider 'court of public opinion') scrutinises the discourse in question. Because discussion of the discourse is not, in its reproduced media form, dialogic or immediately interactive, commentary and analysis interrupt the flow of social action and present the question of 'meaning' as a kind of 'freeze frame' or reconstruction, an exercise temporarily offline from the continuing interests and agendas of the participants.

Put like this, the step-by-step unfolding of the essential stages of a meaning troublespot may appear mechanical. In any given episode, those stages are unlikely to be experienced as if they permit logical dissection. Precise boundaries will not line up neatly and stages will be experienced as overlapping and having blurred edges.

Even this simple outline of a meaning troublespot, however, can help to highlight important differences between the sorts of cases I want to discuss and either the simple model of face-to-face communication or of textual 'objects' placed in the public domain and contemplated from different perspectives. 'Meaning', in my 'meaning troublespots' framework, is constructed in interaction between the different parties, who act strategically in relation to one another against the changing backdrop of a developing interpretive situation. This timeline and apparent fluidity stand in contrast to analysis of a publication, recorded broadcast, single printed-off email, or website visited on a given day, each of which cuts a slice through temporal flow and fixes a snapshot of a particular state of play between the parties at a given moment. On the other hand, at the core of a meaning troublespot there is very often media speech, as much as writing, fixed in a recorded form. Negotiation of verbal or textual meaning places the frozen object derived from speech under intense interpretive scrutiny, in ways that differ fundamentally from the dialogic conditions I outlined at the beginning of this chapter.

## 1.6    Types of interpretive dispute

My category of meaning troublespots will only hold its interest if it is limited to the use I intend for it. The criteria I have put forward are not necessary and sufficient conditions of membership of the class of meaning troublespots, as if conceived in classical concept theory. They are ways of focusing a prototypical category in order to see regularity and contrast between cases that vary in different dimensions: in their scale of publicness; as regards how conflict is expressed; in their duration before people lose interest; in the sorts of evidence available; in the interpretive standards appealed to; and as regards the consequences that follow from them.

It is difficult to specify units of measurement for each of these dimensions. If taken heuristically, however, my criteria will be useful in allowing a case for or against viewing some situation as a meaning troublespot to be assessed in terms of goodness-of-exemplar (GOE) closeness to a set of prototypical features. Multivariate representations of different meaning troublespots, for instance if drawn as spidergrams, would show different areas and shapes; but the trouble-spots would all contain a core of common features.

Meaning troublespots, in my sense, come in different types. They can also be located in relation to each other on a rough scale as regards the intensity of their contestation of meaning (alongside whatever other forces and conflicts drive them and whatever orientations towards conflict are shown in the participants' response styles, such as predisposition towards compromise, appeasement or aggressive domination). From the limit case of disagreement in spontaneous face-to-face conversation (never fully a 'meaning troublespot' in my sense), it is possible to trace other varieties: more formal but still localised interpretive dispute over documents and recorded utterances in institutions; short-term media furore or 'media firestorms', in which the contested point is dissipated away in the flow of subsequent topics (as with disputed points in many broad-cast interviews);[11] disputes amplified by secondary media coverage (e.g. controversies over plays, books, art exhibitions or films, because of how they portray sex, religion or ethnic communities, and sometimes involving widespread public dissatisfaction that takes the form of direct protest such as picketing theatres or cinemas, boycotting goods or burning books);[12] and

---

[11] Jane H. Hill 'Crises of meaning: personalised language ideology in US, media discourses', in Sally Johnson and A. Ensslin (eds.), *Language in the Media. Representations, Identities, Ideologies* (London: Continuum, 2007), p. 13. An example is my own article 'Meaning and public deception: a tale of more than "very, very few people"', *CQ*, 48 (3) (2006), 88–93.

[12] Because no formal procedure for arbitration is involved, arguments on different sides only engage, if at all, through the involvement of third-party, mediating organisations. For efforts in Britain to reconcile the parties during controversy over *The Satanic Verses*, for example, see Commission for Racial Equality, *Law, Blasphemy and the Multi-Faith Society* (London: Commission for Racial Equality, 1990).

beyond these, full-blown legal contestations (such as actions for alleged defamation, obscenity, blasphemy or false advertising) and sustained public controversies (such as those surrounding allegations which in the most serious cases may lead to resignation, imprisonment, suicide, or the possibility of presidential impeachment). Examples of each will be discussed in the chapters which follow.

## 1.7    The problem of interpretive gridlock

For something to be a meaning troublespot, there must be active contestation. In much disagreement about what discourse means, this is nevertheless not what happens. Disgruntled addressees and audiences suffer in quiet exasperation at meanings they think others condone or at least acquiesce in. Sometimes the frustrated person feels disempowered, gagged by being at risk or in need of protection or preferment, and actively avoids confrontation. In other cases, addressees or audiences internalise interpretive conflict, or subordinate their own beliefs or interests for relational benefits with the other party or parties concerned. They may satisfy themselves with a mental 'code book' practice of private translation: 'They *would* say that, wouldn't they? But since A is just code for B, for A read B – but better keep it quiet!'[13] Anger at whatever is conveyed by the discourse may remain nothing more than a climate of tacit discomfort, dislike or disengagement. Many disputes over meaning as a result never become disputes at all. They remain meaning troublespots with the trouble waiting to happen.

Where contestation *is* expressed, what follows is typically a sort of interpretive gridlock.[14] No movement or flexibility seems possible in any direction. Opposing parties are unwilling to concede that the alternative meaning or

---

[13] Code-book translation as a form of interpretation can involve accepted euphemism, such as a 'frank exchange of views' in diplomatic currency meaning a vigorous argument, or, more grotesquely, acceptance of phrases such as 'extraordinary rendition', 'collateral damage', 'ethnic cleansing' or 'final solution'; see Poole, *Unspeak^{TM}*. Satire of such interpretation (and the need for it), especially in relation to political propaganda, can be found in works such as George Orwell's *Animal Farm* or in the idea of Newspeak in *Nineteen Eighty-Four*. In the field of gender differences, see also Jenny Lyn Bader and Bill Brazell, *He Meant, She Meant: The Definitive Male/Female Dictionary* (New York: Warner Books, 1997). For discussion in relation to language functioning generally, see Raymond W. Gibbs, *Intentions in the Experience of Meaning* (Cambridge: Cambridge University Press, 1999), pp. 325–37.

[14] In a different intellectual tradition, the 'interpretive gridlock' I am describing here is very close to what Jean-François Lyotard has called a 'différend': 'As distinguished from a litigation, a différend [differend] would be a case of conflict, between (at least) two parties, that cannot be equitably resolved for lack of a rule of judgment applicable to both arguments. One side's legitimacy does not imply the other's lack of legitimacy. However, applying a single rule of judgment to both in order to settle their différend as though it were merely a litigation would wrong (at least) one of them (and both of them if neither side admits this rule) ... The title of this book suggests (through the generic value of the definite article) that a universal rule of judgment between heterogeneous genres is lacking in general.' See *The Différend: Phrases in Dispute* (Minneapolis: University of Minnesota Press, 1988), p. xi.

significance attributed to the utterance or text is reasonable, or even possible. Even then, disputes are sometimes played down as moments of 'misunderstanding'. But they are only misunderstanding in the specialised sense of failure to see eye to eye, since in such circumstances parties mostly will not concede that they themselves could have misunderstood. Rarely is there a shortage of perceived meaning. Everyone's own interpretation is 'clear' or 'beyond doubt', even while they are locked in heated controversy about alternatives to it. Nor will protagonists in such disputes often accept compromise, such as a settlement recognising that divergent interpretations may be permissible alternatives. They are more likely to insist on vindication of their own interpretation. Failing that, they may seek some form of 'amicable' settlement that may amount to little more than reluctant, face-saving compromise: a way out rather than a way of achieving common ground.

Interpretive contestation can be like traffic gridlock in another respect. Like the gridlock caused by a traffic accident, the priority of those directly involved moves through avoidance of injury, accident investigation, allocation of fault and pursuit of compensation, while for everyone else except drive-by voyeurs, the urgency is to clear the road so everyone else can move on in the continuous traffic flow of everyday discourse.

If interpretive gridlock is to be broken, we need to think again about how we understand meaning. Approaches will be needed that are wider than linguistics or semiotics: approaches that combine grasp of what constitutes credible interpretation with awareness of regulatory provisions and a sense of how discourse fits into larger patterns of social interaction. This is why meaning troublespots as I outline them do not fit neatly either into the established framework of media law topics or into linguistics. The kinds of analysis needed are not traditionally 'hermeneutic' either, in the sense of being concerned with the meaning of remote or opaque texts, such as works from an earlier historical period, or with a general theory of how we understand.[15] Meaning troublespots are less about understanding something that seems out of reach than about settling on a meaning for something understood in too many different ways right in front of us. There is less a lack than a surplus of confidence in meanings being ascribed. Academic accounts of interpretation will contribute to resolving interpretive disputes of this kind only if theoretical insight is combined with attention to practical aspects of behaviour. As a first step, however, we should try something more limited: to describe the different kinds of trouble that arise from communicative events in order to see how questions of meaning fit into them.

---

[15] What makes 'hermenuetics' distinctive from other branches of understanding meaning is traced, with a collection of key texts and extracts, in Kurt Mueller-Vollmer (ed.), *The Hermeneutics Reader: Texts of the German Tradition from the Enlightenment to the Present* (London: Continuum, 1994).

## 1.8     Summary

I began this chapter with an episode of personal, face-to-face interpretive disagreement, before going on to generalise about ways of resolving inter-personal disputes over meaning. I have shown how disputes over meaning in the media complicate the interactional, or 'dialogue', dimension of such dis-agreement in a number of respects. The communications in question involve more complicated event structures, with less straightforward producer and communicator roles, sometimes complicated audience demographics, and dif-ferent textual properties. Procedures involved in managing interpretive disputes may, I concluded, begin from similarities with negotiating meaning in face-to-face interaction. But in important respects they will inevitably differ from how you would expect disagreement to be handled at an interpersonal level.

# 2    Signs of trouble

## 2.1    Introduction

This chapter explores how disputes about media discourse are not all triggered by the same kinds of misunderstanding or disagreement. Some disputes are triggered by features of communicative behaviour, or *use*; others arise as complications with coded or inferred *meaning*; and others again follow from alleged discourse *effects*. This chapter draws some relevant distinctions between these three categories, and discusses the relation between them. Even a simplified three-way categorisation of this kind points to a need to distinguish types of communicative trouble, while acknowledging how far the three aspects are interwoven. I suggest that the three different emphases (use, meaning and effect) echo complementary perspectives of speaker, text and interpreter as a kind of 'interpretive triangle' in any dispute.

## 2.2    Three kinds of trouble

In introducing the term 'meaning troublespot' in Chapter 1, I suggested that whatever resonance this informal concept creates is linked to an implied claim: that related questions of meaning arise in disputes that find themselves in different categories when it comes to legal or regulatory classification. For the people concerned, as well as for their lawyers and in subsequent reporting, a dispute is about something like alleged defamation or product disparagement, negligent mis-statement or injurious falsehood, perjury, incitement to racial hatred, or misleading advertising practices. Yet each 'meaning troublespot' dispute contains a broadly corresponding knot of underlying problems to do with what the contested utterance or text *means*. I am not suggesting that the root significance of disputes about media discourse – or the trouble they cause – is equivalent across different categorics. The opposite is clearly the case. Problems surrounding media discourse take many forms, condensed into the policy aims and definitions of different legal and regulatory measures. What I am suggesting is that we can enhance our understanding of legal contestations of meaning by drawing distinctions between types of *communicative* trouble as well as between types of legal trouble.

To begin, we might say that problems created by media content (rather than more commonly discussed problems of media ownership and institutional structure[1]) are associated with some combination of the uses, meanings and effects of media discourse. These three categories are not precisely defined technical terms, and they are not completely separate from one another. Rather, they are aspects of discourse that may be given different weight or prominence in different kinds of analysis. There is no pre-given or fixed distinction between them. In different intellectual traditions, lines are drawn differently. In behaviourist semantics of the 1950s, for example, meaning was understood as one more kind of 'effect'. This was before emphasis on more specialised, meaning-creating properties of the linguistic system began to shift the focus of most semantic inquiry in the early 1960s.[2] In studies of 'media effects', on the other hand, from roughly the same period onwards (and more recently in different branches of media and cultural studies), often no clearly delineated role is assigned to 'meaning' between media discourse on the one hand and its consequences or personal and social impact on the other.[3] More influential than either of these approaches at present are kinds of audience ethnography. But in ethnographic studies, what I will distinguish as meanings, effects and uses often remain undifferentiated. Attention is given instead to an overall fabric of significance experienced by the interpreter.[4] It will help, therefore, if I begin by outlining the three terms in the senses in which I propose to draw on them.

### 2.2.1    'Use': media communicators behaving badly

When we think of people's *uses* of discourse, we may have in mind any of a further three slightly different but related things.

[1]  For details of law and regulations governing media structures and institutions, see e.g. E. Barendt and L. Hitchens, *Media Law: Cases and Materials* (London: Longman, 2000), chapter 3, pp. 66–114.

[2]  Behaviourist approaches in semantics are described in Lyons, *Semantics*. For linguistic context of the period, see W. T. Gordon, *A History of Semantics* (Amsterdam: Benjamins, 1982). An outstanding exception to what is now mainly a negative view of approaches to meaning in the period is Osgood, Suci and Tannenbaum, *The Measurement of Meaning*.

[3]  On the relation between interpretation and textual effects, see Jean-Jacques Lecercle, *Interpretation as Pragmatics* (London: Macmillan, 1999), esp. chapter 5. Lecercle persuasively suggests that media effects studies have generally overstated the case for direct causation while audience ethnographies have their notions of textual causation far too weak.

[4]  Commonly inspired by Geertz's *The Interpretation of Cultures*, ethnographic approaches to media meaning became popular as 'New Audience Studies'. For a collection reflecting combined influence of Stuart Hall and Pierre Bourdieu as well as Geertz, and charting development from his own *Nationwide* audience to more open-ended ethnography, see Morley, *Television, Audiences and Cultural Studies*. A collection of papers through to 1990 (which seems the end of the main phase of this field's development) is James Hay, Lawrence Grossberg and Ellen Wartella (eds.), *The Audience and Its Landscape* (Boulder, Colo.: Westview Press, 1996).

Firstly there is a general sense of communicative activity. Communicators deploy resources of the language system available to them (or other semiotic systems, such as icons, emoticons, or other conventional visual or audio signs) in order to produce their own new compositions, utterances or texts. Such discourse-in-action is calculated by the user to relate to social setting and designed to meet the needs and interests of one or more recipients. Choices are made within (though they may sometimes deviate from) the grammatical and stylistic options available.

Alongside this frequent, general sense of 'use', however, there is another sense: 'use' that involves not originating but handling and passing on to others, still for a communicative purpose and with varying degrees of creative input, discourse that has been made by someone else. Just as you can talk or compose a text yourself, you can alternatively act as a sort of mouthpiece. You physically relay, replay or otherwise align yourself with some ready-made piece of discourse that you judge to be suitable for a given purpose. You repeat gossip or an anecdote, or e-mail a joke or online birthday card to someone, or put a poster up on a wall to create a particular ambience or signal some loyalty or affiliation you consider an important message about yourself (e.g. about your preferred style of music, a political cause, affiliation to a sports team or cultural milieu). This is still active communication. But now it involves a more obviously 'copy and paste' approach than is associated with choosing and combining signs from your own mental sign-library. Public versions of this transmissive or 'broadcasting' role are *professional* broadcasting roles, including the work of editors, mood music planners in shopping malls, and TV schedulers and publishers, all of whom distribute media content (or alternatively, viewed from a point of view of overproduction and competitive selection, act as gate-keepers of media content). Inevitably this type of use merges with the first type, because it is possible to echo in an adapted form. A lot of discourse that we feel we originate is to some extent 'echoic', even if our creative input varies in degree as we reuse or recycle something. Such discourse is prefabricated not only because the words or individual signs are not of our own making and were already there, as a symbolic field of distinctions waiting to be used, but also because our communications are inspired to varying degrees by genre conventions and whatever we have just heard, seen or read.

Thirdly, there is a kind of 'use' concerned with giving meaning to utterances or texts that have been conveyed by others *to* us. 'Use' is now a kind of cognition: what you might call active reception.[5] Examples include

---

[5] Interpreter 'use' is extended by Umberto Eco to include virtually all unintended meaning. See '*Intentio Lectoris*: the State of the Art', in *The Limits of Interpretation* (Bloomington: Indiana University Press, 1990), pp. 44–63. Confusion between meaning and use is sometimes increased by appeals to Wittgenstein's 'the meaning of a word is its use in the language', or 'what do words signify, if not the kind of use they have' (both from *Philosophical Investigations*, trans. G. E. M. Anscombe (Oxford: Blackwell, 1953)), respectively at 20$^e$ para 43 and 6$^e$ para 10.

motivational uses, such as when you switch to a gardening programme on the radio in order to get you going with the ironing, or play an 'adrenalin anthem' on your iPod to do exercise to, or watch a DVD or read a book in bed to help you get off to sleep. Or you might indulge in fantasy air-guitar or air-conductor performance while listening to music, taking up some imagined performance rather than reception role in relation to what you are hearing. 'Use' in this third sense is a kind of discourse appropriation: it takes over available media content and adapts it to your own interests or needs. Feedback to media producers about such 'use' sometimes reflects predicted patterns; in other cases, it reveals major divergence from uses that were anticipated.

Despite differences between them, the three notions of 'use' distinguished here have a common thread. In each, discourse carries out a strategic role (like a physical action) in some personal or social action in which you are engaged. Combining the three types into a generic notion of 'use' can be unhelpful because it dissolves the distinction between two related but importantly different perspectives that the three sub-classes help to disentangle: whether communication (which involves both a producer and a recipient role) is seen from the viewpoint of the (real or notional) text producer or from the viewpoint of the (actual or possible) text recipient. Producer-perspective 'use' consists of implementing communicative intentions in strategic action. Recipient-perspective 'use', on the other hand, may pay little regard to producer intentions. It may even presuppose that a producer's strategic intentions (as far as these can be known) have been disregarded in order to maximise personal relevance in a communication that is treated as simply one more usable 'object'. This happens, for instance, when media audiences recontextualise published or broadcast material to fit their own interests: when a gay following builds up around a performer likely to have aimed the sexual implication of his or her act principally at straight audience desires; or when audiences find ironic or kitsch pleasures in old-fashioned advertising or films, reworking what was almost certainly anticipated into new, personal or sub-cultural kinds of significance.

How does communicative trouble arise with these three sub-classes of use? Some disputes are about 'use' in the first sense: that of strategic action in deploying signs in a given context. Perhaps the most famous example is the classic misbehaviour of falsely shouting fire in a crowded theatre.[6] Other examples include verbal harassment, committing perjury, texting bullying

---

[6] The 'fire in a crowded theatre' example, influential in US law since its use by Oliver Wendell Holmes in *Schenck v. United States* in 1919, is often inaccurately cited without the essential idea of 'falsely'. For discussion, see Kent Greenawalt, *Speech, Crime and the Uses of Language* (Oxford: Oxford University Press, 1989), pp. 190–4. See also the discussion in Harry Kalven Jr., *A Worthy Tradition: Freedom of Speech in America* (New York: Harper and Row, 1988), pp. 133–4.

messages (or images) to someone on a mobile, spraying graffiti messages on a wall, making threats of physical violence or conspiring to commit a crime.[7]

Complaints about communicative behaviour that involve my second kind of 'use' – relaying or echoing ready-made discourse – are different. One example would be leaking privileged or confidential information (e.g. in cases of insider share dealing or the leaking of commercial intelligence, for instance information about racing car design or budget plans). Other instances take the form of complaints about scheduling and editorial decisions: 'too much airtime was given to the views of extremists'; a disaster movie 'should not have been screened immediately after news about a real train crash'; a TV programme 'should only have been broadcast after the evening watershed'. Broadcasting controversies of this type typically concern alleged misjudgement (or failures of professional integrity) by media editors who bear responsibility for disseminating media content. Dispute over such complaints hangs on issues of responsibility associated with decisions that have been made about whether, and if so how, to represent or publish something.

Sometimes, controversial cases of this second, 'editorial' type involve communicative action considered to be not just ill-judged but actively exploitative or manipulative. One aspect of the outcry about alleged racism in the 2006 UK *Celebrity Big Brother* (the 'Jade Goody / Shilpa Sheti controversy') reflected this, as public commentary grappled with whether the programme makers had, through their casting and later editorial decisions, rigged the programme to show contestants in certain lights. Other disputes about discourse 'use' in this second sense involve editorial dilemmas rather than opportunistic manipulation. Almost simultaneously with the Celebrity Big Brother controversy, families of British soldiers serving in Iraq complained that a decision had been made to announce military fatalities near Basra in a news bulletin before next-of-kin had been notified. The families accepted that the decision was made to avoid any suggestion of secrecy or cover-up. But they felt that one unacceptable consequence had been needless distress to families who feared for relatives and friends possibly involved in the incident in question. In such circumstances the meaning, or 'what is being said' by the discourse, was not in question. Nobody questioned that the announcement's effects were potentially upsetting. Although dispute between the parties was triggered by the possible impact of the announcement, its crux lay in the merit or otherwise of the strategic choice made about what to communicate, when, and how.

In other circumstances again – bringing us closer to the questions of meaning with which I will be concerned in detail later – there are contestations of my third category of 'use', that of recipient-perspective discourse 'use'. This kind

---

[7] Greenawalt, *Speech, Crime and the Uses of Language*, pp. 5–7

of 'use' becomes an object of public debate or controversy when the manner of reception or appropriation of discourse is questioned, usually on moral or political grounds. Disputes arise, for instance, over what children make of what they encounter if given unrestricted web access, or about how members of the public respond to answers acquired in response to freedom of information (FOI) requests.

Overt response is only the tip of an iceberg, however, when it comes to what someone does with a text. Response is a matter both of what sense the interpreter imposes on the text and also of attitudes they hold and affective reactions (including fear, stress, contentment or euphoria) they experience in engaging with it. One currently topical area where unforeseen patterns of use present problems is that of paedophiles allegedly deriving sexual pleasure from perfectly ordinary photographs of children posted on school websites, such as conventional sports team poses or stills from school plays or assemblies. In public debate about such 'use' of photographs (which forms a backdrop to policy decisions about whether school websites should be permitted to post images of children at all), a school's intended behaviour in posting the images is not questioned. Nor is the conventional meaning of the photos. The crux of the discussion lies in the allegation of specialised appropriation, or 'use' in a sense of wilful reinterpretation or 'looking at the photos the wrong way'. If school head teachers are not to be held liable for publishing such images, then responsibility for alleged harm that the photos may do must be located elsewhere, in some aspect of the communicative event other than the act of posting. Paedophile use of pictures of children in order to gain sexual pleasure may be an equivalent *effect*, whether the pictures in question are on a paedophile website or the website of a primary school. But the intentions guiding the different acts (one of posting, the other of 'using') differ fundamentally. Sexual exploitation of conventional images by a viewer – anticipated as the daily stock-in-trade of many newspapers, magazines and forms of advertising – involves cognitive discourse 'use' that depends on active redirection by the recipient of the presumed significance of the image, a calculated redirection that goes beyond what can be understood as 'effect'.

### 2.2.2    Problems of discourse 'effect'

As discourse *effects*, we typically think of when a book or film unsettles you, makes you laugh or sends a shiver down your spine, inspires you to pursue some particular course of action or life direction, or distracts you into temporary escape from day-to-day troubles. Or we might think of when a bureaucratic sign, or piece of technical jargon, intimidates or seems to exclude you, or when someone shouts at their TV when they see something they strongly object to. While not detachable from other dimensions of publication, discourse effects are often legally defined as something distinct, even if they are linked to other dimensions of communication. For example, the legal test for obscenity is that of a 'tendency to deprave and corrupt'; and what seems its opposite, 'aversion', provides a possible defence that the effect on an audience of the allegedly obscene material is to repel rather than deprave, deterring viewers or readers from some line of action or influence rather than encouraging them towards it.

Effects such as being unsettled, frightened, distracted, intimidated or excluded – or for that matter depraved and corrupted – are different from *uses*. You no longer choose whether or how to do something with discourse (including, even if you didn't actively choose to encounter the text, making it mean whatever you want it to mean). The discourse is now doing something to you, quite possibly against your will. Communicative choice for the discourse recipient in such circumstances may be little more than having decided to walk along a particular street where a billboard is on display, or switching TV channel, or clicking through to an unexpected webpage. Someone else's use of discourse becomes its impact or effect on you (subject to intervening processes of interpretation which induce the effect, to be considered below). It doesn't help to think of this aspect of reception as 'meaning' either, because what the text does to you, whether your response is a matter of pleasure, concern, alarm or revulsion, depends on what you already think it says, shows or in some other way conveys. What makes the effect an effect, rather than a meaning, is its emergence from a short-circuited, seemingly unanalysable process (that will differ considerably between written text and images) of cognitive grasp: some preliminary level of processing or understanding.

Effects that are widely considered harmful, and which may in certain cases give rise to a cause of legal action, include where someone feels (or is felt to have been) insulted, traumatised or humiliated by something said to them, or misrepresented in something communicated to others about them. Or the alleged harm may be less an immediate effect than a social consequence: that readers or viewers were led to believe and subsequently act on inaccurate information, for example in buying a savings or pension product on the strength of inaccurate or incomplete financial services information. Such complained-of effects extend, without clear boundary lines, from emotional and cognitive effects to material consequences beyond language, typically involving some kind of loss (loss of money, loss of reputation, loss of self-esteem, loss of customer goodwill). In some legal actions direct proof of real-world effects must be produced, rather than the claimant only having to show how what was conveyed created a certain impression or gave rise to an emotional or cognitive state of discomfort or embarrassment.

Grounds for complaint about discourse 'effects' are always simultaneously, to some extent, about discourse use. Effects in relation to discourse are effects of someone else's communicative behaviour, though the effect cannot be simply read off from the behaviour. An important backdrop to any dispute about effects, accordingly, is the strategic action of the communicator. But the crux in such cases – what the parties claim to be arguing *about*, and so what must be demonstrated – is often less what someone is doing or intended to do than a claimed outcome of what they have done, whether intentionally or not.

Disputes framed in terms of effects are also to some extent about 'meaning'. Media effects are consequences not only of communicator behaviour but of what a discourse conventionally says or implies, even if this doesn't always fit neatly with what appears to have been intended. What makes something an 'effect' complaint rather than an issue of meaning is the possibility that, if you view the meaning of the complained-of discourse differently, then arguably different effects follow. At the same time, a close link between these two dimensions of a communicative event can be found in the fact that evidence for the effect being caused *by the discourse* is to be found in what it is claimed the utterance or text conveys. This 'link to meaning' is relied on to challenge any counter-claim that the effect may have been created by some other agency than the text, such as (particularly damagingly, and sometimes fatally to a complainant's case) his or her own idiosyncratic outlook or prejudiced beliefs.

### 2.2.3    Trouble with 'meaning'

The meaning of an utterance or text, we might say provisionally, lies somewhere *between* the strategic act of choosing a particular form of discourse and the consequences of that discourse for someone who is its recipient. Meaning involves what the discourse says and implies, including the function it would conventionally perform in a given situation. One reason to distinguish meaning from effect, I have suggested, is that the likelihood or predictability of a particular interpretation is more pronounced with meaning than in relation to effects, which may be more variegated and less predictable. Although 'effect' sounds a matter of direct, determinate consequences that follow from a cause, communicative effects vary significantly between members of an audience and are prompted by many things other than the discourse as well as by the discourse itself. By contrast, meanings typically involve some degree of predictability, either because they are conventionally associated with a particular linguistic or other symbolic form, or because in context meaning is prompted as an inference that the interpreter is strongly encouraged or at least highly likely to draw. Further warrant for distinguishing meaning from effect comes from the fact that, in some circumstances, the two are independently variable: you can agree with other people about what an utterance or text means (e.g. the newspaper claim that 'Four British soldiers have been killed in action near Basra') while experiencing devastatingly different effects depending on your wider beliefs or personal circumstances.

In the next chapter I discuss in detail the issue of what a *question* of meaning is, and I explore the underlying problem of what a 'meaning' is in Chapters 4 to 6. Harmful 'meanings', we might say provisionally here, are mentally constructed representations that interpreters entertain, based on conventions of language or other sign systems and on social conventions of use governing those sign systems, which contribute to harmful effects such as those indicated above (e.g. unwarranted distress, loss of money, reputation or self-esteem, etc.). Gradually refining this general notion of meaning, I will argue that meaning questions take a number of different forms rather than just the general interrogative 'what does this mean?', and that these questions invite different kinds of evidence and analysis.

## 2.3    Interaction between communication categories

How robust are the three categories I have outlined? Four scenarios described below illustrate both how interconnected they are and also the sorts of difficulty that arise because categories such as use, meaning and effect are permeable and overlapping; they are distinguishable while not being completely distinct.

*Example 1*    As a starting point, consider the idea that communicative trouble is about standards of behaviour: about what, when and how people communicate. In the political media-storm over New Labour special adviser Jo Moore's widely condemned e-mail urging in 2001 that, for the British government, 9/11 was 'a very good day to get out anything we want to bury', Moore's misdemeanour was generally regarded as an act of misjudgement: a failure of taste and decency.[8] At stake was a proposal to release information on that particular day, rather than what the material in question might mean or what significance or effect releasing it would have. For the purpose of 'burying' things, their significance was already assumed; discourse content was something to be managed as a kind of commodity (or waste product) in the face of a duty of public disclosure, rather than something whose meaning was to be negotiated or debated. In terms of the distinctions drawn in this chapter, issues raised by the episode are accordingly ones of professional judgment involved in strategic behaviour, or *use*.

*Example 2*    Now imagine a contrasting set of circumstances. In this scenario, information is not only not required to be disclosed but not permitted to be disclosed. Where newspapers are legally prevented from disclosing the names of criminal suspects or convicted sex offenders, relevant personal details

---

[8]  See Jones, *The Control Freaks*, pp. 271–303.

are sometimes still presented in news stories, in a way that allows what is called 'jigsaw' identification: the reader can build up, detail-by-detail, a picture of who the alleged offender is. In such circumstances, concerns about how, when and where to publish information are raised, as they were (albeit differently) in the Jo Moore example. In this situation, however, the editorial decision to publish involves questions of meaning as well as questions of strategic 'use'. This is because, in order to decide how serious any misdemeanour in choosing to publish a 'jigsaw' composite of this kind is, it is necessary to consider which personal details were legitimate aspects of the news story; what inferences would have been triggered by particular details in the context in which they were presented; and how far those inferences, considered together, provided a basis for identifying the individual in question. No equivalent issues of close interpretation arose in the Jo Moore episode. In fact most people who expressed shock at the 'burying bad news on 9/11' episode had little knowledge of what the documents to be released contained or how they might be interpreted. In both examples, communicative behaviour (in choosing to communicate in a particular way) is called into question. But the focus or crux of argument is different.

*Example 3*    Sometimes both the communicative behaviour and the meaning are clear, but the nature of the harmful effect, if any, is in doubt. Think of newspaper stories which state, on the strength of claims made by a competition golfer's caddie, or a footballer's agent or a fashion model's stylist, that the celebrity in question is taking time out for a spell in rehab. The 'meaning' here, roughly that 'a (particular) celebrity is taking time out to go into rehab', may be beyond dispute. Even where the meaning is not disputed, however, there may still be considerable debate over what harm follows. Is the 'trouble' that of intruding into the celebrity's privacy (since arguably the alleged addiction is not a legitimate public concern) or that of improperly disclosing information acquired in professional confidence (information which the celebrity in some sense owns)? Each of these possibilities queries the decision to publish. Alternatively, the harm might be viewed as a consequence of publication: possibly the wounding effect of damage to reputation and so, if false, then defamation because of the reduced public esteem in which the celebrity will be held if readers believe that he or she has a drink or drugs problem. The words and images don't say what kind of harm they might cause. The alternative harms that might be alleged differ in terms of what aspect of the communicative event they drew attention to; and if complained of, the causes of action, legal arguments and relevant evidence will be obliged to reflect those differences.

*Example 4*    Finally, consider effectively a reverse case of the situation just considered (which involved uncontroversial meaning linked to potentially different harms). Imagine instead a situation where the alleged harmful effect is beyond doubt: let's say serious damage to competitors caused by alleged false advertising. Suppose that industry sales figures do not support an advertising claim made on behalf of a car manufacturer that their new SUV is the market leader, 'England's favourite 4×4'. In this situation, the alleged harmful effect is likely to be traced back to falsity of meaning: that 'favourite' was a quality or attribute that should have been substantiated by relevant industry figures. A counter-argument might be made, however, that this line of reasoning about 'meaning' is flawed: 'favourite' might be argued not to mean 'most purchased' but something more qualitative, if slightly more nebulous, such as 'especially liked by those who have one and admired by those who don't'. Or alternatively, as will be shown in Chapter 10, the claim might be argued to be merely an empty (and allowable) trade puff, with an almost completely bleached meaning like saying the car is 'wonderful' or 'really special', raising no specific claim to defend at all.

## 2.4     Usefulness of communicative distinctions

Given the complications that run through even the four highly simplified scenarios I have presented, it may sound like hair-splitting to persist with distinctions between my three categories of use, meaning and effect. And yet, as I have presented them, the distinctions are drastically simplified, by comparison with the rich literature in linguistics, philosophy and law that has addressed such matters. So, are my categories too narrow and nit-picking for practical purposes, or are they too broad to meet the particulars of each slightly different set of circumstances?

Faced with such difficulty of conceptualisation, it is useful to revisit the underlying issue: whether it would be simpler – and yet still a fair reflection of how communication functions for the purpose of resolving day-to-day disputes – to settle for a highly general category, say that of 'communicative acts', and not worry about distinguishing finer points of communication such as precisely what constitutes meaning or effect.

Certainly a generic category of communicative acts or 'use' has an attraction. It contrasts neatly with corresponding 'misuse': kinds of communicative behaviour or acts which for some policy reason the law seeks to control. Blasphemy and incitement could be viewed as kinds of physical assault, simply with a linguistic rather than physical MO (or modus operandi); breach of confidence could be thought a kind of theft, in this case of information; and false advertising and misrepresentation might be understood as kinds of (language-based) fraud. Viewing communication for legal purposes as kinds of behaviour or social action has the not negligible merit of simplicity.

Doing without specifically communicative distinctions (such as those between use, meaning and effect) may nevertheless be less attractive than at first appearance. There are important differences as well as similarities between communication and physical action, including the degree of precision communication makes possible in conveying intention and attitude by comparison with physical gesture and other actions. That increased precision allows language (and to a lesser degree other kinds of sign system) to express more nuanced meanings than the significance we can reliably attribute to people's actions. But this same sophistication and precision permits more complex kinds of disguise and manipulation.

There are also four more specific reasons which I believe should be taken into account in making a case for maintaining distinctions between different aspects of communication.

The first is that 'folk' categories corresponding to the types of distinction I have drawn already exist and are widely used. A notion of undifferentiated communicative 'action' would therefore fail to reflect people's intuitions about what is going on in communication. Distinctions between aspects of communication of the type I have outlined are not something dreamt up in media law or linguistics; they are routinely invoked by people thinking and talking about social interaction. Categories such as intention, meaning, style, inference and effect all function (under a variety of descriptions) as elements of 'folk linguistic' terminology. Even where such categories are not precisely formulated or systematic, speaker intuitions and metalanguage can be extremely rich. Appealing to such categories is not, accordingly, an artificial imposition of theoretical categories when adopted for procedures used in dispute resolution that must command public credibility (as well as, in the case of jury trials, those which rely on active public participation). Terms of legal art are anchored if they reflect ordinary language categories and intuitions, even if the technical legal categories are then defined more precisely.

Secondly, disputes gravitate towards particular, contested crux points which only make sense against a backdrop of agreement on other aspects of the communication in question. Even in an intensely hostile dispute, a massive amount of common ground tacitly exists. Most of the words, as well as the relationship between them and what they mean, will go uncontested. Other aspects, ranging from what visual images show through to what atmosphere music creates or what audience a text was aimed at, may also remain uncontroversial. It is almost impossible to conduct a communicative dispute coherently if you query every detail and try to build up areas of mutual understanding word by word and perception by perception, rather than identifying points of disagreement against an accepted background.

Thirdly, a complex division of responsibility is needed, to reflect the roles played by different agents in any given communicative event. If adjudication is to be more than a very blunt instrument, it is essential to establish which responses follow from what is said or shown and which are entertained as a kind of creative appropriation or textual use. In practice, tracing the balance of responsibility between respective roles in creating meaning for most media communications is greatly complicated by the fact that they do not take place between one speaker and one hearer; media texts are typically broadcast or published to larger, internally differentiated groups, whose responses and willingness to believe will vary significantly. A publisher or broadcaster can only be reasonably held responsible for alleged effects that follow from the text itself, rather than on the basis of reactions which have only an oblique relation to conventional meaning.

Finally, distinctions within the idea of communication are needed because modern media law has to narrow down as precisely as possible its definitions of the harms it seeks to control, in order to minimise encroachment on freedom of expression.[9] Historically, in all those countries and periods where it has taken place, separation of communication law from exercise of autocratic power and overt censorship has depended on shifts away from blanket prohibition towards procedures that define liability as precisely as possible, including in relation to sensitive topics (e.g. politics, religion, sexuality). Those procedures are made successful less by enforcing punitive measures to ensure compliance than by encouraging consent to a framework of entitlement based on defined causes of action, standards of evidence, and established lines of defence. Distinguishing different elements of agency and responsibility has played a central role, in the historical development of media law and regulation, in shaping how individual cases will be handled. It has also served a further purpose: that of reducing the number of cases that arise in the first place, by making it possible to limit the scope of legal restriction while still achieving whatever communication policy objectives are pursued.

## 2.5    Communication and social harm

Categories of the sort I have described – whatever their precise detail, but modelled on and extending everyday intuition – form an important bridge between communicative behaviour as commonly understood and formal definitions of social harm as defined in media law. Different legal harms hang on different aspects of communication. Breach of confidence and whistle-blowing, for example, seem primarily matters of discourse 'use' (or at least the 'misuse' of undue disclosure); in each, aspects of meaning and effect play a part in

---

[9] For different ('intrinsic' and 'consequentialist') grounds for frameworks of freedom of expression, see Thomas Emerson, *The System of Freedom of Expression* (New York: Vintage Books, 1970); Greenawalt, *Speech, Crime and the Uses of Language*, pp. 9–39; and Eric Barendt, *Freedom of Speech* (Oxford: Clarendon, 1985). A useful introduction to theories of freedom of expression is Nigel Warburton, *Free Speech: A Very Short Introduction* (Oxford: Oxford University Press, 2009).

argument over what was done but are not the mainspring of an action. Misrepresentation, on the other hand, depends crucially on the issue of 'meaning'. There is no case to answer without an allegation that something amounts to an inaccurate representation; only once that claim is established do other issues matter, such as how intentional any inaccuracy was (e.g. whether it was fraudulent, negligent or innocent) or whether it had a material effect (e.g. by leading someone to make a purchase they would not otherwise have made). Offensiveness, by contrast, is defined principally in relation to 'effect': whether a communication caused distress, trauma or a response of outrage. Only once that is established do questions arise of whether the form, circumstances and intention behind the utterance or text warranted that reaction. Different emphasis between causes of action, as well as between different kinds of appropriate evidence and argument, evaporates if communication is merely described as a kind of undifferentiated social behaviour.

Acknowledging that distinctions are needed in an area, of course, is not the same as knowing how those distinctions should be made. Utterances and texts, as I will have reason to repeat in different contexts, do not come tagged for different attributes or kinds of harm that they may show a propensity to create. Utterances and texts have to be described, contextualised and most importantly interpreted. So distinctions of at least the sophistication of those I have outlined are likely to prove essential, despite the play of ambiguity and some degree of indeterminacy between them.

Finally, it is worth noting that to some extent the categories of use, effect and meaning I have outlined are projections onto the communication process of different *roles* involved in a speech event. Framing disputes in terms of strategic action by producers, for example, foregrounds the discourse producer's intentions. Framing disputes in terms of discourse effects highlights the recipient's or addressee's input, or effort to create meaning. Framing disputes in terms of meaning gives priority to the language or representational codes being used. A spotlight on one or other aspect of what is in every case a multidimensional interpretive dispute serves to place greater significance on that particular role or agency.

## 2.6    Summary

In this chapter, I have described a simplified, three-way classification of different aspects of trouble created in communication. I have emphasised in describing communicative trouble in this way that the three categories interlock in any given case. My focus in the chapters which follow will be on situations in which problems of *meaning* (rather than use or effect) are the crux of contestation. In focusing on meaning in this way, I am not suggesting that what I have called use and effect are less important. Choice of emphasis as a starting point is to some extent a preference on the part of the analyst (and also reflects historical reversals of relative priority among scholars as regards the respective agency of speaker, text and reader in creating meaning[10]). The three-way distinction I have drawn points towards what in later chapters I will call an 'interpretive triangle' of viewpoints on contested meaning. Three possible viewpoints, I will suggest, collide with one another whenever media communication gets into difficulty. Before going on to address tensions between the three corners of this triangle, however, I should explain more fully what constitutes a 'question about meaning' or a 'meaning issue' in the first place.

---

[10] In the essay 'Actions, speech acts, linguistically mediated interactions, and the life world' (1988), Habermas describes three directions in accounts of meaning: intentionalist semantics (Grice); formal semantics (Frege to Dummett); and use theories of meaning (Wittgenstein). 'Each of the three best-known approaches to meaning theory', he comments, 'proceeds from just one of these three ways of meaning that are bundled together, as it were, in the focal point of language; each approach then aims to explain the entire spectrum of meaning in terms of this single function of language.' Jürgen Habermas, *On the Pragmatics of Communication*, ed. Maeve Cooke (Cambridge: Polity, 1999), pp. 228–9.

# 3 Different kinds of meaning question

## 3.1 Introduction

This chapter turns more directly to the form in which questions about meaning are raised. I show how meaning issues are not reducible to a general interrogative: 'what does this mean?' In media disputes and controversies, 'meaning questions' reflect a number of different, more specific categories. Each raises its own questions about what a meaning is and what might count as evidence in support of or against it.

## 3.2 Limits of interpretation

Imagine a reader of George Orwell's *Animal Farm* who believes the book is an entertaining story about personified animals (as many books for children are) but who resists any suggestion that it might be about anything else. Should that reader be encouraged to see that 'the meaning' of the book, drawing on what is sometimes called 'the method of Aesop', lies in how it uses a fictional uprising of pigs and other animals at Manor Farm as a vehicle for political allegory? If so, its meaning is about corruption of revolutionary impulses and the rise of Stalinism, as well as about human hypocrisy in general, rather than about either farms or animals. You might try to persuade such a reader towards those arguably richer meanings by focusing on episodes or themes to which the narrative gives particular prominence. Or you might highlight parallels between what happens in the book and what happened in twentieth-century European political history. Or you might trace the author's stated concerns in this and his other books. Or you might invoke the history of the book's reception. It is possible that by such means you would succeed in persuading the reader that they had got the meaning wrong, or at least that there are other meanings to be had. Such persuasion, it is commonly noted, tends to become more difficult as the historical events themselves recede (as literature teachers often discover with *Gulliver's Travels*).

With fictional works – especially ones that seem to involve allegorical or ironic meanings – meaning emerges as part of an iterative social practice of textual interpretation. There are constantly renewed opportunities for creative reading. Some readings that are put forward may seem more warranted than others, and may enjoy wider support, including in institutional settings such as literary criticism. But each reading aims, by its own lights, at some sort of fresh insight and pleasure, even if critical controversy occasionally ensues. Latitude for reinterpretation extends to cases much less clear-cut than *Animal Farm*. Imagine, for instance, *Tess of the D'Urbervilles* understood as a story about English farming methods. Or what about *Mary Poppins*, considered as an account of class relations in Edwardian London? Even reinterpretations can be reread critically, in order to provoke new insights, as for instance when US film critic David Bordwell organises his chapter on different 'theory-led' readings of Hitchcock under the subtitle 'Seven models of *Psycho*'.[1]

What happens in cases where interpretive variation leads to conflict? On the basis of parallels between historical events and names and events in a novel (especially narrative episodes involving the character Mahound and the Jahilia brothel), one widespread reading of *The Satanic Verses* was that the novel is only a sham work of fiction, having set out to be a dismissive sneer at Islamic beliefs and teaching.[2] Or again, on the strength of resemblances between the character Brian's life and the life of Jesus, *Monty Python's Life of Brian* was held by many to be a blasphemous satire of the New Testament, conveyed by means of a series of easily mapped parallelisms. Yet both texts were admired by others, mostly for quite different reasons.

If these instances of interpretive latitude seem less comfortable than people missing an allegorical reference or going off on some frivolous reading of their own, then what about interpretive disputes that go to court? What of a defamation action, well-known for other reasons, about a minor character in the film *Rasputin, the Mad Monk* – a princess named Princess Natasha – who is raped by Rasputin but who, it was claimed, really represents the claimant, Princess Irina Youssoupoff, wife of an actual historical figure who had been involved in Rasputin's death?[3] Or a TV play about an investigative journalist which was claimed, on the basis of seventeen otherwise gratuitous resemblances (including similar age and build of the main character, and shots of the claimant's flat and local supermarket), to defame the claimant, an actual documentary maker, by imputing that he abandoned his sources and was a

---

[1] David Bordwell, *Making Meaning: Inference and Rhetoric in the Interpretation of Cinema* (Cambridge, Mass.: Harvard University Press, 1989). Bordwell suggests that 'Disputes among interpretive "approaches" renew the institution's group dynamics; heterodox interpretations remain interpretations, and as their conclusions become less shocking, a new rhetoric of recantation, conciliation, and assimilation will absorb their insights', p. 34.

[2] For discussion of the Rushdie affair, see Lisa Appignanesi and Sara Maitland (eds.), *The Rushdie File* (New York: Syracuse University Press and Institute of Contemporary Arts, 1990).

[3] The case *Youssoupoff v. Metro-Goldwyn-Mayer Pictures Ltd* [1934] 50 TLR 581 is more often cited as establishing that film is libel rather than slander. The interpretive issue, apart from whether the film princess genuinely represents the living princess, was whether being raped – if that is what the contested sequence shows – should lower you in the opinion of right-thinking people.

transvestite and shoplifter?[4] Should an interpreter, faced with close resemblances of this third kind, give up a meaning they had arrived at and switch to a meaning held by others somehow more 'in the know'?

### 3.3    Meaning not a single question

These are meaning questions but of a general kind. Each takes the general form, 'Is there a correct meaning and how will I know if I've found it?' Such questions hover between interpretation of a specific utterance or text and more fundamental problems of what a meaning is. They are fairly intractable in this general form.

Usually, interpretive questions about a given utterance or text are framed in narrower, more specific ways. Some of those ways still involve questions about what overall impression the text creates or what significance it has. Others are questions about interpretive crux points: they grapple with the meaning of keywords, phrases or scenes within some larger framework supposed to provide a (less problematic) overall interpretation.

What is more significant than the scale or extent of the discourse being asked about, however, is the focus of the question being asked. Questions at stake in legal dispute about media discourse are usually narrowed down considerably by comparison with a general interpretive invitation. This is so that they can be answered in a way that allows a further issue to be addressed: whether the meaning established meets the test for some alleged offence or infringement (Is it obscene? Is it defamatory? etc.). Perhaps the commonest interpretive question in liberal education is for this reason almost entirely absent from legal debate: whether there are potentially significant meanings hidden from view altogether, but which somehow coexist with the meanings that *have* been identified? Questions about hidden and unsuspected meanings are not usually asked in a legal setting because, unless a meaning has been complained of or is perceived as causing trouble, there is no reason for media law or regulation to show any interest in it.

It is easy to underestimate the range of 'meaning issues' that utterances and texts raise. Some people, on the other hand, query whether there are any meaning issues at all. Instead they contend that questions which *seem* to be about meaning can be reduced either to people's behaviour in arriving at a particular view or to states of affairs in the world which dictate whether any given representation is true or not. As preparation for more detailed analysis of contested meanings in later chapters, in this chapter I therefore list what I take to

---

[4] *Campbell v. BBC* [1990], unreported. See Julie Scott-Bayfield, *Defamation: Law and Practice* (London: FT Law and Tax, 1996), pp. 84–5. For an introductory account of defamation (and of most other areas of English law discussed below), see Frances Quinn, *Law for Journalists* (London: Pearson Education, 2007).

be the main question-types about meaning that occur in media disputes. I begin with questions about reference, then move to various kinds of assertion or claim that are communicated, and end with perhaps the most commonly asked but also most resistant interpretive question: whether something apparently communicated is true. A number of the areas I will outline have been mentioned already. I bring them together here in order to illustrate their range and the main contrasts between them. It should be noted, however, that I am still talking *types*. The questions are not, in the form presented, specific enough to be addressed in relation to a given complaint. In a legal action or complaint procedure, they would be contextualised much further – filled in with particulars – as we will see in later chapters.

### 3.3.1   Who or what is referred to?

This type of question concerns how the objects of discourse, whether people or things, are denoted or described in such a way that they can be accurately identified or referred to. As is clear from cases along the lines of *Youssoupoff v. MGM Pictures Ltd* referred to above, such questions can arise in defamation, where the problem they exhibit is known as 'colloquium'.[5] Such cases may be especially problematic in the genres of faction and docudrama (and are not seen off by conventional disclaimers such as prefacing a comment with 'allegedly'). They include the following main kinds: names for characters chosen seemingly at random but which turn out to be the names of real people (the most cited English legal example is a certain 'Artemus Jones'[6]); satire of recognisable public figures, thinly disguised; and indirect, vague or euphemistic description (e.g. 'a successful football manager with an interest in horse racing'; or 'one of the government's wealthier supporters in the world of PR').

In television and film voice-over, constantly shifting interconnections between what is said and what is shown in the image pose questions about precisely what verbal expressions refer to when they are combined with visual images. A broadcasting standards complaint was upheld, for example, against a crime report programme because of unfair treatment when the complainant, an

---

[5] For explanation of 'colloquium', along with numerous examples (and including discussion of *Youssoupoff v. Metro-Goldwyn-Mayer Pictures Ltd*), see Eric Barendt, 'Defamation and fiction', in Michael Freeman and Andrew Lewis (eds.), *Law and Literature: Current Legal Issues 1999*, vol. 2 (Oxford: Oxford University Press, 1999), pp. 481–98.

[6] 'Artemus Jones' was a fictitious churchwarden in Peckham (London), described in a light-hearted sketch in the *Sunday Chronicle* as enjoying himself at a motor rally in Dieppe 'with a woman who is not his wife, who must be, you know – the other thing!' The name happened to be also that of a barrister in North Wales, who successfully sued for libel (showing among other things the irrelevance of arguments made by the defendant as to intention). See *Hulton v. Jones* [1910] AC 20; [1909] 2 KB 444, and discussion in Barendt 'Defamation and fiction', p. 484; Geoffrey Robertson and Andrew Nicol, *Media Law*, pp. 58–60; Spilsbury, *Media Law*, pp. 73–5.

animal rights activist featured in one episode of the series, objected to footage of her at a demonstration shown as part of a trailer for the whole series. The trailer included narration which made the suggestion that the series would report on major crime stories and would expose 'the mechanics of the criminal mind'. The complainant successfully argued that this labelled her a major criminal.[7] In another case, the general statement 'some CID men take bribes' over a generic, almost picture-library sequence on screen for two and a half seconds of an individual police officer walking down the steps of a police station, was held defamatory of the particular officer shown in the image.[8]

Similar problems arise, as I suggested in Chapter 2, regarding how much detail is enough for criminal suspects such as alleged paedophiles to be considered recognisable (in breach of reporting guidelines) in newspaper and TV news stories that invite 'jigsaw identification'. How many and which details about someone, seemingly given for some other descriptive purpose, have the effect of cumulatively building a picture which will enable a reader to work out who the person being referred to is? And how is likelihood of identification best estimated?

Problems to do with discourse reference also arise with content presented in more extended audio-visual form, for instance in TV documentaries and features. In a standards complaint against a door-stepping documentary about 'quacks cashing in on the hopes and fears of cancer patients', the following question to one interviewee became a focus of contention: 'Why are you trying to peddle a machine which is extremely dangerous?' The issue was not about 'peddling' sales or what makes something 'extremely dangerous', but whether the referring expression 'a machine' alleged risk associated with a machine manufactured not by the interviewee, an equipment wholesaler, but by the complainant, a manufacturer whose electromagnetic therapy machine had been shown, with name and model visible, in an on-screen image much earlier in the programme.[9]

### 3.3.2    What claim is being made?

Questions about precisely what claim is being asserted by an utterance or text arise because indirect forms of communication imply meanings that may not be openly stated but may as a result of inference still be entertained by the interpreter almost as if they had been directly asserted. Claims made in discourse accordingly vary in strength depending not only on explicit hedging devices (such as 'perhaps', 'conceivably', etc.) but also according to the degree

[7]    Barendt and Hitchens, *Media Law*, p. 149.
[8]    Geoffrey Robertson and Andrew Nicol, *Media Law*, 2nd, revised edition (Harmondsworth: Penguin, 1992), p. 60. See also Scott-Bayfield, *Defamation*.
[9]    Complaint to the Broadcasting Complaints Commission from Mr Erik Nielsen regarding an episode of *The Cook Report* (Central Television, 1994), adjudicated June 1996.

of inferential indirectness with which they are made. Where there is uncertainty about what claim is being made, such uncertainty may be created by various discourse features, either in language or in the complicated and continuously changing interaction between word and image in TV or film.

Doubt about precisely what is claimed may be a result of ambiguity or vagueness in wording. When a viewer responded to a TV advert in the lead-up to Christmas that promised 'you get a set of 180 of these icicle fairy lights' but was sent a box with fewer than fifty icicles, she felt dissatisfied with an explanation from the advertiser that each icicle contains three or four LEDs (light emitting diodes), resulting in the advertised number of 'icicle fairy lights'.[10] Problems associated with claims made in advertising of different kinds and strengths have been researched in great detail, for example by Ivan Preston,[11] and are discussed more directly in Chapter 10.

In other cases, a problem of what exactly is claimed arises because of particular interpretive strategies an audience may bring to a given genre or style. How close, for instance, does a parallel between Brian and Jesus have to be for people to interpret what happens to Brian in *Monty Python's Life of Brian* as a claim about what happened to Jesus? And if only some of Brian's characteristics and actions echo the biblical story, then will other fictional characteristics – ones that do not map easily onto the Jesus story, such as the size of Brian's nose – be interpreted not as calculated to reflect but as actively implying things about Jesus?

With non-fictional audio-visual discourse, there is an added problem. Claims appear to be made simply in virtue of something being shown at all. What a photo or video clip denotes can carry a truth-claim (that something exists or existed; that something happened, etc.).[12] Usually, where such claims are relevant, they are verbally reinforced on the soundtrack. But even where this is not the case, particular claims can attach to visual images, for instance in news or documentary (where video material is for this reason sometimes accompanied by disclaimers such as 'reconstruction' or 'library footage') or in adverts, where scenarios illustrate product attributes and capabilities (and are sometimes accompanied by disclaimers such as 'not images of an actual game' in a computer game TV advert). What complicates whether such claims are being put forward or not is that expectations (leading to inferred truth-claims) are activated in some contexts, but not others – without a clear and consistent reason why. The question inevitably then arises: in borderline cases, how does a responsible advertiser or documentary maker, or in due course a viewer, decide one way or the other?

---

[10] Complaint against QVC reported in *Ofcom Advertising Complaints Bulletin*, 8 November 2004.
[11] Ivan Preston, *The Tangled Web They Weave: Truth, Falsity and Advertisers* (Madison: University of Wisconsin Press, 1994).
[12] See Paul Messaris, *Visual Literacy: Image, Mind, & Reality* (Boulder, Colo.: Westview Press, 1994), esp. chapter 4, 'Visual truth, visual lies', pp. 129–60.

### 3.3.3    Is what is claimed fact or opinion?

This type of question concerns whether a statement is properly a statement of fact or a statement of opinion. While complicated theoretically, the distinction between the two can be practically important, since even perverse or extreme opinions may be legitimately expressed where genuinely held and based on relevant available facts. Making a false claim of fact, on the other hand, has serious repercussions in many areas, ranging from defamation, through misrepresentation, insurance claims and false advertising, to perjury. Questions accordingly arise about how the difference between opinion and fact is established.

Questions of fact and opinion are complicated in relation to statements that do not make clear-cut truth-claims about events or situations but may still put forward assertions of comment, conjecture, value or opinion (and so present 'subjective truths'). Where such comment or opinion is presented, including as 'expert' opinion, it is widely assumed to derive its value from being based on established, underlying facts. But the form of expression of opinion of this kind can vary in its closeness to facts on which it is based: opinion may range from loose paraphrase or description, through varying degrees of interpretive commentary, to speculative statement of personal point of view.

In some cases, speculation may be presented in ways that lend themselves to misinterpretation as fact. Equally, there are instances where fact and opinion blend into overblown rhetoric. Consider what is ostensibly an allegation of fact: 'In office, Prime Minister Tony Blair was a murderer.' Is this, as it appears, a factual claim (and hence a potentially serious defamatory allegation about the ex-prime minister)? Deciding this question is something that must be done in context. Note straightaway that a shift is already implicit in the form of the utterance away from a direct factual claim: from specific action or event to generalisation as to disposition or identity (not 'murdered' but 'was a murderer'). This shift introduces an element of subjective interpretation or perspective inherent in the thought process needed to move from evident to general perception; but the generalisation still only holds if based on an underlying factual claim involving murder. In easily imaginable circumstances, however, such an apparent allegation of fact is more convincingly seen as a hyperbolic, rhetorical expression of opinion: an antipathy vigorously expressed and based on beliefs about political decisions leading to deaths that the former prime minister brought about in ordering the invasion of Iraq. If an interpretation based on rhetorical exaggeration can introduce doubt into even a simplified, hypothetical case of this kind, then questions may well arise about how to distinguish factual from opinion claims in more complex actual cases that involve similarly inflamed situations which encourage inflated rhetoric.

### 3.3.4    Is something biased or taken out of context?

Questions about whether some part of an utterance or discourse is taken out of context relate to the problem that, if discourse is removed from its context and placed in a new setting, it may be interpreted in a different, sometimes unfair light. Such questions are therefore essentially ones of whether, and if so how seriously, relevant context is omitted or distorted in a way that encourages meanings to be attributed that would not otherwise be inferred.

One much satirised situation in which 'context stripping' of this kind – sometimes called 'contextomy' – occurs is when extracts from reviews (e.g. of films, theatre or dance performances) are selectively taken and used as promotional material. The words 'a surefire hit' might be chosen, for instance, from the sentence 'a few years ago it would have been a surefire hit'. But quotation is always selective, if not always quite as selective as this example; so the issue is one not of clear-cut flagrant deception but of the degree of permissible risk of a false overall impression being created.

Questions of something being taken out of context are not restricted to potentially misleading blurbs of this kind. With overtly promotional material, the reader or viewer may be expected to exercise a degree of interpretive suspicion. Other areas in which similar problems arise include where quotations are used to support stories in newspaper articles and TV documentaries, as well as selective presentation of information in corporate and political statements and documents. Strategic decisions to communicate selectively may be calculated merely to convey a favourable impression, by being 'wrong in emphasis'. Or they may seem actively to mislead, by showing something in a completely false light. Specific features may be treated at disproportionate length or in special detail. Other details may be exaggerated or depicted with unusually vivid imagery. Contradictory indicators or counter-examples may be simply left out.

Moving up from this level of misleading detail to presentation of whole themes and topics, questions arise about whether one side of an argument is selectively or disproportionately put forward (for instance in arguments about whether, and if so how, impartiality should be achieved in presenting claims about global warming), or whether there is an unfair imbalance in use of close-ups of candidates in an on-screen political debate. Questions about material being selectively used and taken out of context in this way extend from local details that it may seem pedantic to challenge up to the most general issues of media balance and bias.[13]

---

[13] Debates in this area have traditionally been driven by concerns about the marketplace of ideas being restricted to a small number of broadcasters. As channels have multiplied, and with very widespread use of broadband Internet, such concerns are weakened. For broadcasting

### 3.3.5    What reaction is encouraged?

What we take to be the content of utterances cannot always be read off directly as assertion of a series of propositions, even from declarative sentences used to make seemingly straightforward statements. In many cases (some would argue, in all cases), stated propositions are embedded under a marker of attitude towards those propositions (known as a 'propositional attitude'[14]). With asserted material, the attitude that a speaker holds towards the propositions being expressed is one of belief. Because the propositional attitude of belief is so common (it may even underpin the evolution of our communicative abilities[15]), commitment to believing what you assert tends to be taken for granted. In some circumstances, however, an attitude of qualified or restricted commitment to the truth of propositions you are putting forward is also possible – even open scepticism about them.

Types of propositional attitude towards what you communicate other than belief can create irony and other kinds of non-serious communicative behaviour (including banter, story-telling, comic mimicry and jokes). What is conveyed is then less straightforward than a literal interpretation might suggest. This will also be the case if propositions are expressed with different kinds of force, for example used as indirect speech acts of warning, insulting, promising or threatening. Questions may accordingly arise whether something that is said is straightforwardly asserted, intended ironically, or intended as a speech act encouraging some particular kind of response or follow-up action. Interpretation may be a matter of implication and inference, not only of local details within an utterance but in some circumstances, in complex and varying ways, of whole texts. A film might appear to be saying one thing while – in some sections, or throughout – expressing scepticism about that content or treating that content with some shading of doubt or irony. The question then arises, perhaps especially with contested meanings ascribed to novels and media drama: if there is no obvious evidence of a detached, sceptical or humorous attitude on the part of the communicator, then what makes the interpretive judgments that audiences attribute anything more than an impression or prejudice about what attitude they think the text is likely to have adopted towards its subject matter?

Issues of this kind arise not only with postmodern art-works but also in fairly routine advertising. Establishing whether an advert is false and misleading, or

background (prior to the latest phase of public anger at TV fakery), see Brian Winston, *Lies, Damn Lies and Documentaries* (London: British Film Institute, 2000). See also Guy Starkey, *Balance and Bias in Journalism: Representation, Regulation and Democracy* (Basingstoke: Palgrave, 2006). A detailed account of how bias manifests itself, and how it can be analysed, is Barrie Gunter, *Measuring Bias on Television* (Luton: University of Luton Press, 1997).

[14] For propositional attitudes, see John Saeed, *Semantics* (Oxford: Blackwell, 1997), pp. 286–7.

[15] For discussion of this issue, see for example Dan Sperber, *Rethinking Symbolism* (Cambridge: Cambridge University Press, 1975); and Sperber and Wilson, *Relevance*.

(as the ASA Advertising Code allows[16]) *patently* false and therefore not misleading, depends on navigating successfully through questions of this kind, as I
will show in Chapter 10. So may deciding whether an utterance is a statement of
fact or opinion, since the communicator's attitude towards the content must be
assessed alongside the stated content itself. So may deciding whether some
utterances that purport to be statements of opinion are better understood as
attempts to stir up feelings, or incite or solicit action, becoming as a result what
are sometimes called 'inchoate crimes'.[17]

Opening up a gap between form and force in communication requires us to ask in
a more nuanced way how utterances relate to their social context. It also requires
that we think carefully about the intentional behaviour of the author/producer/
editor. In TV coverage of a demonstration, for example, was a placard proclaiming
'Behead the enemies of Islam' a criminal solicitation because of its imperative
form? If so, was the utterance the responsibility of the individual demonstrator and
simply relayed by the broadcaster, or was it a message communicated by proxy by
the broadcaster, if that broadcaster is perceived as sympathetic to the sentiment – or
even without that supposed sympathy? Alternatively, was the placard merely a
rhetorically exaggerated opinion statement in a media war of words, taking its trope
of enemies and death from a perception of Muslim deaths as war casualties to be
equally violently fought against?

### 3.3.6    What follows if you interpret like this?

Questions from this perspective prioritise the likely impact of an utterance or
discourse, and speech acts are viewed from the point of view of the addressee or
person referred to.[18] Typical issues are whether a contested discourse might
embarrass, humiliate or ridicule the addressee or person referred to, so prompt-
ing anger or outrage; or whether it implies something that might cause the
addressee or person referred to to be shunned or lowered in public esteem.

Such questions mix conventions specifically at work in communication (such
as how utterances are typically used or how people are depicted in film or

---

[16]  The first principle of the ASA's code (2.1) is that 'all advertisements should be legal, decent,
honest and truthful'. Less well known is principle 2.8, that 'the Codes are applied in the spirit as
well as in the letter'. See codes at www.asa.org.uk.

[17]  The term 'inchoate' is discussed directly in Emerson, *The System of Freedom of Expression*,
chapter 11, 'Inchoate crimes: solicitation, attempt, conspiracy', pp. 401–12.

[18]  See J. L. Austin, *How To Do Things with Words* (Oxford: Oxford University Press, 1962). Note
that *this* Austin is sometimes confused in legal discussion with the nineteenth-century legal
philosopher John Austin. Legal Austin is prominently referred to throughout work on legal
meaning by the Oxford legal scholar H. L. A. Hart, roughly contemporaneous with the ordinary
language philosopher also at Oxford, J. L. Austin. For discussion of perlocutionary force and
effects, see Thomas, *Meaning in Interaction*, pp. 49–50; Levinson, *Pragmatics*, pp. 236–42. The
issue of distinguishing illocutionary force from perlocutionary force is discussed in more detail
below, in Chapter 11.

television) with speculation as to likely human reactions, social attitudes and behaviour. What is in question is the causal chain from discourse to alleged effect, with meaning viewed as a mediating level of representation between the two. In cases of alleged objectionable or inflammatory discourse (such as discourse held to be pornographic or racially offensive), it is often suggested that the option commonly exists of simply walking away, changing the TV channel, or in some other way ignoring the discourse in question. Even where such an option is available, however, the question arises whether weakly implied meanings are still communicated and left unchallenged: meanings, for instance, to do with the self-worth or future safety of the addressee or person(s) referred to, or even of witnesses who do not intervene. There may also be implied meanings about the scope and acceptability of what it is possible to say or show.

### 3.3.7    Who will read it this way?

This type of question concerns what a media scheduler would call a text's demographic, or the mix of social groups likely in its reception. Relevant questions are less about *who* is likely to read or watch, however, than about *how* that particular audience segment will interpret or have interpreted something.

Questions of this kind are important because of social variation in attitudes and taste. Such variation is relevant not only to general issues of taste and decency (cf. discussions about a TV 'watershed' or 'junk food advertising to children'), but also in terms of more complex problems of interpretation. Because so much interpretation is inferential, questions arise regarding what 'common knowledge' any given audience will activate in making meaning. Such questions affect not only whether a discourse should be interpreted as factual, ironic or pastiche, but also what specific 'innuendo meanings' it might convey. An 'innuendo meaning', as the term is used in defamation, is an interpretation that requires insider knowledge, such as interest-specific, community-specific or generation-specific cultural references (which will vary dramatically, for instance, between the presumed interpretive community for a children's bedtime story on the radio, *Al Jazeera* news, and the sport pages of the the *Daily Telegraph*). The problem of innuendo meaning is discussed in detail in Chapter 9. In its most general forms this type of interpretive question is whether 'virtually anyone told X will hear it as meaning Y', or whether 'only people in group Z, when told X, are likely to hear it as meaning Y'.

### 3.3.8    What does this normally mean?

Questions of this type, if asked about a whole article, programme or web page, come closest to being a general interpretive invitation. The question is restricted only by the 'normally': by the requirement that the meaning should be what the text is likely to mean to an ordinary, average or reasonable interpreter likely to come into contact with it.

The immediate prompt to a highly general question of this type may be something quite specific: a problem to do with obscure words, slang, dialect, idioms or claimed inferences that seem esoteric or obscure. Alternatively, such questions may be the result of the discourse as a whole seeming vague or ambiguous, and so difficult to see the point of. Or they may arise because two conflicting yet to some extent plausible interpretations have become gridlocked, as I have suggested happens at meaning troublespots. Or they may arise simply because a meaning that is completely obvious to everyone else is flatly denied by one of the parties, and it is necessary to establish beyond credible counter-argument what that obvious meaning is.

### 3.3.9    Is it true?

There are various legal harms associated with discourse *not* being true: it may be defamatory; it can falsely advertise something for sale; a complainant may act in reliance on a text or utterance that turns out to be false, for instance if they have sought professional advice but subsequently suffer a loss; or *other* people may act in reliance on an utterance or text (a false report or inaccurate review), then in some way injure the complainant; or something false may shock or traumatise the complainant. With so many possible significances, questions as to truth and falsity feature large in law as well as in the work of regulatory bodies dealing with press and media complaints.

Historically, focus on meaning as a matter of truth and falsity has pulled 'meaning' questions towards events, situations and states of affairs in the world. This tendency is reinforced by the courts, because they are concerned with and can deal with facts more easily than tackling abstract problems of semantics. Facts against which contested utterances are tested can be adduced and proved; so by being thought of as mainly truth-bearing, meaning is directed towards evidential requirements that would be less easily met for other dimensions of meaning. Conveying information (and valuing information as either truthful or leading towards truth by being capable of being disproved) is also central to information-focused notions of the purpose of communication, and an important aspect of established frameworks of freedom of expression.

Questions of meaning are far more often about when something is untrue than when it is true. In its classic form,[19] lying involves a combination of four elements: a speaker intends to create the effect of misleading and in doing so shows lack of

---

[19] There are many illuminating studies of lying and deception, tempting the view that this is an especially rich field. See especially Sissela Bok, *Lying: Moral Choice in Public and Private Life* (Brighton: Harvester Press, 1978). For a cognitive linguistic account, see Eve Sweetser, 'The

sincerity; the utterance functions as a kind of verbal smokescreen, offering a representation at odds with how the speaker herself or himself understands the situation being referred to; the facts of that situation are not accurately reflected in the conventional or likely meaning of the utterance; and the hearer sees a stated or implied meaning but not the intention to deceive behind what is represented. Different combinations of speaker-belief and actual states of affairs result in a patterned set of possible outcomes: honest assertion (where the speaker says what she or he believes to be true); mistakes or errors (where the speaker says something he or she believes to be true but which turns out to be false); unsuccessful lies (where the speaker, uncommonly, intends to mislead but says something that turns out to be true); and lies, which in their canonical form are demonstrably false and insincere statements, communicating what the speaker does not believe.

What distinguishes a prototypical lie from an innocent misrepresentation accordingly cuts across three domains, in each of which we commonly apply the word 'true': a factual domain (what the given situation is); an epistemo-logical domain (what the communicator knows or does not know about that situation); and an ethical or moral domain (of 'honest speaking' or good intention, as opposed to deception). Both the form and the effect of an error and a lie may be identical in a given situation; it is the intent that differentiates the two cases. Asking questions about responsibility for truth in discourse needs to pick its way through these complications.

As regards media discourse in particular, opinion polls suggest that few people conclude, even if media programming isn't crowded with obvious lies, that media deception is rare. Rather, viewers, listeners and readers wonder about borderline cases: different shadings of untruth or disingenuousness. They talk of obscurity or obfuscation; of unreliable statements and seemingly calculated vagueness; of half-truths, tall stories and fibbing; of being economical with the truth and styles of media artifice that create a misleading impression; of 'concealing relevant and providing misleading information'; of things that were 'not materially misleading' but which 'should have been more transparent'; of people shown as occupying roles (such as competitors in quiz shows) that in reality they do not have; and of an array of rhetorical devices including euphemism, exaggeration, inconsistency and omission all seemingly aimed at disguise or avoiding precision about what the communicator believes to be the case. The contemporary, much-debated crisis of confidence in media institu-tions is beyond doubt a crisis of communicators' perceived truthfulness.

definition of lie: an examination of the folk models underlying a prototype', in D. N. Holland and N. Quinn (eds.), *Cultural Models in Language and Thought* (Cambridge: Cambridge University Press, 1987), pp. 43–66. In the wider context of how communication works, see Gibbs, *Intentions in the Experience of Meaning*, pp. 153–60. For a scenario-based empirical study, see L. Coleman and P. Kay, 'Prototype semantics: the English word "lie"', *Language*, 57 (1981), 26–44.

Any actual 'is it true?' question is extremely complex, in that techniques exploiting gradations of directness and indirectness create uncertain scales of implication. 'Misleading' rather than false or untrue discourse alters the conventional balance in lying or deceitful utterances between intention, facts, verbal form and hearer expectation. The hearer's own assumptions and expectations play a greater role in interpreting, but in doing so allow the hearer or reader to be misled. The varying balance between roles must therefore be weighed up in apportioning responsibility, with questions arising about the techniques used in *guiding* interpretation, for example by giving special prominence to features of a story by headlining them or signalling them prominently at the beginning or end of a piece. In such circumstances a communicator is not necessarily someone stating something he or she doesn't believe but just someone who encourages, or even merely allows, a hearer to entertain an idea or belief that the speaker herself/himself doesn't hold but that the hearer is prepared to entertain because of what the speaker has said.[20] Only in limited circumstances will it be possible to answer the question whether something is true on the basis of clear evidence (where the claim put forward can be linked to documents, statistics, photographic evidence or witness statements). In many cases, factual evidence will be inconclusive because the contested claim was vague, suggestive, ambiguous or evasive, and if the utterance was formulated sufficiently carefully there is unlikely to be a smoking gun of public deception.

The most difficult area of questioning provoked by an 'is it true?' approach to meaning lies in a natural follow-up question: whether people feel it matters. Scales of reprehensibility operate in relation even to clear-cut lies. Lies about important subjects may be considered inexcusable while, as Sissela Bok and others have shown, small-scale fibs, so-called harmless lies, placebos, white lies and excuses are not, and may be viewed by some people positively or as inevitable. While questioning of the 'dodgy dossier' and the 45-minute claim about Saddam Hussein's alleged WMDs was widely perceived as an important task of investigative journalism, whatever view was taken subsequently, grappling with minor misrepresentations in media discourse is often viewed as pedantry, less a matter of meaning troublespots than meaning troublemakers.

Scales of seriousness brought to bear on deception come into play in relation to context and genre as well as topic. The crime of perjury, or lying in giving evidence in court, is considered extremely serious by most people. So is

---

[20] In 'The definition of lie' (pp.56–7), Sweetser argues that indirect expressions of this kind transfer responsibility for accepting the truth of an assertion or proposition to the hearer. This is preferable to the speaker because it reduces liability for meaning; for the hearer, such indirectness serves other, complementary purposes: Sweetser claims it is polite, in seeming not to assume control over the hearer's beliefs. The hearer is also encouraged to trust the speaker's lack of intention to insist. This builds up trust that the speaker is not trying to persuade or deceive. The interpreter also trusts her own or his own judgment, having worked for the meaning rather than being told.

misrepresentation by impersonating other people as part of identity theft or fraud. But describing something offered for sale in terms which cannot on any strict interpretation be true begins for many informants to fall in a grey area between strictly false advertising and legitimate puffery. 'Over-polishing a CV' in ways that misrepresent facts at a job interview elicits mixed reaction from groups of informants, varying from indefensible conduct through to understandable determination in a highly competitive employment market.[21]

As the CV example suggests, it is not uncommon for people to tolerate an informal category of justifiable falsehood or forgivable or excusable lies. That category of permissible deception (including fibs and presentational artifice) typically includes simplifying lies to children (as well as, in some political systems and movements, paternalistic lies to whole populations or electorates); comforting lies to the sick and dying; pragmatic lies during a short-term crisis; lies made to proven enemies; lies to protect colleagues, peers and clients; and 'noble lies' told for the greater good of the public, the corporation or the cause.[22] So secondary questions arise in relation to the ethics and politics of lying as well as about whether a text or utterance is true or untrue.[23] 'Is it true?', as a result, is rarely a simple question of truth or falsity. Rather, it is a concoction of issues not only to do with accuracy but also involving: honesty or sincerity (in relation to motive or intention); fairness (in relation to some notionally balanced overall view of a topic); relative priority (in relation to competing interests and demands); and defensibility (in relation to prevailing conditions of communication and action).

Even so, asking the question whether an utterance or text is telling or not telling the truth can still prove irrelevant. Not all discourse puts forward truth-claims (for instance vulgar abuse and many kinds of offensive utterances do not); so some verbal acts can be crimes without actually asserting anything (e.g. threats, conspiracies, and incitements to religious or racial hatred). Yet some genres of discourse which do not put forward truth-claims still offer significant, even defining representations of the world (such as fiction, poems and drama, song lyrics and satire); where the meanings and effects of such texts are disputed, it is not their truth according to some verifiable standard that is in question but some other kind of validity or resonance – perhaps their originality or the balance between, or synthesis of, different positions they present. We fail

---

[21] One media controversy among many in this area concerned a candidate in the 2008 television business competition series *The Apprentice*, who got through to the next week's round as a representative of desirable business qualities despite direct exposure in one episode of his attempt to deceive the panel by faking parts of his CV.

[22] See Bok, *Lying*.

[23] See Bok, *Lying*, including a useful selection of extracts from Augustine, Kant, Machiavelli and others at the end of the book.

to grasp the power or effect of many forms of representation if we treat them as ultimately not meaningful if they do not make truth claims.[24]

## 3.4     Conflicting attitudes towards questions of meaning

'Meaning questions', then, come in different varieties. Bringing them together draws attention to how genuinely varied they are, rather than being simply variants of a common underlying interrogative: 'what does this mean?' There is also, I hope, a further value in listing the different question types. When shown in their variety, the meaning questions offer a reply to scepticism regarding whether 'meaning' is a significant dimension of disputes that present as practical problems about money, reputation, purchasing decisions or power, rather than about the meaning of what someone has said, written or broadcast on a given topic.

Drawing up a checklist of different meaning questions makes it easier to ask how far interpretive debates justify their place in what might be called a 'mine-field' view of meaning: the view that broaching any given meaning question is a bad idea because it will set off secondary explosions of disagreement that it is then difficult to escape. That perceived risk of getting lost in uncertainty about where detonations of contested meaning will come from next contrasts strongly with an apparently opposite, but equally dismissive perception of contested meaning: that if you take a hard-headed look, there are few if any specifically meaning issues to get worked up about, just the facts of the case and the interests of the parties. Acknowledging how extensive and varied meaning questions are may offer a corrective to this view.

Increased awareness of meaning issues is unlikely, however, to encourage many people to want to investigate them. Even where such questions are acknowledged, a common response kicks in: what might be called the 'don't even go there' approach. The minefield image gives reason for caution. Sometimes, however, the view springs from a different perception: that, while you understand most things better by concentrating harder on them, doing the same with meaning only unsettles your spontaneous intuitions. If your imme-diate perception of what is communicated in a given situation is disturbed, then so many alternative ways of looking at what might be meant can crowd in that retreat becomes inevitable. Although seemingly the opposite of the hard-nosed, 'few if any meaning issues' view, this view of uncertainties over meaning multiplying even where there weren't any before leads to the same outcome: a preference for handling media meanings at the level of attitudes and behaviour rather than focusing on processes involved in interpretation.

---

[24] On observation statements and verification, see Hilary Putnam, 'The meaning of "meaning"', in Hilary Putnam, *Mind, Language and Reality: Philosophical Papers*, vol. 2 (Cambridge: Cambridge University Press, 1975), pp. 215–71.

## 3.5      Summary

In this chapter I have suggested that 'meaning issues' arise in disputes and controversies in a number of different forms. The general question 'what does this mean?' is usually too vague to capture the crux of alternative interpretations being contested. Distinguishing different sorts of question that arise about meaning can help to clarify what sorts of evidence and argument are appropriate in any given instance. It can also help in understanding prevailing social attitudes towards whether it is worth investigating meaning at all, rather than addressing disputes and controversies at other levels (e.g. in terms of overall attitudes and behaviour). To see why trying to resolve interpretive disputes without tackling problems of meaning is unlikely to be effective, we must move from considering how meaning becomes a question to examining how meanings are created.

*Part II*

# Making sense of 'meaning'

# 4    Meaning and the appeal to semantics

## 4.1    Introduction

Faced with the challenge of assigning meaning, semantics is an obvious starting point in terms of theory and method. However, this chapter argues that while semantics contributes important insights, the scope and goals of semantics as a field leave it mostly unable to contribute much to arbitrating in or resolving social disputes. This is partly because what is disputed is typically a matter of utterances and texts whose interpretation depends on extensive, situated inference by audiences. Inferential interpretation, as we will see more in Chapter 5, opens up meanings that go far beyond what can be investigated in terms of semantic representation. In this chapter, I establish a number of different understandings of what meaning is.

## 4.2    Meaning not an 'open and shut' case

Near a university campus where I used to work there is a pharmacy, instantly recognisable as you approach because of a large white sign fixed to its gable-end. The sign says 'PHARMACY' and has a large green cross on it. Directly below the word 'pharmacy', in large, upper-case letters, is the word 'OPEN', part of the same metal sign permanently fixed to the brickwork. For much of any 24-hour period, the next thing you see is an iron security grille across the shop's entrance and windows, indicating that the pharmacy is definitely not open for business. In such circumstances, what does the apparently simple word 'OPEN', so prominently fixed to the pharmacy building wall, actually mean?

As an unalterable sign, it seems not to signify, as a potential customer might initially infer, 'now open for business'. Yet 'open for business' would be what you might call the conventional meaning of the word 'open' if used as a shop sign (e.g. when seen hanging on a reversible card inside a shop's glass door). Perhaps if OPEN doesn't mean this, it simply reinforces the attention-attracting sign 'pharmacy', conveying only an indication of 'general willingness to serve' that is roughly equivalent to 'welcome'? Some collocations of the word 'open' lend support to such a meaning. 'Open house', 'open door policy', 'open-minded' and 'open person' all indicate something or someone habitually or temperamentally open, and so receptive rather than necessarily open at the present moment.

But even if that is what 'open' means in this case, is the shop-owner still failing in some kind of communicative responsibility by appearing in this context to encourage the other sense: a belief that the shop is actually open for business (especially as people might be driving round in a hurry in need of medicine)? Or is the fact that the sign is a permanent fixture on a building wall – and so hardly susceptible to being changed each time the shop opens and closes – sufficient reassurance to any reasonable passer-by that there is no intention to mislead. In my experience, groups of informants divide roughly 50:50 between those who consider the fixed-wall 'open' sign a perfectly acceptable instance of modern signage, and those who consider it a mischievous abuse or deception.

One possible approach to understanding what is going on with 'open' here is to look at the word's sense relations: how 'open' relates to other words in its semantic field. These include its synonyms (same meaning), antonyms (opposites), hyponyms (words for kinds or types of whatever the word denotes), meronyms (words for parts of whatever the word denotes) and superordinates (the class of things to which whatever is denoted by the word belongs). We might in this case say, as part of a 'sense' exploration, that 'open' is normally the opposite of 'closed', and that this is part of what gives the word its meaning. Yet in this context 'open' appears, under one interpretation, to mean the same as rather than the opposite of 'closed'. So why should 50 per cent of informants think the use of opposites as synonyms acceptable? There do exist cases where a word can have two meanings pointing in almost opposite directions at the same time (what are sometimes called 'antagonyms', as with 'ordinary', 'idealist' or contemporary 'wicked'); but the anomaly with 'open' here points less to another sense than to a different *whole view* of meaning: a view in which consideration is given to what the speaker intends and what the hearer brings to the creation of meaning rather than expecting to find meaning in the sign itself or in its relations to other signs in a semiotic system. What makes 'open' mean something different may be not so much the word's conventional meaning as some aspect of its use. Introducing an idea of use, and processes of meaning making that involve intention and inference, of course opens up the possibility that hearers will differ from one another as regards what motives they impute to the speaker, and what expectations about 'open' (as well as about discourse in general) they bring to the task of interpretation. Hence, perhaps, the 50:50 split among my informants.

Asking questions about meaning in this way begs a wider question. If implied meanings and inference are involved, then how predictable will a word's meaning be? Inferences will vary. And anyway inferences are something for which the reader or listener must presumably shoulder at least part of the responsibility. With 'open', we may also need to query whether the fixing of the sign to the building's brickwork is part of what the word means. 'Open' may depend for its interpretation on design qualities and manufacture of the wall-sign as well as its location and assumed purpose. Another possibility, linking back to the idea of language as a social system or code, is that the word 'open' is midway in a process of language change: some speakers may use the expression in an extended sense, as in the collocations above, while others do not (or not yet). The innovative, 'normally open' use may stretch the word's conventional meaning until that extended meaning becomes conventionalised, over time, as a change in or addition to the established range of senses. If so, 'open' signs may in future broaden and come to mean something like 'welcome' or 'we very much want your business'... and even 'closed for now, but open in the old sense later'.

## 4.3    Meaning wonderland

Even the apparently trivial case of a one-word shop sign carries us quickly into deep water with meaning. Or changing the image, the example shows, in Michael Dummett's expression, how high the sea of language runs.[1] How variable, though, can the meaning of any given sign be? And what implications follow from such variability as regards either our general concept of meaning or our grasp of meaning in a given case? More particularly, what degree of responsibility do speaker and hearer bear in respect of meaning? Such issues will inevitably arise wherever, as here (and as deconstruction has shown), words can be unpicked to reveal instability in what normally appear to be stable systems of interpretation.

In relation to public *disputes* over meaning, some further issues need to be explored. Why, if meaning is something fixed and stable, should disputes occur at all? Any 'meaning in/meaning out', fixed-channel model of communication as a code carrying messages between people should predict that there will only rarely be *meaning* breakdown. You might expect moments where the code is misunderstood (e.g. with children, with non-native speakers, or in cases of language pathology); and you might expect moments where there is clear-cut, intended manipulation or deception, in cases of outright lying. But instead we seem faced with animated and highly focused disputes over alternative accounts of meaning in which many contradictory meanings – but still not *all* meanings – may be claimed as possible.

My aim in pursuing these questions is not purely academic or theoretical. Some account is needed of how competing meanings come to be put forward at what I have called 'meaning troublespots'. If disputes which may ultimately be

---

[1]  A number of metaphorical fields recur in thinking about meaning, including sea and deep or dangerous water, woods and forests, and darkness and battles. Michael Dummett's key essays on meaning are collected as *The Seas of Language* (Oxford: Oxford University Press, 1993), and Ogden and Richards refer to 'The Enchanted Wood of Words' in *The Meaning of Meaning*, p. 138.

less about meaning than about conflicting interests are to be viewed as still in an important sense problems to do with meaning, then it is essential to refine the sense of what meaning *is* and what regularities or rules it is subject to.

I chose the 'open' example because single words, rather than extended texts or complex, mixed media or multimodal discourse, are a good place to start. Apart from the scale and apparent simplicity of individual words, they are the level of communication at which people tend to place most faith in stable meaning. The level of the individual word is the level at which it is usually felt easiest to declare with confidence that a given meaning for a word is 'correct' or 'incorrect', partly because word meanings can be checked against the interpreter's own mental lexicon (i.e. against their own intuitions about language) or in a public resource such as a dictionary. With the possible exception of specialised dictionaries of symbols (e.g. of religious symbols), it is rare to find equivalent confidence displayed regarding meanings for images or whole films or novels. With more extended discourse, people seem more ready to accept that some process of meaning *making* is needed to establish what something means, and that there may not be a conclusive answer. What makes the 'open' sign discussed above thought-provoking is that, as a one-word message, it seems initially obvious what it should mean.

'Open' turned out, though, not to be a case like Humpty Dumpty's behaviour towards Alice in Lewis Carroll's *Through the Looking-Glass*. Remember that Humpty famously rebukes Alice with his assertion, 'in rather a scornful tone', that 'when I use a word it means just what I choose it to mean – neither more nor less'. Humpty assigns to words meanings he likes rather than meanings other people will recognise (e.g. 'glory' for Humpty means 'a nice knock-down argument' and 'impenetrability', rather more obscurely, means 'we've had enough of that subject, and it would be just as well if you'd mention what you mean to do next, as I suppose you don't mean to stop here all the rest of your life'[2]). For semanticists, much of the interest in this often-quoted passage lies in how it demonstrates the need for social convention or agreement in establishing what signs mean. If we abandon the security of linguistic convention, in a sort of looking-glass world, then what follows is absurdity or madness. But linking of words and perverse individual choices of meaning like Humpty's is not what is happening in my 'open' example. What is in question is use of an expression in a way that modifies its core meaning in a new direction. Altered use puts the resulting contextual or situated meaning in tension with the established, con ventional meaning. 'Bending' words in this way can be creative, developing extended or figurative senses that lead, by way of gradually changing propor-tions between use of the alternative senses, towards longer-term semantic

---

[2] Lewis Carroll [1871], *Through the Looking-Glass and What Alice Found There*, illustrated by Helen Oxenbury (London: Walker Books, 2005), chapter 6.

change. By contrast 'twisting' words is a common description applied to lying, verbal deception and interpretive recalcitrance. Part of what we need to understand, accordingly, if we are to see how meaning conflicts arise, is what makes twisting different from bending: how tensions between meanings in a given context can be created, for good or ill, as a by-product of communication's inherent creative potential.

### 4.3.1   Fixed and variable meaning

The interpretive challenge presented by the word 'open' suggests that 'dictionary meaning', even for a single word, may very much underdetermine interpretation in a given context. Even if attempts are made to push problems of meanings that exceed definition out of mind, those problems resurface whenever pressure is applied to what is being communicated.

This can happen even when people are grappling with matters of life and death. In a radio interview at the end of a murder trial, for example, the grandmother of a man who had pleaded guilty to stabbing six people to death in three different cities claimed through her sobs, 'he is not a murderer'. In apparent frustration at other people's incomprehension, she is heard continuing to say over and over, 'he is not a murderer'. As her grandson was taken away to begin his sentence, what could she mean by this statement, beyond expressing her own sense of shock and humiliation? Almost certainly, the grandmother was not contesting a core meaning of 'murderer' as a combination of basic meaning components, 'intend' + 'cause' + 'die'.[3] Since neither the facts of 'cause' or 'die' had been contested, the grandmother seemed pained and confused by something else: most likely by whether 'intend' really is inherent in 'murderer', rather than 'murderer' in legal terms involving some less fixed compound of capability, responsibility and intent. If 'murder' involves debatable states of mind, however, and is affected by mitigating circumstances that distinguish 'murder' from 'manslaughter' and other kinds of killing with diminished responsibility, then the word's meaning seems less easily defined than the core conceptual meaning suggests, and which will be applied to her thereafter as relative of a 'murderer'. Uncertainties and changing beliefs about justice and

---

[3] Note that Fodor has commented extensively on 'murder'. Even in 1970 he was suggesting (for very different reasons from the social dimensions indicated here) that definition is not just building with features. See Jerry Fodor, 'Three reasons for not deriving kill from cause to die', *Linguistic Inquiry*, 1 (4) (1970), 429–38. For an alternative account, see Lecercle, *Interpretation as Pragmatics*, p. 130. David Crystal provides a short history of meanings of 'murder', with particular reference to the relationships between Normans and Anglo-Saxons in medieval England, in *The Stories of English* (Harmondsworth: Penguin, 2005), pp. 125–6.

punishment may affect the meaning of 'murder', and so of 'murderer', in ways that are not reducible to 'semantic primes'.[4]

Construing even individual words on a given occasion of use is not a matter of taking a meaning off-the-shelf but rather a miniature version of the more open-ended, context-sensitive process of interpreting a whole utterance or longer text. It is therefore questionable how useful it is to think of the meaning of an expression, let alone the meaning of a whole newspaper article, novel, TV programme or film, as being fully *in the words*, or in a combination of words and pictures or multimodal texture, rather than at least partly in how the particular form of expression – whether word, web page or DVD – is shaped by the interpreter to produce that meaning. In everyday communication, few people query characterisation of meaning as something you create by applying common sense and understanding of the world in addition to your familiarity with a particular language or set of representational conventions. In fact, to invest too much faith in the idea that you can grasp communication by appealing only to the meanings of signs in a fixed code risks a kind of woodenness of response and in worst cases a kind of psychosis.

But it will not always feel like that. When the flow of meaning making is for some reason interrupted, different models of meaning surface: meaning prescribed by dictionaries, fixed in texts, endorsed by reference books and determined by authorities. It is not so surprising that the idea of meaning slipping beyond our grasp should be a worrying prospect, except in sheltered circumstances such as games, puns and jokes, since meaning is something we *need* to control at least sufficiently to avoid absurdity and madness. In legal contexts in particular, a view of meaning that legitimised meaning variation on any scale would magnify problems already faced in deciding what a legitimate interpretation is, making the day-to-day business of determining meanings in court or regulatory tribunals extremely difficult.

## 4.4 Meanings of meaning

Pondering 'the meaning of meaning' as the world of events and actions rushes by invites scepticism, even derision. The situation is hardly helped, either, by the recursive possibility: pondering 'the meaning of the meaning of meaning', and so on. But the complexity inherent in meaning is not easily sidestepped, on either an everyday or a theoretical level. Ignoring complexity in how meanings

---

[4] 'Features' and 'social' are not the only ways of approaching definition. For discussion of sense boundaries and construal of word meaning, see William Croft and D. Alan Cruse, *Cognitive Linguistics* (Cambridge: Cambridge University Press, 2004), pp. 109–40. On connections between definition and social (including legal) argument, see Roy Harris and Christopher Hutton, *Definition in Theory and Practice: Language, Lexicography and the Law* (London: Continuum, 2007).

are created and conveyed leads only to simplistic appeals to spurious authority. Yet it is easy to share a sense of caution in setting off down the theoretical road where multiple meanings are concerned. When notions of stable or correct meaning are questioned, the door can seem flung open to overblown claims that meaning cannot be ascertained at all, that analysis leads only into an abyss of non-meaning, and that persuasion succeeds or fails only by the sheer force of someone's rhetorical will-to-power. If investigations of meaning are to contribute to understanding interpretive disputes, they need to steer a route between these opposing positions.

### 4.4.1    Types of meaning

Where the purpose of investigating meaning is theoretical (for instance in linguistics, psychology or anthropology), most inquiries narrow down their field of investigation at the outset. They do not study meaning in general but instead a specialised field such as linguistic, psychological or anthropological meaning. Within any chosen field, they then often narrow down further. For instance, the focus of linguistic meaning may be on truth-conditional meaning; in philosophy of language, it may be on questions of reference or the theory of names. Disciplines conduct valuable research without being diverted down side avenues or into endless meta-questions partly because each takes for itself a more precise object of knowledge and set of investigative methods. By contrast, to explore meaning in a wider discussion of social trouble requires broader – inevitably less detailed – engagement with what people typically understand by meaning. Without such breadth, any given meaning problem is likely to be held to fall outside a theoretical frame placed on it; and if the questions always fall somewhere outside the precise field anyone claims to know about, then academic contributions to understanding meaning will seem merely an irrelevance or even an impediment.

Trying to grasp 'meaning' as a general concept can be like St Augustine's famous reflection on the concept of time, 'If no one asks me, I know; if anyone asks and I try to explain, I don't know.'[5] This similarity between describing time and describing meaning was noted by Ludwig Wittgenstein in his discussion of the elusiveness of meaning in language use and difficulties facing us in 'clearing misunderstandings away'.[6] Wittgenstein used the analogy to explore how the meanings of propositions that seem to stand for thoughts function as many

---

[5]  'Quid est ergo tempus? si nemo ex me quaerat scio; si quaerenti explicare velim, nescio'; see
    St Augustine, *The Confessions* (London: Hendrickson Christian Classics, 2004), book II, ch. 14, no. 7.

[6]  Wittgenstein, *Philosophical Investigations* 42[e] para 89. In an early article, Levinson showed how
    different 'language games' in Wittgenstein's sense, and constraints imposed on language use by
    different kinds of activity, affect many aspects of meaning, not only speech-act type. See Stephen
    Levinson, 'Activity types and language', *Linguistics*, 17 (1979), 365–99.

different sorts of tools in an open-ended number of 'language games', or different kinds of use that allow words to perform a wide range of purposes and to mean something in one practical context that is often quite different from what, in some other context, they seem to say.

Given the sorts of difficulty identified above with what meaning is for any given semiotic symbol, it may help to start thinking about meaning further back. Many writers, for example, have found it useful to sort meaning into types (often as a preliminary to discussing one particular type). One of the most famous examples of such classification in the English tradition (in their case not early in discussion but emerging within it) is Ogden and Richards's categorisation, in *The Meaning of Meaning*, of sixteen types of meaning, with sub-groups judged as being of differing degrees of importance.[7] Classification into types in this way vividly shows how pervasive meaning issues are. Such categories can nevertheless seem distinctions imposed from above or outside: a philosopher's construct rather than categories within language users' own understanding. An alternative way of seeing the range of different kinds of meaning is therefore worth considering, which looks at verbs that describe how we express or articulate meaning: not only 'mean' itself, but also 'convey', 'evoke', 'entail', 'signify', 'refer', 'express', 'intimate', 'insinuate', 'imply', 'indicate', 'denote', 'connote', 'signal', and many others. Together, such verbs show a tightly interwoven range of ordinary language understandings of what 'mean' means.

'Mean' itself, as linguists and psychologists have shown,[8] suggests a number of different notions of meaning (alongside its other, distinct senses of 'unkind' and 'average'). 'Mean' can describe how something is a symptom or clue that helps us see something else (clouds 'mean' a storm is coming; someone's new car may 'mean' they've been promoted at work); it can suggest significance or importance (we speak of an opportunity 'meaning' a lot); it can suggest purpose or justification (the 'meaning' of life); it can show intention or determination (I didn't 'mean' to do it); it can signal what somebody intended by something they communicated (her sudden expression 'meant' it was time to go); and it can indicate what an expression conventionally means, as a kind of gloss ('claustrophobic' means being 'afraid to go out'). The senses overlap, but each opens out into a larger perspective on what meaning is, how it is conveyed, and how it will be understood.

Uses of 'mean' can play on these well-established nuances between senses. Consider Oscar Wilde's Miss Prism, for example. When she is famously made

---

[7] Ogden and Richards, *The Meaning of Meaning*. Hilary Putnam's later article of the same name (in his *Mind, Language and Reality*) outlines a particular theoretical view of meaning rather than offering a broad review of different approaches to meaning.

[8] See James Hurford, Brendan Heasley and Michael Smith, *Semantics: A Coursebook* (Cambridge: Cambridge University Press, 2007), pp. 1–14; Gibbs, *Intentions in the Experience of Meaning*, pp. 42–4.

to say of her own novel, 'The good ended happily, and the bad unhappily. That is what Fiction means',[9] she evokes a number of these senses in commenting on what fiction 'means': a sense that fiction entails these outcomes; that these outcomes are what makes fiction significant; and – wittily because contrasting with the complexity or pretension of definitions of a literary genre – that the fate of the good and bad characters is sufficient gloss for what the term 'fiction' denotes. All these intersecting senses are then enveloped by the main comic effect: that this is the meaning of fiction because things are very different when it comes to real life.

Refracting 'mean' and its derivative 'meaning' into multiple senses in this way can begin to seem merely like the word feeding on itself, however. Within the range of senses, it is therefore worth narrowing things down to a smaller number of clusters that will be drawn on in the chapters that follow.

There is a broad notion of meaning – broader than the one typically at work in linguistics – which might be called the 'significance' sense. In this sense, meaning is part of more general mental or cognitive states (and 'meaning' roughly means 'meaningfulness'). Where the word is used in this way in relation to a text or utterance, this sense – 'the meaning of life' sense[10] – conveys a notion of meaning in which a 'source discourse' is woven or appropriated into the self as belief, feeling and identity, a view which contrasts with meaning as a process of mental modelling that simply leads you to entertain some specific mental representation. Meaningfulness follows on from discourse processing in many cases by embedding the output of that processing in general patterns of cognition and emotion, in a process that is explored in more detail in Chapters 5 and 6.

Narrower than this, there is a cluster of what we might call 'semantic' or 'semiotic' senses. These denote the resources and mechanisms of systems of signs (linguistic, visual, gestural, etc.). In this group of senses, meaning-making is about processes through which linguistic utterances, images, and text–image and multimedia combinations convey recognisable, describable ideas.[11]

Within *this* 'semiotic' meaning, there are then more specialised, theoretical senses, developed to account for particular ways of building models to explain how different processes combine to construct representations we call meaning. In specialised schools of thought, the word 'meaning' may refer to just one aspect of these processes (as in the linguist's separation of semantic from

---

[9] *The Importance of Being Earnest*, Act II.

[10] Terry Eagleton's *The Meaning of Life* (Oxford: Oxford University Press, 2007) relates meaning to different philosophical and cultural frameworks for finding significance in life, and so to questions of identity, value and social direction. On different understandings of 'meaning', see esp. pp. 56–96.

[11] The distinction drawn here between conceptual and wider social meaning is considerably simplified. See discussion in later chapters, and the account in Geoffrey Leech, *Semantics: The Study of Meaning*, 2nd edition (Harmondsworth: Penguin, 1974).

pragmatic processes, or philosophical use of the expression 'meaning and reference', in which 'reference', sometimes an aspect of meaning, is recast as something that contrasts with 'meaning').

What does such proliferation of theoretical senses of 'meaning' achieve? The various senses allow a view of the production of meaning as an analysable complex of processes underpinning communication or representation. They define domains and mechanisms that can be shown to be needed in accounting for the overall capability we have to use language and other representational systems as precise means of communication. Because overall meaning consists of different sub-systems of meaning production working together (as illustrated dramatically in the Miss Prism quotation above), we need to open out the different senses for consideration, or in I. A. Richards's image to refract meaning into different beams within overall Total Meaning.[12] In disputes in particular, where there is disagreement about what something means, it is only such separation of different aspects of meaning – at whatever level of impression or technicality it takes place – that allows the crux of disagreement to be identified.

### 4.4.2     Unbearable abstractness of meaning?

Model building in relation to meaning makes possible new ways of analysing particular meanings, as well as building a conceptual map of meaning overall. Such work can lessen the sense that meaning evaporates when forced into attention, and so reduces what you might call Wittgenstein's 'St Augustine effect'. However, as judges and media regulators routinely point out, resolving *disputes* over meaning is a practical rather than theoretical matter. If we wait for satisfying answers to theoretical questions about meaning, it is unlikely that urgently needed settlements will be reached anytime soon.

In this spirit, dismissive references are sometimes made in judgments and debates about media regulation to 'mere semantics' or 'falling into semantics'. A risk is perceived, in seeking to illuminate questions of meaning, of discussion becoming over-complicated or even futile, by being too 'abstract'. That caution is understandable but hides an important distinction. In relation to meaning, abstraction is not just losing sight of the problem or getting lost in theory; it is also a question about what level of meaning is being sought. Meaning can be understood at different levels of abstractness, with differing implications as regards how useful the resulting notion of meaning will be when it comes to

---

[12] 'Whether we know and intend it or not, we are all jugglers when we converse, keeping the billiard balls in the air while we balance the cue on our nose. Whether we are active, as in speech or writing, or passive, as readers or listeners, the Total Meaning we are engaged with is, almost always, a blend, a combination of several contributory meanings of different types.' I. A. Richards, *Practical Criticism* (London: Routledge and Kegan Paul, 1929), p. 180.

engaging with contested interpretations. Level of abstraction is a *dimension* of meaning as well as a problem in discussing it. How you frame the questions about meaning that you ask guides what kind of answer you get. Compare the following three levels of abstractness in meaning, ranging from resources available in a given communicative or semiotic code through to reporting specific cognitive effects experienced by a particular person.

1. Meaning can be what a word, sentence or text might hypothetically or potentially mean. Meaning in this context is considered away from any actual circumstances of utterance or exhibition (and so without taking social context or background knowledge into account). In this sense, meaning is analysed as a propensity in some 'default', hypothetical set of circumstances (this is the level of dictionary meanings, semantic representations and general descriptions of semiotic codes, 'in the abstract').

2. Meaning can be what the same linguistic or textual form would mean if uttered in a specified set of circumstances and interpreted using interpretive strategies typically brought to bear in communication (this is broadly the province of pragmatics, or – since an equivalent distinction between levels is not usually drawn in semiotics – part of general semiotics).

3. Meaning can be what the same linguistic or textual form *did* mean on a given occasion for an interpreter (this is more the province of histories of reception, some branches of hermeneutics, and audience ethnography).

The three levels are reflected in the concerns of different research specialisms. What matters here, however – certainly as regards situations in which conflicting meanings are contested – is how the different levels interrelate in any given discussion and what counts as evidence for each.

This last point about evidence is crucial. For the 'semantic' level, *linguistic* or semiotic context (the surrounding words or signs), along with intuitions of the interpreter, will be what matters. With pragmatic meaning (meaning as created by a typical person following conventional interpretive strategies in a specified, situation type), appeal will be made both to intuitions and to the context of utterance (the situation and actors involved): what they would know, what they would think the other person knows, etc. In the third case, of a specific person's already produced interpretation, evidence for a claimed meaning seems available only from the mouth or pen of the person who experienced it.

In theoretical inquiry into meaning, 'possible' interpretations (and alternatively interpretations that 'don't go through') are not studied in and for themselves. They function as examples and counter-examples in investigating specific theoretical questions. Reversing the direction, you get prediction: a particular strategy, coupled with a given utterance and a specified context, allows you to anticipate what readings are *likely* to be produced. In practical disputes, by contrast, questions are mostly formulated in relation to some meaning that, it is claimed, has already been derived (i.e. the particular meaning complained of, or pleaded as

having been derived: e.g. 'on hearing this, the listener became convinced that...').
The issue to be resolved is whether that meaning was plausibly or reasonably
derived from the combination of the discourse presented and the circumstances in
which it was presented. In deciding between alternative accounts of meaning, it is
the interrelation between levels of meaning production that matters: between the
code, the inferences drawn or likely to be drawn, and the context.

Because there is a need for discussion across these different levels, there can
be a clash between the different senses of abstraction here: whether 'abstract'
(as a criticism of semantics in media disputes) means merely over-complicated
and abstruse, or whether it means one specific way of modelling what meaning
is (i.e. comparing meaning in a given case with patterns of meaning across a set
of cases). Where this happens, the difference is more than a local misunderstanding, or 'semantic quibble'.

## 4.5    Problems with applying semantics in interpretive disputes

Even with goodwill on all sides, how useful is discussion drawing on semantics
in understanding and resolving interpretive disputes?

There is a long-standing tradition of believing that clarifying the meanings of
key terms involved in disputes will significantly help solve them. But most
disputes, I have suggested, are about conflicts that discourse 'represents' in the
limited sense of defining and presenting them in a particular way or from a given
point of view. The conflicts themselves exist simultaneously in other manifes-
tations as well as language (or visual representation). To the extent that such
conflicts present themselves as questions of 'meaning', therefore, it is necessary
to take into account how communication is functioning as a kind of social action
within the dispute (what is said, by whom, on what occasion, and to whom)
alongside the capability of expressions and utterances to represent beliefs and
states of affairs. The semanticist's dream of solving the world's problems at the
level of meaning and representation remains inevitably largely that: a dream.

In modern use, semantics is less a general theory of meaning than a technical
specialism not only within a theory of communication but within a theory of
meaning. It has its own specific project, standards and methods. During the
word's history, 'semantics' has shifted from seventeenth-century origins in
understanding the weather, through nineteenth-century use as a broad term for
investigating meaning in general, through to its current, more specialised
senses. Semantics now typically investigates what someone can be held to
know when they know the meaning of a word or sentence of a given language.[13]

---

[13] Examples of theoretical work in semantics within clearly formulated frameworks include Ruth
Kempson, *Semantics* (Cambridge: Cambridge University Press, 1977) and Ronnie Cann, *Formal
Semantics: An Introduction* (Cambridge: Cambridge University Press, 1993).

Given this aim, semantic theories take a restricted range of topics for explanation (including properties such as synonymy, converseness, implication, ambiguity, tautology, contradiction or entailment), and base their findings on evidence from language acquisition, how the mind is able to process meaning, and cases of dysfunction and pathology. Many semantics textbooks end with sections that open out into other approaches to meaning such as pragmatics and discourse analysis; and in cognitive semantics, boundaries between linguistic meaning and general cognition are not drawn so tightly.[14] But what defines semantic theory is its ability to make generalisations and account for apparent counter-examples and exceptions within an explicitly delineated theoretical model. The field is not concerned to explain every detail of what is going on in any specific act of communication. If the history of semantic interventions in the public sphere has not been a successful one, therefore, this is partly because of inappropriate expectations placed on semantics as a field of inquiry.

Drafting his dictionary of cultural keywords, *Keywords: A Vocabulary of Culture and Society*, during the 1950s and 1960s, and aware of the social problem-solving aspiration of the earlier General Semantics movement (a name for work by writers in the 1930s and 1940s including Korzybski, Chase and Hayakawa), Raymond Williams noted in his 'Introduction' a crucial limitation of work on meaning. 'I do not share the optimism, or the theories which underlie it', he writes, 'of that popular kind of inter-war and surviving semantics which supposed that clarification of difficult words would help in the resolution of disputes conducted in their terms and often evidently confused by them.'[15] Similar pessimism is expressed by the semanticist John Lyons in his account of the General Semantics movement as involving a concern 'to make people aware of the alleged dangers of treating words as something more than conventional and rather inadequate symbols for things'. Lyons concludes, somewhat dismissively, that the movement might be more appropriately known as 'therapeutic semantics'.[16]

## 4.6    Summary

In this chapter, I have looked at complexities in the word 'mean' and in ideas of meaning. I have outlined a number of dimensions of meaning, and drawn attention to traditions of work, including the neglected tradition of General

---

[14] Croft and Cruse, *Cognitive Linguistics*.

[15] Williams, *Keywords*, p. 24. Particularly notable among works of General Semantics are Chase, *The Tyranny of Words*, and Hayakawa, *Language in Thought and Action*.

[16] Lyons, *Semantics*, p. 98. Leech, *Semantics*, pp. 40–58. A number of the examples that Leech links to different types of meaning here are keywords for Williams. Cautioning against Hayakawa's arguments in *Language in Thought and Action*, Leech is also close to Williams on the risk of cultivating 'an over-optimistic faith in the curative power of semantics', p. 57.

Semantics, that have attempted to argue a case for raising the profile of discussion of meaning in different areas of social practice.

If a more productive approach to debating meanings in contested situations is to be found than is possible in this tradition, it will be necessary to move beyond ideas of meaning associated with semantics. This is not because semantics has failed but because the field of semantics has different, more specialised aims. Understanding the social circulation of meaning in the media must begin by clarifying what approach to thinking about meaning is called for. Fundamental differences exist between approaches: between theories of the meaning potential of individual expressions and sentences; theories of utterance or text meaning and the strategies that produce such meaning; and accounts of how people have interpreted given utterances or texts on particular occasions. Investigating disputed meaning will only move beyond (mostly unheeded appeals to) semantics by disentangling differences between these approaches. We must rethink the questions being asked rather than simply choosing between answers to the existing questions.

# 5     Interpretive variation

## 5.1     Introduction

In Chapter 4 I suggested that it can be unrealistic to nurse expectations about the usefulness of 'semantics' in resolving public controversies over meaning. The result is likely to be only disappointment at that field's different objectives and approach. It seems preferable to acknowledge the range of processes beyond the semantic that contribute to overall meaning effects. In considering media discourse from this enlarged viewpoint, I suggest in this chapter that it is better to *start* with the fact of interpretive variation, rather than working from an idealised template of fixed meaning and then acknowledging situational factors and variable inference when they become inescapable. Inferential meanings are not arbitrary or random, however. Insofar as they are meanings of the discourse, rather than thoughts loosely associated with it, inferences are constrained by pragmatic considerations. Such considerations ensure that not all interpretations will be regarded as equally plausible or legitimate.

## 5.2     Should a hundred meanings blossom?

Consider a commonplace statement. If a hundred people watch a film in a cinema, they will end up with a hundred different meanings for that film. This can be a rhetorical point worth making in the face of the alternative idea that meaning is fixed and uniform. At the same time, such a bald statement of massive interpretive variation is vague in at least two respects. Firstly, it fails to distinguish whether there are boundaries as regards what kinds of reaction to a discourse will count as its meaning. Secondly, the statement neglects differences within the effects lumped together to create the apparent interpretive diversity.

In order to overcome such vagueness, a more precise account is needed: one which describes meaning as something actively produced by interpretation (rather than merely read off from an inherent meaning of signs) and yet not something unbounded or ineffable. To develop such an account of meaning, it is not enough to invoke some sort of undirected spread outwards from discourse into many different kinds of reaction and response. Rather, meaning must be considered as a mix of varying but still specific, interrelated kinds of effect. If we take this wider view of the range of processes in play and the interaction between them, we can also illuminate debate about the differences between 'variant readings' and 'misreading' that I.A.Richards, standing out among thinkers on meaning in the 1950s, was already lamenting as a neglected aspect of investigation into interpretive validity.[1]

## 5.2.1    Natural and communicated meaning

To disentangle different aspects of meaning, we should first distinguish between kinds of meaning that are communicated and kinds that are not. Not everything typically thought of as meaning is 'communicated'; and many people would argue that not everything that is communicated is meaning.

Our interpretation of some signs, we have seen in the previous chapter, follows from our ability as humans to infer causes from effects and effects from causes. This is part of our cognition but not narrowly part of communication or representation (except in massively anthropomorphised visions of the world in which you consider everything you think of as a message to you from some divine Other). It is our general cognition that enables us to interpret a cloud to mean rain, a weathervane to indicate wind direction, or a dented car to mean it has been in an accident. C. S. Peirce formalised this notion (which had for centuries permeated ideas about communication) by describing signs of this kind, within the three-way classification of signs he distilled from his many other, far more elaborate classifications, as 'indexical' signs.[2] Slightly later, contrasting this kind of indexical sign with the sorts of sign mostly used in language, the philosopher Paul Grice characterised the meaning such signs produce as 'natural meaning', which he contrasts with what he calls 'non-natural' or communicated meaning.[3]

Such a distinction has consequences as regards our initial idea that a hundred people in a cinema create as many different meanings as there are people. If we include *all* the inferences that members of an audience draw – for instance inferences from the state of the seats to the state of British cinema, or inferences from rubbish in the aisles from a previous screening to the degree of interest of the film's narrative – then we have in mind diversity in the audience's thoughts; but we are using 'meaning' in a highly generalised sense. Such inferences are 'meaning' in that people attribute significance to their experience by interpreting the world around them continuously throughout their waking hours (and

[1] I.A.Richards, 'Variant readings and misreading', in Thomas Sebeok (ed.), *Style in Language* (Boston, Mass.: MIT Press, 1960), pp. 241–52.

[2] For C.S.Peirce's classification of signs, see Lyons, *Semantics*, pp. 99–109.

[3] 'Meaning', in Paul Grice, *Studies in the Way of Words* (Cambridge, Mass.: Harvard University Press, 1989), pp. 213–23.

possibly also while asleep). But in choosing to call this meaning, we in effect decide not to differentiate within our overall stream of consciousness the more specialised processes involved in construing what the film says.

As well as drawing inferences about the world, we make inferences about the behaviour of other people around us. In making sense of that behaviour, we employ mind-reading capabilities that form part of a more general 'theory of mind' that includes a capacity for metarepresentation that we rely on extensively in occupying the same social space as others and coordinating activity with them.[4] We attribute mental states to other people as showing that they are engaged in purposive action, and so give meanings to people's behaviour as having been intended by them, without however believing that they necessarily intended to communicate some particular meaning by that behaviour *to us*. This is the case, for instance, if we notice a row of holes in the earth in someone's garden as we walk past and infer that those holes have been dug for the purpose of putting plants into, or if we interpret someone's adopted posture as a strategy to achieve maximum leverage in picking up a heavy bag. What if we focus on *this* type of inference in assessing an audience's reactions to the film? If, in the cinema, the person in the seat in front keeps looking at their watch, we might infer that they need to leave soon or possibly that they are bored with what they are watching. Such inferences are no longer about cause and effect in the world but are about human states of mind and intentions. In most circumstances, though, there is still no reason to suppose that the person in question is trying to communicate a message to the person in the row behind.

More specific again than this kind of mind reading, we infer meanings that we *do* take to be intentionally communicated to us. We attribute to someone else (or to some other communicating source, such as a collectively authored or produced text) both an intention to communicate and also a narrower intention to convey some particular meaning *by* communicating. The particular meaning we arrive at comes partly from the form of the expression, and partly by combining the conventional meaning we find in that form of expression with two other things: first, extra assumptions related to aspects of context that the presumed communicator could anticipate we would be aware of; and second, a general intention on the part of the presumed communicator to draw our attention both to the form of the message and to those relevant aspects of context. In practice, therefore, we are helped towards the meaning we arrive at by a presumption that the utterance was shaped by the communicator to be relevant to us in

---

[4] For an introduction to different kinds and levels of intention, see Gibbs, *Intentions in the Experience of Meaning*, pp. 21–39. On different levels in creating meaning in communication, see D. Wilson and D. Sperber, 'Linguistic form and relevance', *Lingua*, 90 (1993), 1–25. For ideas of 'theory of mind' and 'metarepresentation', see Dan Sperber (ed.), *Metarepresentations: A Multidisciplinary Perspective* (Oxford: Oxford University Press, 2000).

circumstances that are manifest to each of us. This presumption ensures that, if we follow interpretive strategies that might have been anticipated, we will quickly and easily get to the particular meaning, whereas other meanings we might in principle create for the utterance or text are far less likely, because they will be less rewarding and more effort to construct.[5]

In formal interpretive settings (such as commenting on the film that the hundred people have seen in a seminar, or a lawyer construing a statute that treats some aspect of the film, or a religious scholar analysing a religious text that may be thought to comment on the film's subject matter), spontaneous processes of discourse interpretation of this sort are supplemented by doctrines and heuristics learnt as a specialised interpretive craft for the given field (as the film critic David Bordwell has shown, in the book referred to in Chapter 3, in exemplary detail for the field of interpreting films itself ).[6]

How do these distinctions advance our understanding of how much interpretive variation to expect? Even if we take into account only communicated meanings, not all the other kinds of meaning I have pushed out to the margins for the moment, we still find considerable interpretive variation. But now we are concerned specifically with variation between interpretations that are a result of how the discourse is construed – meanings attributed to its organisation as a discourse – rather than more general thoughts about how people behave or how the world is. It is this inner circle of variant meanings that causes most trouble in disputes, because it resists explanation as simply the result of us all being different people or having different social interests. It is also the area of meaning for which the communicator or text producer is likely to be thought most responsible.

To narrow meaning down as I have done is not to suggest that the other kinds of meaning have no role to play. But it *is* to suggest that those meanings are different in important respects, especially when it comes to who is responsible for them. In discussing contested meaning, it is important to distinguish between what seem to be meanings of the discourse for which communicator and addressee share some complicated, combined responsibility, and other kinds of significance to be found in the situation around it.

## 5.3     Code and inference

Communicated meaning of the kind I have described consists of two major processes. An act of decoding of linguistic, visual or audio-visual material provides an input to inferential interpretation (what in I. A. Richards's 1950s diagram of the 'canonical speech situation' could only be shown between the

---

[5] For theoretical discussion, see Sperber and Wilson, *Relevance.*     [6] Bordwell, *Making Meaning.*

decoding stage and the destination of the signal as the letters 'DV', standing for 'development' or 'what most fully takes into account the situation the utterance is meeting'[7]). The precise boundary between code and inference, as well as how code and inference interact, continues to be hotly debated. But the main differences between the two processes seem largely beyond doubt, and the question of differences between variant readings and misreading should be seen in this light.[8]

For linguistic discourse, decoding is principally a matter of deriving propositions from the form of utterances. With images, decoding involves organising the perceptual stimulus into a representation of what is denoted in the image-field: what Barthes and others, varying an already complicated terminology, have described as arriving at an image's 'denotation'.[9] With audio-visual texts such as television or films, decoding involves a combination of both these processes. Meaning is carved out of particular choices made in representing whatever is said or shown, in what sequence and from what angle, along with whatever sound effects and accompanying music are used. The semiotic codes of verbal discourse, images and audio-visual discourse are different kinds of sign system, with different conventional properties; but despite their differences, this decoding stage of interpretation (which is already shot through with elements of inference such as those involved in disambiguation and reference assignment) seems to differ less between interpreters than the inferential stage which in Richards's fumbling term 'develops' the output of decoding. At the decoding level, the conventional pairing of sign and meaning that Humpty's assertion denied has genuine force: symbolic conventions with differing degrees of stability anchor a sign's meaning and oblige regularity of interpretation because of the cultural patterns of equivalence and contrast of which the linguistic and visual signs are conventionally capable, before this particular use of them.

Even at the decoding level, however, there will still be some difference of received meaning. As we have seen with examples in previous chapters, it is difficult to contain meaning within a stable decoding framework even for a single word, let alone for a longer text. If a word is cited in the abstract (in a notionally 'default' situation of use), its meaning potential is so open-ended that competing possible senses flood in, depending on whatever fanciful circumstances you care

---

[7] For I.A.Richards's diagram of communication, see 'Variant readings and misreading', p. 242; the discussion of 'situations' is on p. 251.

[8] Walter Kintsch emphasises that the term 'inference' should be (but commonly is not) reserved for non automatic generation rather than retrieval processes in text comprehension. See *Comprehension: A Paradigm for Cognition* (Cambridge: Cambridge University Press, 1998), pp. 189–93.

[9] In media and cultural studies, denotation is often discussed as defined by Barthes, in *Mythologies* (London: Paladin, 1973 [1957]). For linguistic accounts, see Lyons, *Semantics*, pp. 206–15, as well as clear distinctions in Gillian Brown, *Speakers, Listeners, and Communication: Explorations in Discourse Analysis* (Cambridge: Cambridge University Press, 1995), pp. 58–62.

to make up. As soon as that same word is specified as being used in a given situation, its meaning becomes contextually narrowed and more resistant to alternative readings; but oddly as soon as a situation of use is specified, the word then begins to attract contextually specific inferences triggered by background knowledge, beliefs and associations. Such polysemy does not necessarily create a meaning 'problem'. Meaning beyond pairings of sign and meaning according to a code is only problematic for frameworks that do not recognise non-conventional processes in meaning creation. In such frameworks, inferential aspects of meaning must be accounted for as part of the capability of the signs themselves, rather than being created by interpreters.

The general picture emerges of limited variation at the level of decoding and greater variation at the inferential level. To judge intuitively from causes of legal action and patterns of complaints to regulatory bodies, this pattern in variation is reflected in the kinds of interpretive dispute about meaning that occur. Disputes tend to be less about the immediate, decoded meaning of what is said or shown than about a superstructure of inferences that the basic decoding level is expected to bear.

This aspect of interpretive variation, in terms of processing levels, needs also to be seen in relation to a different kind of variation: that between how interpretation takes place for different media. Between media, contrastingly, there seems to be *greater* variation at the decoding level than at the inferential level. There is more difference between how you initially read or hear linguistic discourse and how you look at a picture or watch a film than in the processes of inference you go on to apply to the initial representations you produce in different ways from the different media forms. Inference works on mental representations of what is said or shown, it has been influentially argued by some cognitive scientists, once they pass from specialised input modules of the brain into a set of central cognitive processes.[10] Inferences combine output from mode-specific or module-specific representations with already held beliefs, attitudes, knowledge and understanding of the situation in which the communication took place, in a process which integrates different sources of material and is for this reason similar across different media experiences. As a result, in terms of interpretive differences between media, there seems to be a convergence in meaning-making between initial diversity of decoding processes across media and greater commonality at the inferential level.

Do these similarities and differences have any consequences? The patterns I have described may be why conflicts over meaning in media disputes, even given the largely image-based character of contemporary media, are conducted

---

[10] Debates over cognitive specialisation in relation to language are largely concerned with the degree of the mind's 'modularity', and often take the form of responses to Jerry Fodor's *The Modularity of Mind* (Cambridge, Mass.: MIT Press, 1983).

to an otherwise surprising extent by using verbal summaries of what has been depicted. A documentary or fiction film is summarised in terms of what it shows in its own, medium-specific way; the effect of that summarised depiction is then debated as a matter of inferences that may have given rise to the alleged effect. Bringing together the two dimensions of variation (variation at interpretive levels and variation between different media), it ends up seeming possible, by means of description and summary, to describe visual or audio-visual discourse sufficiently precisely to guide discussion of how contested effects may be conveyed.

## 5.4    Creativity and risk

The account I have presented of how meanings are produced is of course schematic and considerably simplified. It is also theoretically controversial in at least some of its detail. I hope nevertheless that my description will serve to query discussion of disputes over meaning that takes as its model of communication a fixed code that is used to transport a clearly delineated message through a channel from communicator to addressee. In its place, I prefer to see communication treated as presentation of evidence of an intention to communicate which generates one or more inferable meanings (alongside other implications that the interpreter may derive but which were not intentionally communicated). Interpretation, in this view, is more a struggle engaged in by interpreters to create meaning, and meaning is not something fixed but something continuously augmented and modified in the situation in which the meaning-making takes place.[11]

Some degree of interpretive variation inevitably follows from such an account. But there is no suggestion that, if we loosen our hold on fixed meaning, we will automatically get a hundred different interpretations from our cinema audience or drop into an abyss of interpretive free-play.

Why no free-play or abyss? Because with most utterances, or with utterances joined up to form longer stretches of discourse, there is commonly one main meaning, or primary focus of meaning, that presents itself as relevant and will usually be derived by most people in the target audience, albeit with a penumbra of local interpretations and associations around it. While alternative interpretations can certainly be produced – and still others contrived with different degrees of ingenuity – those interpretations are likely to remain for the most part at the margins in terms of uptake and recognition. Interpretations from the

---

[11]  This formulation is close to Gillian Brown's description of meaning based on Bartlett's work in psychology; see 'Modes of understanding', in Gillian Brown, Kirsten Malmkjaer, Alastair Pollitt and John Williams (eds.), *Language and Understanding* (Oxford: Oxford University Press, 1994), p. 10.

margins can be teased out and shown to destabilise the 'mostly perceived' meaning, but the commonly perceived interpretation is likely to be constructed first, even by interpreters who go on to reject or criticise it.

With long texts, especially multi-media texts, interim meanings are produced as well as higher-order constructs derived from the interim meanings to produce an overall representation of what the text means. Even in cases of considerable complexity such as film interpretation, it is still usual for the hundred cinema goers to come out of the cinema in agreement about who did what to whom, which characters are alive at the end, how the plot resolved (if it did), and often also about what the film's main themes were and the point of view adopted in relation to those themes. Films that challenge this kind of consensual production of meaning achieve their greater variation and indeterminacy of interpretation not because the given discourse is polysemous in principle but because they work creatively against an anticipated interpretive struggle to impose coherence on it.[12]

Agreement on some aspects of a film's meaning and significance may be less likely (as Anita and Bobby discovered in Chapter 1). In interpreting a film – or a poem, painting or piece of music – interpreters derive not only the one or more general meanings on which agreement with the other ninety-nine people is likely, but also many other personalised meanings and judgments that combine what the film says with what the interpreter already thinks. These meanings involve associations, resonances and comparisons of many different kinds. Such meanings are less strongly implicated by the organisation of material in the film itself; but there may still be evidence in support of them. Other meanings again may depend on thoughts and associations that are prompted but unsupported by textual evidence; these will still be interesting and pleasurable – and are largely or entirely the interpreter's own work.

Making meaning in this way is a far more open-ended process than that predicted by transmission of meaning by code along a conduit between speaker and hearer. Arguably, much of the interest and pleasure in interpreting discourse follows from this combined, 'code and inference' capability, activated in different ways according to the situation that the interpreter is in and the function the discourse is expected to serve. This same potential of meaning, however, also makes misinterpretation more likely, and begins to explain the puzzle mentioned earlier: why, if meaning is encoded and transmitted from speaker to an addressee who then decodes it, should interpretive variation occur, except as background 'noise' in the system – let alone disputes that seem not a matter of

---

[12] Stanley Fish famously illustrates his idea that 'meanings are the property neither of fixed and stable texts nor of free and independent readers but of interpretive communities' with an anecdote about how a group of literature students could confidently and coherently read notes on a blackboard left from an earlier class as a poem, 'How to recognise a poem when you see one', in Stanley Fish, *Is There a Text in This Class?* (Cambridge, Mass.: Harvard University Press, 1981), pp. 322–37.

interpretive opportunism but of genuinely conflicting understandings? Potential for misinterpretation is increased because, in the film example, the hundred cinema goers bring different beliefs, memories, aspirations and knowledge about the world (and about cinema) to the screening. They combine what is said and shown in the film with different contextual assumptions and derive different kinds of significance, including sometimes going off in completely different directions. The full range of inferences that audience members are likely to draw is almost impossible for the text producer to anticipate, even if some of the main communicated effects will be highly probable. Communication is in this sense an activity fundamentally associated with risk. Interpretive disagreement over public or media discourse is not just a matter of unintended meanings being attributed to discourse but of divergent or contingent meanings being ascribed and treated as if they *were* intended.

## 5.5    Boundaries of legitimate inference

Outlining a field of meanings that allows for more variation than a 'fixed code' model need not be permissive of any interpretation at all. We only need to recognise that there are different kinds of meaning within an overall social field of response. The field of meaning and response needs to be defined more clearly; but in doing this we face two related difficulties.

The first is to establish where boundaries to what can be called 'meaning' should be set. Not everything that an interpreter thinks should be taken as the responsibility of the text or text producer, rather than as a creation of the interpreter's own thoughts and feelings. Within the different kinds of reaction to a discourse that are reported, for instance in read-aloud protocols or informant interviews, we should be confident in saying when meaning shades off into other kinds of response, thought or affect.

The second task is to consider how different kinds of meaning relate to one another *within* the designated field, a field that ranges from conventionalised (coded) meaning potential of individual words and signs – apparent or literal meaning – through to vague impressions, associations and reactions.

One schema commonly used in organising different kinds of meaning in this sort of interpretive field is spatial: levels of meaning are distinguished, as well as relative closeness, vertically, of a given meaning to the form by which it is evoked. Such a model invites the question whether there is a 'lower' edge to what can be called meaning, close to the discourse form itself, and whether there is an 'upper' or outer edge of what can be called meaning, at some remove from discourse form and including potentially quite long-range meaning effects – but still before meaning effects seem wilful or wholly created by the interpreter. In between these two limits would fall the range of meaning effects for which the text producer might be thought accountable, possibly to different degrees related to the different levels. I return to issues raised by the metaphor of 'spatialisation' in the next chapter, relating such imagery more closely to psychological processes.

### 5.5.1   'Beef is safe'

Before discussing how meanings are produced depending on human psychological capabilities, however, I want to describe some of the many different sorts of meaning that a media audience might derive from what appears initially to be a simple message. For this purpose, I have chosen a widely circulated 'top line' or 'headline message' conveyed as public reassurance by the Government's Chief Medical Officer, Sir Kenneth Calman, in 1993 (and then repeated in 1995) concerning the risk to health posed by the BSE epidemic in cattle, or 'mad cow disease'.[13] Sir Kenneth Calman's announcement was widely perceived subsequently as a government PR gaffe during a crisis for UK beef production. I am not concerned here with policy aspects of the announcement but with steps by which different kinds of meaning were attributed to a widely reported key phrase of this sort, in this case the announcement: 'beef is safe'.

With varying amounts of surrounding detail in different reports and interviews, the prominent (and almost certainly carefully chosen) headline words 'beef is safe' were relayed to a national and international media audience. That audience included general consumers, workers in the meat industry and the health industry, people in the media, parents of children, children themselves, and people of different religions with different attitudes towards eating meat as well as different political beliefs about governments and public information. The succinct media headline message was transmitted by means of more than one channel but inevitably led in its varied reception to simplification and crude distortion. What *did* the central message, 'beef is safe', mean?

Tracing different kinds of meaning constructed from (or for) these three monosyllabic words, I suggest, points less to their dictionary meanings than towards a more open-ended circulation of inferential interpretations. Closest to the words themselves, 'beef is safe' means something like 'whatever is denoted by the word beef has the property of being whatever is meant by safe'. This is hardly a helpful interpretation. But that construction is a necessary building block towards more rewarding meanings. The reformulation in terms of what is denoted establishes the general distinction, associated with Alfred Tarski,[14]

---

[13] Sir Kenneth Calman is a Scottish doctor who spent much of his career in hospitals and universities. He was Chief Medical Officer at the Department of Health, 1991–8. For details of the beef scare, see www.bseinquiry.gov.uk/report.htm.

[14] Alfred Tarski, 'The semantic conception of truth' [1944], in Leonard Linsky (ed.), *Semantics and the Philosophy of Language: A Collection of Readings* (Urbana: University of Illinois Press,

between object language and metalanguage and allows movement, for this particular utterance, from the form of the utterance towards a belief that the message 'beef is safe' will be true if and only if beef, as something in the world rather than in language, is safe. Notwithstanding the importance of this move in the development of semantics, virtually no one would want to offer this reformulation as the meaning that the audience found in Sir Kenneth Calman's announcement.

We can move from the meaning potential of the words used into entries in our mental lexicon for those words, and so to concepts. We might then say that the type of meat known as beef is harmless or not injurious to health. But this seems still simply a gloss. What then? We might ask what kind of statement 'Beef is safe' is. It is not a referring statement in the way that 'the beef I bought yesterday is safe' would be; it doesn't pick out a specific entity and say something about it. 'Beef' is a non-count noun (it doesn't exist in the plural, 'beefs'), and it occurs here without an article ('a' or 'the'). So 'beef is safe' is a general statement, that beef *in general* is harmless or not injurious to health. To be interpreted, however, that general statement must be contextually narrowed – even if it doesn't refer to one particular piece of meat – to exclude self-evidently toxic, contaminated or decayed beef, or beef left in the boot of the car for the past month. Such beef presumably isn't safe. Some contextually relevant scope for beef must be inferred even in a 'general' statement.

'Beef is safe' takes on its meaning by being embedded in a specific act of utterance: Sir Kenneth Calman *says* beef is safe. The speaker in this case is not someone interviewed for a media vox pop; he is someone presented as a scientific authority, the government's Chief Medical Officer. Sir Kenneth Calman speaks *ex officio*, with his words weighted accordingly. If his authority is felt sufficient by a given interpreter, then the embedded proposition 'beef is safe' is 'disquoted', or adopted into the interpreter's own belief system as 'beef is safe' (it *is* safe, Sir Kenneth Calman says so), rather than stored as a belief that depends on being ratified or authorised by the speaker (beef is safe, but only *if* the speaker who told me this is right in what he or she is saying). What an utterance means depends to some extent, accordingly, on the particular hearer's inferences about the knowledge and intentions of the speaker.

With this necessary ground clearing, we arrive at the beginning of interesting divergence in interpretations of Sir Kenneth Calman's announcement. The process of getting to this threshold level of interpretation may seem laborious in relation to just three words. In practice, it would all happen instantaneously, as if automatically, with the resulting interpretation still seeming 'close' to the words uttered.

1972), pp. 13–47. Tarski's metalanguage point is related to his effort to resolve the 'Liar Paradox' ('Epimenides' Paradox'); see Michael Clark, *Paradoxes from A to Z* (London: Routledge, 2002), pp. 99–106.

The interpretive moves which follow, by contrast, seem less automatic. They draw on other kinds of thought process. 'Beef is safe' invites inferences in response to a further implicit question that the interpreter addresses: why is Sir Kenneth Calman telling me this? A search for relevant meanings beyond the proposition that 'beef is safe' is triggered. That search combines the meaning arrived at so far with the interpreter's own beliefs, memories, associations and desires. Many different inferences might be derived. Without pursuing here the issue of which inferences are most likely, and why, some indicative possibilities are:

- I only feel comfortable eating meat that is safe; *beef is safe*; I can feel comfortable eating beef.
- I only buy foods that are safe; *beef is safe*; I'll now buy beef.
- Governments are responsible for ensuring public safety, including about health; *beef is safe*; so the government has fulfilled this part of its responsibility for ensuring public safety.

If the assumptions on which such inferences are based are sufficiently accessible, they will be activated early during a search for relevant interpretation. The resulting inference is likely to be taken as having been intended by the speaker (and so considered a meaning communicated by the utterance).

But what if different background assumptions combine with the utterance? Assumptions will certainly vary significantly across an audience of millions for a widely reported, public 'headline' statement of this kind. From other assumptions, different inferences may be drawn that may or may not have been intended by the speaker. The likelihood of such inferences will depend on how accessible and easily activated the assumption is on which the inference is based:

- Things can only ever be relatively, not completely safe; *beef is safe*; so beef is only relatively safe, not completely safe.
- Governments give you as upbeat an account as possible when things go wrong; *beef is safe* tells me nothing is wrong with beef; so there may or may not be a problem with the safety of beef.
- Government scientific advisers provide precise, scientific assessments; *beef is safe* is a scientific assessment; so beef is safe to the standard of a scientific assessment.

Alongside inferences of this second, general kind, there will also be – differently (and to different extents within the audience) – more obviously irrelevant implications prompted by 'beef is safe'. Such implications seem more an activation of beliefs that the hearer already has than meanings derived *from* the utterance. Examples might include:

- Vague ideas can't explain health issues in a complicated world; *beef is safe* is a vague idea; telling me beef is safe doesn't help me understand this situation.
- You might get run over by a bus tomorrow so what does it matter then what you ate?

- Thank God I'm vegetarian.

At this range from the utterance, we arguably leave the field of discourse meaning and enter a more general domain of reaction, extrapolation, creative commentary or response. A major challenge in understanding meaning, there-fore – especially when it is contested – lies in distinguishing between interpre-tations that seem fully (even unavoidably) warranted by the utterance or text; interpretations that seem plausible or reasonable (but which you could miss); and interpretations that seem fanciful, extravagant or extraneous.


## 5.6    Public circulation of meaning

Faced with such a wide range of possible interpretive responses – from repre-sentations close to the words themselves through to responses which seem merely contingent – we should ask again whether a media statement like 'beef is safe' has a single meaning. If so, how is that meaning best described. If we simply say there are millions of different interpretations of 'beef is safe', by analogy with our hundred people in the cinema above, we might conceivably be accurate ethno-graphically speaking. But if we leave meaning production undifferentiated to that extent, then saying that texts prompt many different meanings says very little. In particular, we fail to say anything useful about who is responsible for which aspects of which meaning – and saying something useful about that becomes essential when people argue over meaning and begin to lay blame.

The diffusion of incrementally different meanings I have sketched for 'beef is safe', in a highly simplified way, often goes unrecognised. In fact, this turned out to be the case with 'beef is safe' itself. Some time after his influential statement, Sir Kenneth Calman was called to give evidence to an inquiry into the Government's handling of BSE. During his testimony, he was asked to clarify how his earlier statements, that he had encouraged Government to be more open about the dangers of beef, could be reconciled with his public announcement that 'beef is safe'. Sir Kenneth told the inquiry that, as a medical researcher, he was much concerned with the meaning of the word 'safe'. 'In ordinary usage "safe"', Sir Kenneth said, 'does not necessarily mean no risk.' He added that 'no risk' was certainly not what the word meant to him. Calman's account of 'beef is safe' here, which suggests that his comment served to draw attention to risk assessment, may seem complacent given the scope of possible interpretations outlined above. More surprising, however, is Sir Kenneth's appeal to 'ordinary *usage*' (i.e. a way of *talking about* risk rather than a scientific means of measuring and evaluating it). Focusing his self-justification on 'usage' seems to imply that the meaning of 'safe' lies in a stable (in this case, arguably counter-intuitive) meaning of the word, rather than in inferential interpretations that his chosen words prepared the ground for. Sir Kenneth Calman's statement may be thought disingenuous. But if so, the basis of that criticism lies less in his misjudgement of a particular meaning for the word 'safe' than in his failure to see the risk, in media communication, of considering it safe to assume a particular, stable meaning.

Fuller context than is provided in my description would be needed to reach a fair judgment on how responsible or irresponsible the pronouncement that beef is safe was. 'Beef is safe' was a 'top line' Government information announcement. It lent itself – and was almost certainly *chosen* to lend itself – to quotation and reproduction. It would be rash, however, to look at the utterance in isolation and judge its integrity or otherwise. A wider, contextualised account, partly linguistic and partly social, would be needed.

Public communication in the media is complex strategic action, rhetorically directed at mixed audiences and towards a variety of effects anticipated as likely in different target groups. Among other considerations, the speaker-persona foregrounds expressions and statements that seem likely to be selected as headlines, soundbites and quotations, and plans for varying levels of attention, awareness and interest on the part of different audience groups. Some public relations professionals have maintained that the problem with Sir Kenneth Calman's announcement was less the message itself than the identity of the messenger. The same message, it may be felt, would have been interpreted differently, and more favourably, if it had the source credibility of a sympathetic third-party ally, more detached from Government than its own Chief Medical Officer.

What seems beyond doubt is that the creation of meaning in the media in such circumstances is only partly the meaning potential of the signs used. It is also created by the communicator's anticipation of strategies that interpreters bring to those signs in a given setting. Such interaction between strategies and forms takes place with all discourse, and is the basis of pragmatic accounts of language use. But there is special complexity in the shadowboxing of media-amplified announcements, as can be easily shown for the 'beef is safe' case. Just consider an account of possible interpretations along the lines developed above for 'beef is safe', if the Government's Chief Medical Officer had gone on television and announced, 'beef is not safe'.

## 5.7    Summary

In this chapter, I have looked at interpretive variation in ways that seek to reflect the complexity of media audiences. I have emphasised the role played by inference in attributing meaning, and suggested that it is possible to track inferential interpretation through its various, alternative paths. In media controversies, I conclude, communicators and audiences are to varying degrees aware of the complexity of the media communication events in which they are involved. They frequently, though not always, take the mediated character of those communication events into account in arriving at the inferences they draw.

# 6    Time-based meaning

## 6.1    Introduction

In this chapter, I describe how attributing meaning involves cognitive processes that take time and effort. Meanings are also retained in memory for
limited and differing periods. I suggest that such processes, and the gradual
absorption of textual meaning into patterns of belief and attitude, must be
taken into account in deciding which aspects of meaning text-producers
should be held responsible for.

## 6.2    Meaning in the mind

In Chapter 5, a spatial metaphor was used as a way of exploring the different
kinds of meaning that seem to exist. The metaphorical schema I adopted
allowed meanings to be thought of in terms of their 'proximity' to the words
or signs from which they are derived or their distance or 'range' from those
words or signs. Extending the spatial analogy, I visualised a 'lower edge' of
repetition or close paraphrase of the utterance or text and an 'outer edge' of
cognitive effects that are still typically recognised as meaning, before responses
shade off into general belief or attitude. The spatial image (of distance and
range) is a variant, I suggested, of a long-established trope: that of 'levels' of
meaning. As with the image of 'levels', my spatial metaphor begs the question
of what exactly is represented by 'distance' or 'range'. Is relative distance a
matter of complexity of the meaning produced: a sort of layering of meanings,
one level superimposed on another in tiers of complexity (as thinkers in what
might be called the 'Ogden and Richards' tradition, with its origins in the
psychology of Wundt, seem to have believed creates meanings of increased
significance)? Or is relative distance a matter of stages or sequence of processing, and so a procedural matter irrespective of the complexity of the output
meaning (with literal meaning constructed first, then figurative and other
implied meanings, which need not be any more complex or profound, derived
afterwards)?

Even raising such questions in this loose, intuitive form draws attention to an
aspect of meaning hardly touched on so far: that of 'psychological reality' in
meaning production. The general question can be asked another way. How far

should meaning production be investigated as a matter of processes that can be plausibly carried out with available psychological abilities, rather than as something abstract or inherent in a collective, social system of representation? This issue has been raised, in a different context, in the two previous chapters. There, I suggested that it is important to distinguish between meaning as abstract symbolic potential and meaning as mental representation by specific interpreters in given situations. A hundred people in a cinema may or may not interpret the same text differently in some respect, but we might now add that one thing is beyond doubt: that each person's act of interpretation is achieved by means of that person's individual mental processes. The appearance of collective 'group meaning', or overall audience effect, is a result of patterned accumulation of individual interpretations distributed across a large number of individual mental states: not meaning as intrinsically a single, social object but meaning as a construct based on resemblances between many slightly different instances.

The two general views of meaning at stake here – meaning as symbolic potential and as cognitive event – are of course not completely separate from one another. There is an overlap between what takes place in the minds of different people presented with the same discourse, so it is possible to generalise across individual psychological processes in the direction of social patterns, and to see meaning as something identifiable in general terms that is distributed (sometimes unevenly) across a population. Such generalisation is essential in theory construction, which relies on regularities rather than the specifics of individual cases. Such generalisation is also essential in directing discussion of meaning towards kinds of social analysis, including for the purpose of determining public policy. If we are to investigate interpretations arrived at by particular readers or viewers on given occasions, however – the approach principally adopted in dealing with complaints in media law and regulation – then claims about meaning should be at least consistent with cognitive processes from which they follow.

To analyse those connections, it is necessary to consider how meaning is created from another point of view. At the subjective level, meaning production is a cognitive or psychological process. It relies on an infrastructure of cognitive capacities whose essential role is instantly revealed if they are impaired by injury, illness or age. Meaning production also shares another property with other kinds of specific event rather than with abstract or ideal types: it uses up energy and takes time.

## 6.3     When does a meaning become a meaning?

It may take only milliseconds to recognise and retrieve a meaning for a word or phrase, and not much longer to integrate the processing of a short stretch of discourse as a coherent mental model, draw inferences from it, and incorporate it within a framework of already held knowledge and beliefs. But it takes longer for that interpretation – still recognisable as a mental construct derived from a source text or utterance – to be evaluated, reflected on, or tested against experience. Interpreting in this sense is an activity that takes up not only energy and time, but different *amounts* of energy and time depending on what view of meaning you adopt.

But how long? One obvious starting place in understanding the time-course of meaning production is to consider how long it takes your eyes to scan backwards and forwards across lines of text, or to listen to an utterance, or to process an image such as a photograph or frame of film. In psychological studies of discourse comprehension, considerable interest is shown in such durations, for example how long it takes to recognise individual words, or to retrieve clusters of knowledge items from long-term memory, or to perform specified tasks based on images. The time it takes to recognise words *as* words – very roughly 250–350 ms – can be measured experimentally in word recognition experiments. Other variables can then be manipulated (e.g. priming the process of recognition by first causing related material to be brought into short-term memory, so making some words more accessible than others), in order to discover how words are connected to one another in the mental lexicon, or to investigate other mechanisms at work in what is sometimes called a 'constructionist' phase of comprehension.[1] Recognition speeds under given conditions can be compared with different, typically slower speeds involved in other mental processes including elaborative inferences, mental modelling of situations and scenarios, and problem-solving. Relative speed associated with a specified task is taken to reflect processing complexity – time taken reflecting amount of work done. So time calculations help to identify stages in processing and contribute to our understanding of mechanisms at work in discourse comprehension. Meaning, we surmise, is what is produced as you perform this combination of tasks, or at least very soon after.

With longer stretches of discourse – articles, books, films – the reception process lasts minutes or hours rather than seconds. Modelling that process calls for more than one single, decisive step and must be iterative and cumulative. Meaning is produced as you go along for individual units (words, images, individual utterances as part of a soundtrack), then stored in buffers and restructured in memory by being summarised as episodes, themes, significant contrasts. Information is also retrieved from long-term memory to create bridging inferences, extended by other inferences that go beyond simply creating discourse coherence into deriving new thoughts – all this as the input

---

[1] Kintsch, *Comprehension*.

process (of turning the pages, or the disk playing) continues. If you put your book down or pause your DVD, meaning production will be interrupted, at least in any direct relation to the text. In memory, however, you have already created provisional networks of links, themes and expectations that are structured but will now remain incomplete, leaving open the question of where the discourse was going and how those structures might have been updated or modified, as well as how in due course they might have achieved completion or closure.

### 6.3.1    Online and offline inferences

If discourse processes of this kind require work, how much meaning do people take the trouble to create? Given sufficient time and incentive, the psychologist Walter Kintsch and others have shown, there is almost no limit to the range of inferences interpreters will draw from a discourse. This no doubt helps account for the massive amount of interpretive variation and debate that tends to occur in formalised interpretive settings (such as seminars, seminaries and courtrooms). But if the time available is limited, a different picture emerges.

Experiments using simple narratives containing a range of tested inference cues have been devised to identify what kinds of inference interpreters typically draw, and at what stage in their processing. Readers of simple short stories have been shown (by Arthur Graesser, for instance, working with various collaborators[2]) to derive automatically only a relatively small number of different classes of inference: referential inferences (linking discourse entities to each other in the text); causal inferences (relating material to what has already taken place in the story and with consequences that may follow); and inferences from actions or description to presumed circumstances or conditions. For Kintsch, some of these inferences are hardly inferences at all; they would be better described as specialised kinds of information retrieval from long-term memory. And some such inferences, Kintsch suggests, are more likely than others (for instance interpreters can be shown to be more likely to make antecedent causal inferences than consequent causal inferences). Beyond this small number of inference types, however, further classes of inference also seem to be optionally drawn: inferences that go beyond local coherence to a sort of superorderinate discourse structure. Such inferences include ideas about characters' long-range goals, inferences to significant themes within the discourse, and inferences regarding the author's intention and likely interpreters' reactions. Psychological studies investigating such inferential work under experimental

---

[2]  Arthur Graesser and Rolf Zwaan, 'Inference generation and the construction of situation models', in C.A. Weaver, Suzanne Mannes and Charles Fletcher (eds.), *Discourse Comprehension: Essays in Honor of Walter Kintsch* (Hillsdale, NJ: Lawrence Erlbaum Associates, 1995), pp. 117–40, esp. p. 125. See also Kintsch, *Comprehension*, pp. 193–9.

conditions open up important perspectives on how meaning is produced, including how far discourse comprehension proceeds by incremental interpretation and how far by kinds of 'just-enough' shallow processing. What is significant here is simply the broad outline of findings by psychologists such as Kintsch, Graesser and others, in particular the basic distinctions they draw between three kinds of inference: inferences automatically derived as part of spontaneous, immediate comprehension; other inferences that seem to be only sometimes generated, with irregular patterns of distribution in groups of experimental subjects; and other inferences again that can be elicited but appear not to be drawn spontaneously.

Why does any of this matter? The significance of the time-course involved in interpretation is that it points to differences between kinds of meaning generated spontaneously in the course of reading or watching (so-called online inferences) and other, reflective inferences drawn where the interpreter is given a longer time, and perhaps additional incentive, to construct a meaning for a discourse, especially to review it as a whole rather than interpret it as an unfolding sequence of steps. Interpreting within a continuing event or situation produces different results from reflecting on interpretation *after* that event or situation. For psychologists, such differences raise questions about the kinds of mental process at work in the two different cases.[3]

For media regulators, as we will see, the same basic insight poses a different, practical question: which reading of a contested discourse – since readings are unlikely to remain constant, even for one person – is properly the meaning to be judged? An initial interpretation, constructed and experienced in a given situation in real time? Or a more careful unpicking of discourse details as a later process that has inevitably lost the interactive and unfolding nature of the earlier interpretive moment? This question is usually answered in law in a robust manner: the meaning to be established is the first, or earliest interpretation (it is a 'fact' of the original reception situation). This is despite the likelihood that – as I will suggest in the next chapter – this meaning can be difficult to identify with any degree of confidence.

## 6.4    Closure and continuing dialogue

Complexity of the psychological processes at work in interpretation presents a theoretical challenge to media regulation. But that challenge might *only* be theoretical. The task facing media regulation of content is a practical rather than

---

[3] A fascinating introduction to psychological processes involved in reading, which discusses both the neuroscience and social consequences of literacy (and relates both to changes associated with contemporary 'information societies'), is Maryanne Wolf, *Proust and the Squid: The Story and Science of the Reading Brain* (New York: HarperCollins, 2007).

theoretical one: that of maintaining public order, resolving disputes, and apportioning responsibility and resources. Purely theoretical niceties in relation to
meaning will be irrelevant. There is reason to think, however, that the issues
outlined above may not be only theoretical. Complications with meaning as a
time-based process do lead to practical dilemmas. To see how this happens, it is
necessary to consider further how meanings to be adjudicated in any given
dispute are identified and brought into comparison with one another.

When someone finishes reading a whole book or viewing a whole film, it is
common to speak of further strengthening or modification of their interpretation
that continues to take place: a process of interpreters consolidating their ideas or
changing their mind. There may be little opportunity to talk during a film or
while reading a book. But after reading or watching there is often some sort of
interpretive follow-up, including by means of dialogue with others (as we saw
with Anita and Bobby on their way home from the film in Chapter 1). Ideas
formed during a text's reception are queried or linked more closely together;
contrasts are accentuated; themes and points emerge. Some details to which
little significance was attached in an initial response take on greater importance;
others lose some of their impact or shock when first encountered. Gradually, an
initial interpretation loses some of its distinctiveness as a meaning derived from
the particular utterance or discourse and is embedded in the interpreter's beliefs
and attitudes. The ideas or feelings in question may still be associated with the
particular discourse. But the meaning has been appropriated into the interpreter's subjectivity. Processing the specific stretch of discourse gives way to
another aspect of 'meaning': meaning as meaningfulness or personal
significance.

Reading or viewing in company, in social groups with their own internal
networks and social dynamics, increases the influence of other people on any
one person's interpretation. Some degree of joint production of meaning
through dialogue commonly takes place, whether that dialogue has a
one-sided form, led by an authority figure such as a priest or teacher, or develops
as informal, peer-group conversation. In such situations, what becomes significant is not only that meaning-making is, as discourse ethnographers have
shown, a shared and continuous process. Further, because interpretation of
media discourse in a group involves dialogue about a discourse that has already
been interpreted individually, rather than a process of coordinating participation
in an experience or task still underway,[4] a new layer of secondary or
'meta-'representation is introduced. That extra layer of representation consists
in part of other people's *attitudes* towards the particular meanings being discussed as well as towards meaning-making in general. The various mental

---

[4] As in Gillian Brown's comprehension research tasks. See Brown, *Speakers, Listeners, and
Communication*.

representations of the discourse that are being sifted and combined into an overall view are tested against interpretive constructions created by other people, with such dialogue inevitably reflecting values and power relations within the interpreting group. Moderation of other people's interpretation by leaders or figures of disproportionate influence in such groups can lead interpreters to view a discourse differently depending on who they watch or listen with, and who they talk to afterwards. The process also contributes to how people move in and out of membership of what have been called different interpretive communities.[5] In some circumstances, the extra layers of attitude towards meaning may even dominate over earlier processing activity. This type of social stabilisation of meaning becomes prevalent if, for instance, people are certain they won't find a TV programme suitable even before they've watched it, or feel convinced in condemning a novel, film or art exhibition as obscene or blasphemous, or in some other way offensive, without ever needing to see it.

## 6.5 Meaning approximation

Disputes over meaning are resolved by one of three main outcomes: the anger or grievance at the contested interpretation is relieved by a judgment in favour of one party and against the other (or others); or common ground is found in a meaning the parties can to some extent agree on; or the parties agree to differ, and settle and walk away without any resolution. By the time disputes reach court, the third of these alternatives is less likely, because by that stage such an outcome may be both publicly humiliating and also expensive. To achieve either of the other two outcomes, arbitration requires a process to establish a single meaning.

In order to weigh up the relative merits of competing meanings, however, it is necessary to know what those meanings are first. This involves stabilising and stating them, for instance in a written complaint form or legal pleading. A specific 'audit point' for meaning in what I have described as a flow of interpretation and reflection must therefore be decided on: when and where was the meaning felt, and by whom? It is not self-evident, however, what the appropriate time-point for meaning is or on what basis that should be decided. Three main possibilities exist.

In principle, 'the meaning' might be considered to consist only of those responses reported *during* exposure to a discourse, by analogy with experimental procedures used in discourse comprehension studies. Besides the obvious impracticality of such a procedure, this way of identifying meanings makes little

---

[5] The idea of 'interpretive communities' aims to acknowledge patterns in interpretations that vary in predictable ways, depending on how meanings are arrived at, while rejecting the idea of fixed or inherent meaning. See Fish, *Is There a Text in This Class?*

sense: a procedure for elicitation or reporting could only be initiated *after* a discourse had already been felt worthy of complaint; by then, creating a new interpretive experience to capture 'raw interpretation' would require new experimental subjects, defeating the aim of dealing with the immediate experience of the legal protagonists themselves. The only alternative to this would be some kind of bizarre, on-the-spot self-reporting, like a think-aloud protocol or interpretive diary.

Alternatively, meaning could be judged to be whatever representation is constructed during a film's final credits, or on closing a book: a sort of summing up of the process of meaning-making at the point of closure that the discourse itself seems to offer. But such an 'audit point' for meaning presents similar difficulties to those of contrived 'online' comprehension experiments. By the time anyone knows they want to report an account of their response, the particular interpretive moment has passed.

Or meaning might be considered to be mental experience of a discourse 'recollected in tranquillity'. This more reflective view of what a discourse means – with meaning now including the significance created for the discourse by the continuing flow of life and dialogue subsequently, as much as by specific mental representations 'at the time' – results in complaints being based on reactions formulated only after a time-lag. Such accounts of interpretation deal no longer with effects created at the time but with those created cumulatively and later. Those later interpretations may retain some of the freshness and immediacy of first impact, but people often describe their comprehension process as leading to a 'meaning you end up with', as if meaning settles and is enriched, as well as being filtered or forgotten, by being gradually absorbed as personal meaningfulness.

The question of a suitable audit point for meaning is not purely theoretical. Choices have to be made that have real consequences, and judges and media regulators themselves tend to take a firm view. The interpretation in question should be that of the original context of publication or broadcast. The moment of interpretation resembles other actions that come up for judgment before the law (a robbery, a murder, or a contested financial transaction). What is to be assessed is the impact that the film or book or advert had when it was watched, or when the label was first read on the packet, or when someone opened their newspaper on a Sunday morning. Despite priority being given to this original meaning-creating experience, however, it is only a later reconstruction of such experiences that receives scrutiny. Legal consideration of meaning involves a kind of replay. The contested discourse is given a full airing, but that airing inevitably admits inferences and influences available after the fact which would not, and possibly could not, have been entertained at the time. This backward look in the direction of what interpretation might have been like at an earlier moment is reflected in awkward frequency in legal discussion of hypotheticals such as 'would have...' in arguments on all sides. The classic hermeneutic problem persists: of being interested in a meaning as experienced at one historical moment while constructing it at another.

## 6.6     Given time and attention

Dilemmas concerning time in meaning-making may appear purely academic debating points here too, rather than practical concerns in resolving any given dispute. What matters, it may be contended, is not so much struggling to be precise about which exact meaning is the one to be decided as a 'best endeavours' approach to settling a situation or at least calming the parties down. In this practical view, meaning arbitration is a rhetorical knocking of heads together rather than semantic truth-discovery (and in such circumstances, the spatial schema for meaning adopted above should accommodate another kind of meaning: the 'near-enough' meaning).

Whatever protestations are made, however, that time-course issues in meaning are merely theoretical snares, to be ignored for practical purposes, such questions do sometimes bite as practical problems for media law and regulation, as well as being implicit in the structure of legal adjudication. Two particular contexts stand out. Firstly, such issues become relevant where a process of interpretation is for some reason interrupted; in those circumstances, the court or regulator must decide what time-frame to invoke for expected completion or closure of the meaning in question and what to do about meanings half-formed in the meantime. Secondly, the issues are relevant where varying degrees of time and attention are given to an interpretive process; in those circumstances, the court or regulator must decide between radically divergent interpretations that are likely to be put forward as a result. Consider an example of each of these types of situation.

### 6.6.1    Interrupted interpretation: 'Nothing good ever came out of America'

When interpretation is interrupted, a practical problem arises of clarifying the time-frame for meaning to be created: how long is the interpreter expected to wait for the 'complete meaning'? In principle, such problems could arise wherever texts unfold over a series of episodes. So this could be a problem with any TV or radio series (and with some serials). Each episode of a narrative series brings some plot lines to an end, continues others, and introduces still others. Themes are extended across episodes; and events that are depicted in one episode – including violent or sexually explicit events that might well give rise to complaint – are often contextualised only in another. Deciding what the relevant meaning of any given scene is, therefore, or of any particular episode, requires choice of an appropriate interpretive horizon. There may be very good reasons why meaning should not be expected to be self-contained within a 15-minute programme segment before the next advert break, but it might seem less reasonable to carry over a 'hung' meaning between episodes that make up a long-running series or to justify an effect in a film by urging an audience to wait for fuller contextualisation or explication in the sequel. Responses to such issues are built on complex but often tacit views taken of who or what creates meaning, how, when, and for whom.

As an example, consider a poster campaign at 120 sites advertising a new digital TV channel, 'Five US' (which screens American drama, comedy, films and talk shows). The campaign, in 2006, began with an initial, mystery or 'teaser' poster, which carried no brand name or logo, and only one line of text: 'Nothing good ever came out of America.' One week later a second poster appeared at the same sites (plus a further 200 other sites) with the line 'Who says nothing good ever came out of America?' accompanied by the brand name of the TV company plus names of some of the imported shows on offer. In the meantime, however, complaints had been received about the first poster by the Advertising Standards Authority, including some from US citizens.[6] The complainants claimed that the first poster conveyed an unfair, anti-American attitude, was offensive and racist towards Americans, and could incite violence in areas where tension already existed.

Leaving aside other technical issues, discussion centred on whether the first poster should have been required to put forward a complete, self-contained meaning in order to satisfy the advertising code, rather than making a rhetorical claim at odds with the advertisers' actual view in order to overturn that view in the second poster. Some people must have seen the first poster but missed the second, complainants argued; they would have formed their interpretation exclusively on the basis of what was said and shown in the first. The advertisers argued, by contrast, that 'most people would have recognised the first poster as incomplete and would have delayed making a judgment until the entire message was clear'.

Can meaning be responsibly held in abeyance in this way from one week to the next in anticipation of later posters in a campaign, as needed for this sort of 'teaser' poster? If it can, then the meaning to be judged against advertising standards is whatever meaning is created for the series as a whole. If it can't, then the first poster's announcement – which the advertisers themselves considered 'an opinionated statement that was designed not to be considered in isolation but as a precursor to follow up posters' – should provide the self-contained meaning to be judged against the code. Allowing interpretation of a series of communications over time carries an implication, however: other

---

[6] A total of ninety-nine complaints against a poster campaign mounted by Five US (Channel 5 television), reported December 2006, www.asa.org.uk.

material would need to be evaluated on the same grounds of whether it could be argued to relate to some more extended discourse strand of which it forms a part. This would open up awkward cases, if generalised to other areas of regulation: how far should one day's newspaper allegation be viewed as only one step in a scrics or strand, not to be taken in isolation but contextualised or balanced later, for instance, in a continuing campaign waged by the newspaper? How close together in time should programmes or items such as reports or documentaries be, if they are to achieve balance of broadcast output on a controversial theme? How long should be allowed to elapse between a programme or article complained of and a 'right of reply' piece required by a regulator, if one is to be interpreted in relation to the other? There is no shortage of questions, or of practical proposals in relation to those questions. Each takes an implicit view on a more rarely formulated, underlying question: what constitutes an appropriate time-frame for meaning in what is always a continuous process of interpretation?[7]

### 6.6.2 Porn-heads in the newspaper

My second example is also about incomplete interpretation. But it only involves a single text. Interpreting even a single text takes time, though not the same amount of time for each person. Reading print discourse can mean skimming for general meaning or scanning for specific information perhaps as often as attention to a whole text, which can anyway be either casual or careful. Listening to the radio goes on in noisy workplaces while people do many other things as well as in quiet rooms where people listen attentively. The many different *uses* of discourse beg the question: what is the necessary standard of attention in interpretation, beyond which frivolous misunderstanding of a discourse will no longer be seriously entertained as the communicator's responsibility? Communicators should presumably not be held responsible for meanings produced by interpreters who don't pay any attention. But what about interpreters who do pay some attention, but may or may not read or view the whole discourse complained of? Or interpreters who pay full attention, but only engage with part of the discourse (for instance a newspaper story headline or the largest print on the label, or the main image and caption while driving past a poster, or the first five minutes of a film – each a common set of reception conditions)? Deciding what should count as the threshold of a meaning to be taken seriously calls for consideration of the different circumstances in which processing and interpretation take place.

In an influential 1995 libel case, *Charleston v. News Group Newspapers Ltd*, the newspaper the *News of the World* published (as part of a report on a

---

[7] On the time-frame dimension involved in achieving impartiality, see Robertson and Nicol, *Media Law*, pp. 601–3.

new computer game) photos of the faces of two well-known *Neighbours* actors, with their faces superimposed on the bodies of other people depicted in pornographic poses. The photos and headline implied that the actors had willingly adopted the poses, while the captions and full text made it plain that this was a contrived visual effect.

The case went in favour of the newspaper and against the complainant, who had failed to show defamation. Explaining his opinion at appeal, Lord Nicholls of Birkenhead emphasised how everyone reads selectively, scanning headlines and turning pages, with readers pausing at different points to read an article and leaving some articles unread. He also addressed the question of whether a headline, taken alone or with an attached picture, could still be defamatory if the text of the article as a whole removes the defamatory imputation. Since some newspaper readers only see the banner headline and glance at the picture, without reading the accompanying article, in their mind the reputation of the complainants might be damaged. But Lord Nicholls went on to argue that English defamation law requires a single standard of meaning – not multiple interpretations, either simultaneously or at successive moments – in order to determine whether an article is defamatory: a standard embodied, as we will see in Chapters 8 and 9, in the 'ordinary reader' of that newspaper. Such a standard, Lord Nicholls acknowledged, is a yardstick. Readers of mass circulation newspapers 'vary enormously in how they read articles and how they interpret what they read', with the result that 'some readers understand in a defamatory sense words which by the single standard of the ordinary reader would not be judged defamatory, and vice versa'.

Having acknowledged that the yardstick involves simplification, Lord Nicholls went on to argue that in this case the ordinary reader would not have failed to read captions accompanying the pictures which made clear that the complainants' faces had been superimposed on other actors' bodies. Those captions encouraged the ordinary reader to infer that the complainants had not actually been indulging in the activities shown in the pictures. Other details of text and layout were offered as evidence of what the ordinary reader would have noticed and inferred. Switching back from the idiom of the constructed legal fiction of the ordinary reader to an apparent act of interpretation at a specific time and on a given date, Lord Nicholls felt able to declare confidently that, 'when the ordinary reader put down the *News of the World* on 15 March 1992, he or she would have thought none the worse of the two actors'.[8]

---

[8] Lord Nicholls in *Charleston v. News Group Newspapers Ltd* [1995] 2 AC 65, at 73–4 (HL). Context for this quotation is provided in the longer extract discussed in Barendt and Hitchens, *Media Law*, pp. 354–6.

## 6.7 This will mean more later

In each of the two examples just described, meaning was viewed principally as 'discourse processing' or comprehension: what the reader may or may not have comprehended at the time, or over a period. Less attention was given to the 'significance' dimension of meaning. As we have seen, however, meaning can also be viewed in this less event-like way. If meaning is understood as a process of gradual appropriation and augmentation of significance, then much longer time-spans than those discussed so far open up. Emphasis must be placed on how meaning accumulates and is absorbed into or adopted by the self, modifying beliefs and acting as a guide to ways of living. The timeline for such signification is much longer, arguably a lifetime.

Early in *Seven Types of Ambiguity*, the poet and literary critic William Empson offers an analysis of different possible meanings for the line in Shakespeare's Sonnet 73, 'bare ruined choirs, where late the sweet birds sang'. He points to a sort of digestion of meaning which he describes as the meaning 'people are thinking of when they say "this poet will mean more to you when you have had more experience of life"'.[9] Empson acknowledges that such meaning may be 'hardly in reach of the analyst at all'. But he goes on to distinguish between information that in principle can be made available to explicate such a meaning (which he says is irrelevant to the Shakespeare line, because the problem is not one of background knowledge) and a sense of being 'at home' in a structure of meaning, or having a disposition or readiness to apprehend a certain kind of meaning – a view of meaning within Empson's account of verbal ambiguity that has unexpected affinities with the larger 'fore-structures of meaning' envisaged in Gadamer's hermeneutics.[10]

'Readiness' for a meaning seems both a personal and a community matter: a question of personal growth and self-formation, and at the same time a public climate for taking on board particular ways of representing given topics. As a dimension of time in meaning, of course, this might also raise only theoretical problems. Arguably the most relevant practical questions associated with it are ones where a text is considered controversial at the time of its publication or exhibition – it may be considered obscene, blasphemous, or in some other way offensive – but where an argument can be made that it conveys meanings or significance of a kind likely to be grasped only over a longer period of reception. Deciding what to do about anticipated meanings in the future rather than demonstrated meanings from the past involves setting aside immediate tensions

---

[9] William Empson, *Seven Types of Ambiguity* (London: Chatto and Windus, 1930), pp. 21–2.

[10] Starting from his discussion of Heidegger, Hans-Georg Gadamer examines the role played by 'fore-structures' or historical conditions of understanding in Part II of *Truth and Method*, 2nd edition, trans. Joel Weinsheimer and Donald Marshall (London: Sheed and Ward, 1989).

in order to assess what the longer-term significance may be. In such circumstances, what might be called the 'stakeholders' in meaning are not only present readers and viewers – who may be intolerant in either their praise or their condemnation – but also interpreters in the future. It is necessary to speculate about a much longer timeline of future interpretation if freedom of expression concerns in relation to such texts are to be met.

The historical record of literary and media censorship in most countries offers many examples of interpretations that have changed radically over extended periods, and of regulation or censorship interrupting texts' reception because of a damagingly near horizon of interpretive values. It is a question worth asking, therefore, how far, by restricting or censoring a text at one point in time, its future meanings and meaningfulness are unwisely closed off, even before there is a chance for alternative kinds of possible significance to be explored. The practical issue is whether a presently entertained interpretation – for instance, that a discourse misrepresents its subject or represents it in an unacceptable and harmful way – should restrict further circulation of that text, or how far trust should be placed in some future but as yet unknown set of interpretive circumstances in which the same discourse may make a different kind of sense. The author Salman Rushdie took the opportunity presented by writing a short essay sixteen years after the *Satanic Verses* controversy to meditate on the question of restricting circulation of possible interpretations and the importance of making currently sensitive material available to later generations. He called his essay simply 'Coming after us'.[11]

### 6.8     Summary

In this chapter, I have shown why it is necessary in evaluating conflicting accounts of meaning to consider not only what meaning is, but the cognitive processes involved in *attributing* meaning. I suggest that such processes must be taken into account in deciding which aspects of meaning text-producers should be held responsible for.

I have also suggested that time plays an important role in determining meaning, on three contrasting timescales.

1.  A timescale concerned with crystallisation of a perception of meaning in the instant of comprehension. What we usually refer to as the meaning of an expression or stretch of discourse is often treated as a timeless, abstract idea rather than a localised representation. But such meanings take the form either of an expressed output such as a written review or spoken commentary, or of

---

[11] Salman Rushdie, 'Coming after us', in Lisa Appignanesi and Sava Maitland (eds.), *Free Expression Is No Offense* (Harmondsworth: Penguin, 2005), pp. 21–6. The essay begins with the arresting sentence (p. 21), 'I never thought of myself as a writer about religion until a religion came after me.'

a quickly formed mental representation such as a thought, belief, attitude or memory trace. If we are to anchor accounts of meaning in the processes by which meanings are made, then accounts of interpretation need to explore the time taken to process segments of discourse 'in real time', and to distinguish between such 'online' processes and later reconstructions of meaning.

2. A timescale of links backwards in time, between the cognitive point of interpretation and the past. Such links are implicit in the structure and content of long-term memory which is activated as assumptions used in inferring meanings. The knowledge-base mobilised in creating new meanings is a network of already derived and stored beliefs within which the relevance of any new representation must find its place. What appears to be an instantaneous act of discourse processing reaches *backwards* in time, in that patterns and contrasts in the interpreter's system of beliefs – what might be called the person's system of acquired personal meanings – are gathered over time through socialisation, with traces left from cumulative, earlier perception and understanding of words, images and other symbolic resources.

3. A timescale projected into the future of interpretation, both by the self and by others. The after-effect of discourse processing is a slow absorption of meanings that have been processed, distilling from comprehension new kinds of significance or allowing the processed meaning of the discourse gradually to fade away. This the 'it will mean more later' view of meaning opens out the timescale of meaning-making measured in seconds into foreseeable *future* time, for which current interpretations are provisional resources for use in future circumstances that can be anticipated but are as yet unknown.

*Part III*

Verbal disputes and approaches to resolving them

# 7     Meaning as a knockout competition

## 7.1     Introduction

In this chapter and in Chapter 8, I consider how disputes over meaning are handled, *as disputes*: what roles are played by the parties; how the parties engage with one another; and what standards are appealed to in efforts made by third parties to arrive at decisions. This chapter begins with ideas of 'argument' and develops an account of how disputes over meaning often combine perceived cooperation with underlying conflict of intention and interest. Taking up the theme of time from Chapter 6, I also show how media law and regulation procedures create distinctive, 'after-the-fact' adjudicative speech events, even as they seek to evaluate interpretations that, it is claimed, were ascribed 'at the time'. Overall, I show how complainant and defendant work over earlier versions of meaning in order to accentuate their own claims. In doing so, they pull meaning in different directions. Meanwhile, a judge, jury or adjudicating body seeks to decide '*the* meaning'.

## 7.2     Fighting over meaning

In the red corner, complainants and accusers (often individuals, but they can also be companies or institutions): 'widespread and systematic deception of millions of viewers'; 'a farrago of half-truths'; 'a grotesque manipulation of the facts'; 'a pyramid of piffle'; 'a pile of claptrap'; 'a tissue of serious factual inaccuracies'; 'simply vicious vapourings and a vile tissue of lies'; 'a piece of window-dressing designed to deceive'; 'a view that cannot have been honestly held'; 'flagrantly outrageous remarks'; 'a series of half-truths, distortions and what appear to some as not so much amnesia as lies'.

And in the blue corner, defendants and apologists (often, though not always, newspapers, media companies or institutions): 'comment on a topic of public concern'; 'the language was not excessive'; 'the piece was clearly marked as opinion'; 'comment was only offered on the basis of non-disputed facts'; 'a fair account in all key respects'; 'fair in that an opportunity was given to the plaintiff to reply to the comments which are now complained of'.

Holding the ring, the courts and regulatory bodies. Beyond the official bodies, the court of public opinion, with its own history within the body politic and changing view of proceedings – perhaps increasingly all part of a media-fuelled spectator sport.

Or switch the image slightly. We now have, on the ropes: the early 1960s Government Minister John Profumo's famous line when challenged on his relationship with a prostitute one of whose other customers was a Russian spy, 'there was nothing inappropriate in my relationship with Miss Keeler';[1] President Bill Clinton's 'I want you to listen to me, I'm going to say this again, I did not have sexual relations with that woman, Miss Lewinsky';[2] or, shrugging off challenges to the British Government's claims about an imminent threat from Saddam Hussein's WMDs, an anonymous civil servant's withering, 'silly fuss over words and details'.[3] Pursued for the killer punch in the other corner by: investigative newshounds, pressure groups and opposing barristers, as well as in some cases by ambulance chasers and gold diggers. When out for the count, the seemingly gracious, saving euphemisms are offered: 'There had been a miscommunication'; 'I gave a reply that wasn't untrue but was clearly misleading'; 'I'm sorry I caused misunderstanding'; 'I'm sorry I showed a lack of candour.' Or alternatively the more defiant, 'this isn't the occasion to play the truth game'.

My boxing scenario suitably reflects the adversarial nature of disputes over the meanings conveyed by media discourse, at least in British and US courts. Based on the early history of libel law, a duelling analogy might also have been justified: semantics at dawn. As far as they can, though, legal processes follow painstaking procedures in arriving at their decisions: statements of claim, written rebuttals, preliminary hearings in chambers, systematic presentation of evidence, measured decisions and leave to appeal. Even so, when the procedures become an object of satire – as ritualised slanging matches in costume, or protagonists tearing chunks out of each other rather than converging on a sensible settlement – the image can seem more one of Punch and Judy.

With regulatory bodies, the adversarial nature of debating meaning is less obviously pugilistic. Complaints are made. Responses and evidence are requested from the broadcaster or newspaper. That evidence is considered by

---

[1] For a fuller account, see 'John Profumo', in Matthew Parris and Kevin Maguire, *Great Parliamentary Scandals: Five Centuries of Calumny, Smear and Innuendo* (London: Robson Books, 1995), pp. 156–81. For wider analysis of political scandal, see Thompson, *Political Scandal.*

[2] 'I know that my public comments and my silence about this matter gave a false impression. I misled people, including even my wife', said President Clinton in a four-minute TV address from the White House in 1998. For discussion of lies, true statements which lead to false inferences, and outright lies, as well as the argument that debates over meaning may have been a matter of 'angels on the head of a pin' in this controversy, see Lawrence Solan, 'The Clinton scandal: some lessons from linguistics', in Janet Cotterill (ed.), *Language in the Legal Process* (Basingstoke: Palgrave, 2002), pp. 180–95.

[3] Osborne, *The Rise of Political Lying*, pp. 184–218.

the complainant. Adjudication is made by an expert panel, sometimes with the help of a meeting or brief tribunal. A service standard is promised and monitored. Views differ on whether this type of extrajudicial process is as effective as open confrontation in court. Either way, arbitration must engage with the parties' self-interest, as well as the material consequences of any given interpretation; what the protagonists say cannot be just accepted at face value. This is especially important where complainants are not members of the general public but commercial rivals, as is common with complaints about comparative advertising and malicious falsehood.

In media law and regulation, the meaning of a discourse that is being contested is not a seminar topic. Meaning is something to be fought over; and judges and juries do not research meaning, they decide it. As arguments are bartered and points conceded about the merits of competing interpretations, different angles on meaning also become weapons to fight with. To reach an outcome, legal or regulatory proceedings must fix a legally defining meaning as the basis for calculating any damaging effects it has caused, and so what the verdict should be (guiding, where appropriate, the award of damages and costs, as well as in some cases imprisonment of the defendant).

## 7.3    Argument culture

Such processes are not without their critics, including as regards how language is handled in stressed, legal confrontations. The staging or framing of verbal interaction as head-to-head argument prompted the sociolinguist Deborah Tannen, for example, to write her critical account of 'argument', *The Argument Culture*.[4] Tannen suggests that in Western countries confrontation is unnecessarily ritualised; combat and 'battle' are too widely adopted as metaphors for social interaction; and an 'automatic warlike stance' is too readily adopted. Tannen's objection is not to fighting in any circumstances. She only objects to the pervasiveness of the idea that there are two sides to every argument, and to the extension of that idea into a belief that we should then fight those two sides out to the finish. The proper balance of many discussions, she argues, is lost in this way of proceeding and genuine debate or real 'argument' is curtailed. She calls the 'battle' approach to resolving issues 'agonism', borrowing the term from the classical Greek word for contest.

'Agonism' is clearly the basis of adversarial systems of justice such as those adopted in Britain and the USA. Such systems are usually justified on the grounds that they provide a dialectical structure for presentation, testing and rebuttal of arguments, and are for that reason the best way to arrive at a fair

---

[4]  Deborah Tannen, *The Argument Culture: Changing the Way We Argue* (New York: Virago, 1999).

verdict. But the question arises: how appropriate is this adversarial process to the particular challenge, discussed in previous chapters, of dealing with *meaning*?

## 7.4    Need for counselling in a meaning triangle

Consider again why it should be necessary to fight over meaning at all. If the meaning of an utterance or text is fixed by the semiotic codes in which it is expressed, then we might expect only rare disputes, in exceptional cases. There would be instances of deception and fraud, but these would be caused by malicious or inappropriate *use* of discourse in a given situation rather than by disagreement about what something means. It is only if there is significant (and credible) interpretive divergence that the authority of textually determined or consensual meaning should break down.

As we saw in Chapter 5, however, there *is* some justification for a view that meaning variation may be considerable. The meanings of words and visual signs – especially when used in longer stretches of discourse – are not rigidly fixed. Instead, a range of contextual triggers prompt meaning variation at different levels. At a certain point, such variation ceases to be socially comfortable 'difference' and tips over into disputable incompatibility, either unintentional or as the result of malicious intent – or sometimes a volatile cocktail of the two.

Meaning is never just meaning, but always meaning for someone. In disputes, the incompatible meanings that are put forward must be seen in relation to people's frameworks of belief, self-image, sense of what is right or appropriate, and professional or commercial self-interest. An interpreter's response to an utterance or text may be largely based on how favourably any of these factors comes through in the meaning they choose to ascribe. If an addressee feels misrepresented, injured or in some other way offended, on the other hand, he or she may decide there are grounds for disputing whatever is considered to have been communicated. This is what makes contestation of meaning more than interpretive variation. It involves sense of injury rather than merely disagreement or perception from a different point of view; there must be some sense of having been misled, misreported, misrepresented, defamed or insulted. That sense of grievance is then formulated as a specific complaint or 'cause of action'. For complaints based on such perceptions of injury to need to be settled by a formal procedure of some kind, rather than being resolved by apology or agreement to disagree, the person accused of causing the offence must dispute that the words do bear, or are capable of bearing, the interpretation alleged.

But how did the differences of interpretation that cause the problem ever creep in? Because of the combined role of code and inference in how meanings are arrived at, it was argued in Chapter 5, the meanings at issue in any dispute are the result of a complex division of labour. Some meaning effects are produced primarily by conventions of the code; some arise because of the need to ascribe a communicator's intention; and other meaning effects are the result of creative inferential interpretation by the receiver. The structure of an interpretive situation as a result is a kind of meaning triangle.

There is a tradition of thinking about meaning in terms of triangles, most famously C. S. Peirce's, and Ogden and Richards's, triangles used to describe the symbolic properties of an individual sign. The triangle I propose to describe here, by contrast, is about interpretive roles and agency, and is concerned with very different aspects of meaning from those explored by Peirce or Ogden and Richards.[5]

Imagine a triangle whose three corners represent the different agencies I have identified as being at work in constructions of meaning. The apex is the linguistic code. At bottom left is the communicator's intention. At the triangle's bottom right-hand corner, attribution of meaning by the receiver. The extent to which one or other of these agencies takes precedence over the other two guides (or, from another point of view, distorts) the resulting meaning. The triangle is not stable or static. It can be pulled or stretched in different directions when there is interpretive disagreement. If absolute priority is given to the meaning attributed by the receiver, then in an adversarial or agonistic conflict over meaning the complainant will win. She or he is accepted as having perceived or felt whatever is claimed. If, however, absolute priority is given to the meaning intended by the communicator, then the defendant will win. She or he will deny having intended the alleged meaning. If absolute priority is given to the meaning provided by the code, then there should never have been a dispute in the first place; any dispute that *has* arisen could have been resolved by checking the code, for instance by looking up what was said in a dictionary, phrase book, or code book of symbols.

It is worth stating the obvious. Conflict resolution over meaning cannot work by simply picking between the three alternatives. Absolute precedence cannot just be given to any one of the three agencies. Meaning must be found in what is a more complex division of labour. Communication is open-ended, inferential and creative; that propensity cannot be closed back down whenever

---

[5] The Ogden and Richards sign triangle can be found in *The Meaning of Meaning*, p. 11. Lyons summarises similar accounts and presents triadic relations in signification in his own triangle, in *Semantics*, p. 96. For pedagogic use of triangles that are not about individual signs but which indicate relations between text, producer and consumer, with meaning in the middle, see for instance the diagram in Andrew Beck, Peter Bennett and Peter Wall, *Communication Studies: The Essential Introduction* (London: Routledge, 2002), p. 25. My account of a 'meaning triangle' is an elaboration in linguistic terms of explanations given by defamation specialist Patrick Moloney QC to juries, clients, pupils and other interested parties about how meaning is contested (personal communication).

there is a struggle over meaning by fiat, suddenly appealing to one-sided authority whether of the speaker, the hearer or the code. Instead, in order to maintain public order at the level of discourse some interpretive construct must be devised to stand in for the supposed (but absent) fixity of the code, while giving due recognition to intentional and inferential dimensions. Judge and jury, or the regulatory body's panel, perform this role that conventions of the code fulfil in a fixed-meaning model of communication. Confronted with pulling and stretching in different directions, their task is to ascertain meaning.

Roles can now be added to the accounts of meaning at each corner of the triangle. Each corner designates someone's version of what the contested utterance or text means, someone who tries to pull the outcome towards one particular corner. The defendant is at the bottom left-hand corner. The complainant is bottom right. Presiding at the apex, and standing in for the conventional stability of the code, the relevant legal authority weighs up arguments and evidence in relation to legal tests prescribed for each offence, and decides where the meaning of the discourse complained of should lie within the area of the triangle.

### 7.4.1     Legal action replay

Viewed in this way, the legal or regulatory situation is a specialised communicative event, one in which different formulated meanings supported by different corners of the triangle are pleaded, scrutinised and haggled over. It is not a simple event, however, and has different levels or layers.

Consider court proceedings as the exemplary case. In court, there are the protagonists themselves, complainant and defendant, with their irreconcilable interpretations of the contested utterance or text. Their interpretations, as we saw in Chapter 6, are not 'objects' fixed by a single interpretive act but an accumulation of repeated acts of processing influenced by subsequent dialogue and advice, layered on top of initial engagement with the utterance or text complained of as either its producer or receiver. These accumulated interpretations are replayed in a form organised to meet as far as possible the court's expectations. The voice given to those reconstructed meanings is only partly that of the protagonists themselves. Lawyers do much of the talking, reporting and amplifying the protagonists' interpretations and grievance on their behalf, even though the lawyers were not involved in either the original production or reception of the discourse and are acting on the basis of second-hand representations of what was communicated and understood there. Listening to the evidence, the judge, jury or expert panel are also 'outsiders' to the earlier communicative event. But they have become definitive in deciding what it meant.

Why should this matter? Isn't the complexity of the courtroom communicative event simply an elaborately described routine occurrence: people talking about what went on earlier, with mediation by a bystander asked to offer an independent view? I want to suggest that there is an important difference.

Meaning is more elusive and malleable than the facts of events such as a burglary or road accident. One important feature of feedback loops in conversation, I suggested in Chapter 1, is that they are more or less immediate. Much of the relevant context – including surrounding frameworks of topicality and allusion – is still in place, available to help settle vagueness or local misunderstanding. Interpretation in a courtroom, by contrast, deals with discourse most of whose original context has been replaced by new and different contextual assumptions. These new contextual assumptions inevitably have the potential to redirect the inferences likely to be drawn by those now considering the contested material for the first time. Efforts can be made by the court to specify the meanings to be tested as far as possible, by having them stated clearly in writing in the pleadings. But if meaning is always 'meaning for someone', then the split character of the communicative situation inevitably reframes interpretation of the earlier discourse. Opposing lawyers help to establish a meaning that will suit their client's interest by encouraging the interpretation they themselves put forward and building scepticism about their opponent's meaning. 'The meaning' is now judged less against expectations of the earlier addressee or audience, in a 'thick' context of situated reception at the time, than replayed to the court for analytic purposes and rationalised in relation to interpretive expectations of a hypothetical addressee, who must be projected back into the original circumstances.

This projection across split contexts may be difficult. But conflicts over meaning do need to be resolved. The depth of anger, pain and outrage occasionally provoked by discourse puts this beyond question. Difficulties outlined here may therefore be a practical difficulty that courts and regulatory bodies must contend with. The courts may in turn view their adjudicative role on meaning with differing degrees of confidence or enthusiasm, especially where their task is exacerbated because (like a dictionary defining the meaning of a word by using other words) every extra procedure developed to clarify meaning gets further caught up in a web of supplementary words that raise their own meaning questions. In these difficult circumstances, courts have to interpret in a sense favourable to one or other aggrieved party, in order to bring litigation to a close. They also have an unenviable extra role thrust on them: the symbolic role of being the designated body responsible for deciding what meaning is.

### 7.4.2    *Only the meanings pleaded*

Complexities of the kind I am tracing in the communicative event structure of legal discussions of meaning may seem to make the work of courts and regulatory authorities somewhere between daunting and impossible. But there is another way of looking at things, in which legal arbitration appears more straightforward. An adversarial approach to meaning, seen from this different perspective, may even have advantages over other kinds of interpretive debate.

In a legal setting, it is only necessary to be concerned with the particular meanings or aspects of meaning put forward for deliberation. Most communication takes place without ever being complained of. It does not require legal construction or comment. A lot of discourse that *is* complained of never reaches court either, because the parties agree a practical settlement at an early stage. These two factors considerably reduce the amount and kind of meaning questions that need to be resolved in a formal, legal setting. Even with contested meanings that do reach court, interpretive work is selective. If the pleadings for a given action do not propose a particular interpretation, there is no need to consider it. No one wants a comprehensive account of the meaning effects of the discourse, only arbitration between the two (or more) meanings pleaded as being in contention. From this perspective, the interpretive task is less a matter of exhaustive discourse analysis than of selecting the least implausible reading from the ones on the menu.

In practice, this narrower approach to investigating meaning marginalises attention to many of the more complex effects created by audio, audio-visual and multimedia discourse, for example photographs, TV, film and web pages. Few people would question that precise details of colour, as well as sound effects, visual composition of a shot, and details of costume and *mise en scène* all contribute to overall signification; but such details tend not to become a focus for legal argument unless for some highly specific reason they suddenly become interpretively significant. Even if they do, such effects are still likely to be accounted for in an interpretive generalisation about overall impression that is accepted (or at least not challenged) on either side. Broadly the same applies as regards the affective dimensions of meaning and aesthetic properties and effects that texts give rise to. The 'feeling' or emotive potential of the discourse, which can be difficult to describe with precision, is treated as making itself felt as an overall impression left by the discourse. Many of the crux points, even with complaints about TV and film, are often (as I argued in Chapter 5) summarised in language and treated as if they involved linguistic meaning or types of meaning that can be grasped at a level of idealisation or abstraction.

## 7.5     Conflict and cooperation

In the face of so much conflict and contestation, it might be queried why linguistics and philosophy appear more concerned with communicative 'cooperation' than with communicative *struggle*. Is such a preference, out of reach of ugly, day-to-day confrontation, simply an academic article of faith reflected in Tannen's distaste for agonism? Why should Grice emphasise the notion of a 'Cooperative Principle', for instance, or Habermas make an appeal to 'mutual understanding' within his framework of Universal Pragmatics?[6] Shouldn't the agonistic concerns of courts and regulatory authorities push analysis of communication at least as much towards conflict?

There is something in this criticism, but different understandings of cooperation and conflict in communication are sometimes confused when it is made. Conflict and cooperation are not alternatives to each other in communication but often work together, albeit at different levels. Conflict is actual and experienced; cooperation can be actual too, but it is also hypothesised, even in cases of overt conflict, as a mechanism in how either comprehension or misunderstanding is created. Habermas's idea of 'mutual understanding' is a model of what communication *could* be (and for Habermas should be), put forward as an essential concept in modelling strategies at work in our efforts at achieving whatever understanding we do manage. Grice's account of a Cooperative Principle is similarly not a failure to see that conflict happens, but rather a principle that is hypothesised as the basis of the reasoning Grice believes allows us to fill in gaps between what is overtly said and what must be inferred if we are to understand what someone is getting at by using a particular form of words in a given context.[7]

Somewhat ironically, cooperation in Grice's theoretical sense plays a significant role in creating many meaning conflicts. Suppose you are angry with someone and want to be disparaging about that person to other people. You may choose to represent the person in some way that will allow your audience to see your intended meaning straightaway, because it is explicit in what you chose to say. Alternatively, you might veil your disparaging meaning in an indirect or oblique form of expression. If your utterance is well judged in relation to the situation, its meaning will still appear spontaneously enough to your audience because they instantly infer it; but your meaning is now only predictable (and can only be explained as something *you* anticipated) on the basis of some underlying interpretive mechanism or process in addition to the conventional meanings of your chosen words. What Grice and others have argued is that communication often only achieves its goal, even if that goal is ultimately to create a misleading effect, if it is processed as having been conveyed in a cooperative way.

---

[6] On the Gricean Cooperative Principle, see Grice, *Studies in the Way of Words*, pp. 22–40. For Habermas's Universal Pragmatics, see his 'What Is Universal Pragmatics?', in *On the Pragmatics of Communication*, pp. 21–103. For contextualisation of these ideas, see Cummings, *Pragmatics*.

[7] Sperber and Wilson's use of the concept of 'relevance' in place of 'cooperation' shows how interpretation can follow a principle of self-interest compatible with evolutionary accounts of human cognition rather than Grice's postulated notion of cooperation. Sperber and Wilson, *Relevance*.

In communication, then, cooperation and conflict work together. What is said may initially fail, against an expected standard of direct cooperation (e.g. because of Grice's Maxim of Quality, which forms part of his specification of how the Cooperative Principle works, according to which you should say and only say what you take to be the case). Your indirect expression 'flouts' this principle by saying something at odds with what you are likely to believe to be the case. But communication still succeeds at an inferential level because, on the strength of an expectation of Gricean cooperation, your addressee draws inferences to fill the gap and make your utterance seem cooperative again (such procedures being essential, for instance, with figurative language and irony). This mechanism of inference explains utterances that appear not to be cooperative but actually are. But now consider indirect, conflictual kinds of discourse. The same wheel that is spun to create implied meanings by restoring presumed cooperativeness can be spun again: the presumption of inference-level cooperation can be exploited for hostile or antagonistic purposes by the speaker. She or he chooses a form of words that covertly violates the Cooperative Principle, misdirecting the hearer towards false inferences that the hearers will draw in trying to restore presumed cooperativeness. In these circumstances, an utterance may appear initially not to be cooperative, then have a cooperative reading imposed on it by inference, only to be actually functioning *against* cooperation by misdirecting the addressee towards an interpretation which the speaker intends to be misleading.[8] Such complex layering of our communicative resources of choice of utterance, invited inference and hearer expectation is a core mechanism of spin, as well as many shades of mendacity, misinformation and other kinds of deception described in previous chapters.

## 7.6     Caught up in the act

How can efforts to resolve meaning disputes in media law and regulation cope with complex games of meaning bluff on this scale? Because arbitration typically deals with complaints after the fact (rather than with prior censorship or injunction), such questions are a matter of defining and evaluating meanings pleaded as being in contention in a dispute, rather than trying to restrict deceitful or manipulative behaviour before it happens. Two main strategies are employed to hold in place what would otherwise be a continuous kaleidoscopic image of claimed meanings: first, specification of the meanings in contention as precisely as possible; and second, clarification of the level of meaning within the communicative act that is being analysed. Each of these efforts towards definition is worth looking at more closely.

---

[8] See Grice, *Studies in the Way of Words*, p. 30. For exposition and illustration, see Thomas, *Meaning in Interaction*, pp. 65–78.

## 7.6.1    Opposing statements of meaning

Legal procedures attempt as far as possible to restrict continuously changing accounts of meaning. Careful formulation of statements of meaning is not just a way of expediting business or a ceremonial style of formality. It is also a response to the slippery and multidimensional character of meaning likely to be at stake in any contested situation. In day-to-day conversation, interpreters rarely evaluate meaning by dissecting it after the fact, as they must in a complaint adjudication or legal action. We do sometimes respond to what people say by directly querying or contesting what they meant; more commonly, though, we respond by spontaneous uptake, acting on what was said and adding something – however direct or oblique – to the topic rather than stepping outside the frame of dialogue to comment, metalingually, on its meaning. This is partly what makes conversation a continuous, shared production of meaning. Only where there is unexpected disruption in the onward flow do conversationalists ask for some kind of playback, or shift into a sort of repair strategy involving comment about language rather than addressing the subject matter in hand.

Conflicting meanings can only be examined, however, once it has been established what they are. So shifting to a metalingual level is a starting point in legal or regulatory discussion. Courts and regulatory bodies require meanings being claimed to be presented in fixed and explicit, generally written form, so that they can be scrutinised and evaluated. Meanings must be spelt out in pleadings or in a complaint submission that states them in the form of paraphrase (sometimes labelled and numbered, as Meaning 1, 2a, 2b, etc.). Interpretations that originated as spontaneous mental representations are in this process objectified, and take the new form of further or extra discourse about the contested discourse. When lawyers, judges and juries determine meanings, they respond to a combination of the original contested discourse with extra interpretive or 'metalingual' commentary on it, in a process that brings together meanings from different moments and situations and deals in ready-mades: here's a meaning I prepared earlier.

A meaning that provides the basis of an allegation which is presented in this way (rather than the contested utterance or text itself, which can be reinterpreted afresh whenever anyone chooses to) provides the baseline for argument. It will be referred back to, responded to and argued against in the unfolding process of the dispute. If the representations to be debated were only stored in people's minds, they would remain malleable and continuously susceptible to modification or drift in the course of argument, as people shift their ground depending on how things are going. The laborious task of establishing paraphrases or glosses of alleged meanings is undertaken in complaint adjudication and legal actions in order to stabilise as far as possible exactly what representations of the contested utterance or text are in contention.

### 7.6.2     Clarifying meaning level within a communicative act

With the meanings in contention in place, the process of contesting utterance meaning can start. This may take the form of face-to-face interaction or a more formal process of adjudication, and proceeds through a series of moves or turns that make up a drama of claim and counter-claim. The moves are codified to some extent. In courtrooms, there is likely to be question followed by answer, allegation followed by rebuttal, presentation of alternative accounts of a situation or readings of an expression, along with many other forms of the cut and thrust of verbal claim and challenge. Forward movement is propelled by moves or turns consisting of spoken claim and counter-claim, if the situation is dialogic, or of procedural steps made in written statements of claim, rebuttal and questioning within a complaint adjudication or legal action.

Development from turn to turn, or move to move, is achieved by either of two general strategies. Most commonly in a conversation, as I have said, a response turn involves some particular uptake in relation to meaning attributed to the previous utterance: it builds on what was said with further elaboration or introduction of new but related material (it may give a reason, explain the context, add an example or offer a counter-argument, etc.). Where the link between moves or turns is weak, the second adjacent turn will appear to be a digression, or will mark some other kind of discontinuity (sometimes appearing irrelevant or perverse rather than incoherent behaviour, departing from expectations governing the verbal situation). Alternatively, however, the response move can freeze the dialogue, and shift into metalingual commentary; it then offers a comment on or evaluation of the previous move, for example claiming that, as understood, it is false, simplistic, outrageous, scandalous, inaccurate or aggressive. A move of this type does not extend the meaning of the previous turn but interrupts dialogue in order to challenge it. While not the usual strategy, this critical meta-commentary is essential in evaluating statements, interrogating positions put forward by others, and so conducting public debate.

Such 'freeze-frame' metalingual comments offer insights into how interpretive disagreement works in general, as well as how it is managed in a legal or regulatory setting. Any verbal act is a combination of a 'content' and a particular force with which the act of utterance presents that content. Sometimes this double level in communicative acts is notated as $F(p)$, or a force acting on a core of propositional content.[9] When someone steps outside the flow of ongoing

---

[9] The distinction between illocutionary force, F, and propositional content, p, as well as how they work together in utterances, $F(p)$, is well explained in John Searle, 'A Taxonomy of Illocutionary Acts', in *Expression and Meaning: Studies in the Theory of Speech Acts* (Cambridge: Cambridge University Press, 1979), pp. 1–29. See also detailed discussion below, Chapter 11.

discourse in order to query or challenge what has been said, his or her meta-lingual comment can either refer to the proposition or content (i.e. the p) or it can refer to the force of the utterance as a verbal act (i.e. the F, for example how it is functioning as an act of allegation, accusation, threat, etc.). Incidentally, in a more precise account it might also be noted how the metalingual comment can be about the force, as a calculated, conventional effect on the addressee; or alternatively how it can be a comment on the expressive function for the speaker himself or herself, as in the comment that something was 'an emotional out-burst' (a phrase which ascribes significance of the behaviour to the speaker rather than to the addressee).

Opening up these levels offers a glimpse of possibilities in intercutting between them. A speaker can refer back to what has been said (whether in spontaneous conversation or in a more formal setting) by choosing between a set of patterned choices:

> (A) a reply which extends the topic (in my sense of continuing or
>      extending the dialogue on the prevailing topic)

or

> (B) a metalingual, freeze-frame evaluation or comment.

Each of these moves can in turn refer to either (C) the propositional content conveyed by the act; or (D) the communicative act itself, especially its force.

As an example of these permutations, consider a situation that arose during the Arms to Iraq scandal between 1990 and 1992 (and in the subsequent Sir Richard Scott inquiry into it in 1996). In the course of that scandal, a number of allegations were put by journalists to the Minister for Procurement of the time, Alan Clark. Although differing in their detail, the substance of the allegations was a claim that the minister was involved in selling arms to Iraq which could be used for military purposes, despite an embargo on doing so being in place at the time. The journalists' questions focused on an allegation of improper or possi-bly even illegal conduct. Their content was effectively that the minister was aware of or connived in selling arms to Iraq in contravention of the embargo. Obliged to comment in some way on such allegations – and leaving aside outlier options that simply block dialogue altogether, such as not making himself available for interview or saying 'no comment' – the minister had four main options as a basis for formulating his reply. These might be described as follows:

> **Combination A + C:** a response move that keeps to topic (A) rather
>      than stepping outside the frame to contest the act of alleging, and (C)
>      rebuts or challenges its content: e.g. 'The political situation in Iraq
>      required that, as far as we could, we should give active support to a
>      friendly government.'
>
> **Combination A + D:** a response move that keeps to topic (A) rather
>      than stepping outside the frame to contest the utterance of alleging,

and (D) rebuts or challenges its communicative force: e.g. 'If acting in the country's best interest only leads to accusations of improper conduct, then our commercial arrangements for dealing with Iraq are seriously flawed.'

**Combination B + C:** a comment (B) directed towards the previous utterance as an act which (C) rebuts or challenges its content: e.g. 'What you are alleging is completely untrue.'

**Combination B + D:** a comment (B) directed towards the previous utterance as an act which (D) challenges the force of that earlier utterance: e.g. 'It's scandalous to allege anything of the kind.'

In the situation of which this is a simplified account, Alan Clark's on-the-record reply to the question put to him along these lines was this: 'I have a complete and total answer to these allegations, which are rubbish, trash and sensational.'[10] What is fascinating about this reply, and many others like it before and since, is that it appears to deny the content (by calling what is alleged 'rubbish' and 'trash') while alternatively dismissing the speech act of alleging that content rather than the content itself (since 'rubbish' is something not worth saying as much as it is something that is untrue). Two years later, in a legal action against three executives from the arms exporter Matrix Churchill, Alan Clark was obliged to confess that ministers had not been straight about arms sales and the trial collapsed. In addition to admitting, somewhat ironically, that he had been 'economical with the actualité', he commented, 'I had to indulge in a fiction, and invite them [UK companies exporting to Iraq] to participate in a fiction.'[11] In the meantime, rhetorical play between levels of meaning in the communicative act in his on-the-record media response had served as plausible denial in an earlier chapter in that fiction.

## 7.7     Clever footwork between meanings

In the adversarial setting of a semantic 'boxing ring', the meaning relations I have described are always available for use in strategic manoeuvring. Speakers facing media questions have an extra diversionary tactic available to them alongside the customary advice to 'deny everything': they can respond either to utterance content – some situation in the world that has been referred to,

---

[10] The accusations to Alan Clark were made formally by Liberal Democrat MP Sir Russel Johnston in December 1990.

[11] See Osborne, *The Rise of Political Lying*, pp. 19–20. The French reference incorporated into 'economical with the actualité' may be seen as a conscious echo of Sir Robert Armstrong's contention, during his evidence in the Peter Wright Spycatcher trial, that he had been 'economical with the truth'. For detailed analysis of 'economical with the truth' as a euphemism for committing a professional lie, see Alan Durant, 'On the interpretation of allusions and other innuendo meanings in libel actions: the value of semantic and pragmatic evidence', *Forensic Linguistics*, 3 (2) (1996), 195–210.

which may be true or false – or to characteristics such as degree of appropriateness, politeness, insult or threat involved in the utterance that represents the state of affairs. For example, if door-stepped with the traditional philosophical conundrum, 'Have you stopped beating your wife?', an interviewee can either reply 'I never touched her' (addressing the proposition underlying the interrogative) or alternatively 'That's an outrageous accusation' (addressing the communicative force of the imputation being made).

Direct responses to utterance content are distinctive in being susceptible to judgment in terms of truth and falsity. Responses or comments that engage with the force or effect of a communicative act, if ever held to account, must be assessed according to some other standard of interpretive validity. How these different meaning relations, and standards suited to them, are addressed in legal interpretation is a topic for the next chapter. What is striking in day-to-day media communication is how easily switching between levels offers a body swerve to interviewees in tight corners. A cartoon in a satirical magazine vividly captures how blurring the different levels deflects attention from the crux of a contested situation without ensnaring the speaker in a recorded lie. The cartoon[12] shows the footballer David Beckham at a pre-Euro 2004 press conference using clever footwork in response to media allegations that he had an affair with his Spanish PA Rebecca Loos during his time at Real Madrid. A slightly flustered cartoon Beckham announces to the assembled press, 'The allegations against me are scurrilous, ludicrous, shocking and lots of other words that almost, but not quite, mean "false".'

## 7.8    Summary

In this chapter I have shown how contestation of meaning in the media fits into Tannen's wider notion of our 'argument culture'. Drawing on the work of Grice, I have also shown how disputes over meaning often involve a combination of perceived cooperation and underlying conflicts of intention and interest. I have described how a distinctive, 'after-the-fact' adjudicative speech event is created in media law and regulatory procedures, even as those procedures try to evaluate interpretations that it is claimed were ascribed 'at the time'. To link the different time-points, I suggested, discussion of what is meant reconstructs earlier meanings in a kind of interpretive 'legal action replay'. Such reconstruction cannot, however, avoid introducing fresh presuppositions and assumptions, which trigger new and potentially different inferences from those likely to have been drawn at the time.

---

[12] *Private Eye*, 21 March 2003.

# 8    Standards of interpretation

## 8.1    Introduction

A variety of standards exists in different areas of media law and regulation for fixing what the 'authorised meaning' of a contested discourse should be. These standards are outlined in this chapter. There are conceptual standards such as 'truth' and 'validity'. There are also standards based on notional, model readers, including the meaning attributed by an 'ordinary reader', by an 'average consumer', and by the (generic) 'reasonable man'. I show how normative interpretive guidance of both kinds reflects procedural as well as interpretive needs. But both kinds of interpretive standard, I suggest, also carry cultural baggage and can present difficulties of coherence and consistency.

## 8.2    Adjudicating meanings is different from interpreting

By 'standard' in interpretive disputes is meant the basis or criterion of whatever judgment is made in assigning a definitive meaning to a contested utterance or text. That standard is invoked on an indefinite number of occasions, whenever a decision needs to be made in a particular court action, or when a regulatory authority investigates a complaint. In principle, the process of deciding meaning in such a context is straightforward. Decide what is conveyed by the utterance or text, then decide whether that meaning meets the relevant legal test for the alleged offence or cause of action. When dealing with two meanings pleaded in contention, decide which meaning is right and which is not.

Unsurprisingly, things are not as straightforward as this. Largely this is because deciding on an authoritative meaning is different from analysing meaning in the ways I have mostly done in earlier chapters. It is not a matter of explicating a meaning that has been ascribed (by outlining intuitive or reported interpretations and showing how they arise). Rather than opening up meanings, a normative or prescriptive view is taken: closing meaning down to what interpretation *should* be derived (or should have been derived, on some earlier occasion of publication and reception). A further reason that deciding on an authoritative meaning for a contested text or utterance is difficult is that it is unclear, until specified, what confers legitimacy on any decision as to correct meaning beyond the power to insist. Interpretation *can* be imposed, like a parent or potentate knowing the meaning of other people's communications better than they do, and settling quarrels on that basis. If the authority in question is sufficient (whether it is parental, political, religious or legal), then little room is left for discussion once judgment has been pronounced. But where adjudication of meaning seeks legitimacy on the basis of wider assent and recognition among those who are subject to the outcome, as in modern systems of law and regulation, then some 'interpretive standard' or criterion of what it is that warrants a particular meaning must be adopted.

At its simplest, an interpretive standard offers generalised grounds for judgment that, as I indicated in the previous chapter, go beyond the positions or interests of the parties, as a kind of 'meaning umpire'. The main constraint, in an adversarial setting such as a court or with a complaint to a regulatory body, is that the standard should have a basis apart from either the 'intended' meaning maintained by a defendant or the 'experienced' meaning felt (and then advanced as the basis of a complaint) by a complainant. What can confer the 'more than' that allows an adjudicated meaning to be 'more than' a third subjective voice? In particular, what makes an official adjudicator's meaning more legitimate than those pleaded by the parties themselves, who, being more directly engaged in the actual circumstances, are in some respects better placed to know what was meant?

As a way into exploring how adjudications are arrived at, this chapter begins by reviewing different ways that decisions *might* be made. It then examines a number of different interpretive standards in use by courts and regulators. In these descriptions, I relate issues in determining validity of meaning to the account of meaning-making I have developed in earlier chapters. By way of conclusion, I consider how far meaning in media disputes is a matter of interpretive judgments that are independent of any particular offence (the 'meaning' of an utterance is its meaning, regardless of what offence is alleged) and how far it is a matter of rhetorical import in a specific set of circumstances. This question takes us back to the 'processing' and 'significance' dimensions of meaning outlined in Chapter 4. It also prepares for more detailed discussion of the particular areas of media law and regulation chosen as case studies in Chapters 9–11.

## 8.3     Sources of interpretive authority

Because there is such a range of possible criteria for interpretation, it is worth starting with a list of alternative, *potential* ways of deciding on a correct or definitive meaning. Adjudicators (judge, jury or regulatory panel) could, at least in principle, work on any – or alternatively some combination – of the principles indicated here.

1  Decide, as an *exercise of authority*, what the contested discourse means regardless of what the complainant, defendant, or anyone else says.

2  Ask each of the members of a jury or panel to draw on their intuitions and then *collectively arrive at a consensus* as to meaning.

3  Ask an *expert in meaning* who, as a different sort of exercise of authority, explains what the contested discourse means.

4  Establish what the correct meaning is *by applying logic and reason* to the question of how people should think.

5  Establish the meaning *everyone* would arrive at.

6  Establish the meaning *most people* would arrive at.

7  Establish the meaning *everyone in the target audience for the text* (however that is estimated) would arrive at.

8  Establish the meaning *most people in the target audience* (however that is estimated) would arrive at.

9  Establish the meaning that *a sufficient number of people* in the target audience would arrive at, with 'sufficient' defined by some further criterion (a significant proportion, a substantial proportion, '30–50 per cent', some number that is not numerically negligible but much less than half, etc.).

10  Establish the meaning *likely to be attributed by someone vulnerable or easily influenced*, for instance someone in need of protection from the practice the law is trying to control (e.g. vulnerable to being misled, threatened, groomed on the Internet, mis-sold something, depraved and corrupted, etc.).

11  Establish the meaning *likely to be attributed by someone sufficiently well informed* not to be led astray by excessive persuasion, and who is not given to wilful misinterpretation.

12  Establish the meaning *likely to be arrived at by a typical audience representative*, with 'typical' characterised by some further, defined set of attributes ('ordinariness', 'averageness', 'reasonableness', etc.).

13  Commission a *survey or focus group* to establish meaning empirically, based on a larger language-community sample than a jury.

Listing these alternatives illustrates how wide the range of possible approaches is. None of the listed approaches is simply a frivolous list-filler or act of faith, either, like saying toss a coin or consult the *I Ching*. It is possible to find in legal history or current practice examples of each being used as the basis for some interpretive test, or advocated as a credible alternative.

The sheer range of alternative approaches draws attention to the nature and extent of choices that must be made. It also begs historical and critical questions. Why have certain approaches been adopted rather than others? Why are some approaches used only exceptionally or only in some jurisdictions? What policy motives justify different standards in different areas of law, fields of regulation, or periods of legal history? For instance, why has the average consumer gradually replaced the credulous consumer as an advertising standard? And why does the reader assumed in advertising law read more cautiously than the reader in defamation law – with what implications as regards the interpretive standard required for 'trade libel' somewhere between the two?

## 8.4     What creates a 'standard'?

To see what makes an interpretive *standard* different from a particular interpretive judgment, consider the process of attributing meaning applied to the following textbook example[1] of an alleged defamatory statement (a statement that might have been published in the course of a TV or radio news programme, on a news website, in a blog or in a newspaper). Suppose it is stated that:

(U)  'The owner of the Celebration Café has been charged with an offence under the Food Act 1984.'

First, we must set out what is involved in interpreting here. The published text is what we might think of as the initial utterance, which we can call U. This published text or utterance, U, represents in a particular way (through its choice of words, sentence pattern and point of view) a claimed state of affairs in the world, A. We need to say 'in a particular way' because a variety of related forms (e.g. different sentences consisting of near-synonyms or adopting a different word order for emphasis) could have expressed 'the same thought', as U2, U3, U4, etc. Significantly different interpretations (I) can be placed on U as published, however, including the following:

(Ii)    'The owner of the Celebration Café has been charged with an offence...' (a face-value interpretation)

(Iii)   'The owner of the Celebration Café is suspected of committing an offence...' (an inference from charge to suspicion)

(Iiii)  'The owner of the Celebration Café has committed an offence...' (an inference from charge to guilt).

Each of these interpretations (Ii–iii) is a meaning likely to be distinguished in standard law textbooks as possibly attributable to the published statement, U. That statement (leaving aside complexities of different senses given in law, linguistics and philosophy to the term 'statement') in turn purports to represent the state of affairs in the world, A.

As regards the statement's meaning, two kinds of relation now exist. First, a relation between each of the interpretations Ii–iii and the state of affairs, A, that the statement U denotes. Each of these relations (Ii/A, Iii/A) could be true or false as a matter of fact, and evidence in support or against each might be presented.

---

[1]  This example is adapted from Sallie Spilsbury, *Media Law* (London: Cavendish, 2000), p. 64. But the general idea of a scale of inference from suspicion, to charge, or to committing an offence underlies the actual case of *Lewis v. Telegraph* [1964] AC 234. That case concerned an article in two national newspapers alleging a 'fraud squad probe' inquiring into the affairs of a city firm of which the complainant was chairman.

Second, a relation between each of the interpretations (Ii–iii) and the published utterance (Ii/U, Iii/U, etc.). If we wish to characterise this second set of meaning relationships, we need a more open-ended interpretive vocabulary than that of truth and falsity. You might think, for example, that it is reckless to infer guilt from charge (i.e. you feel only a face-value interpretation, Ii, is warranted), perhaps because you believe that someone is innocent until proven guilty. Or alternatively you might think that it is justified to infer guilt from charge (interpretation Iiii), perhaps because you believe there is no smoke without fire. Alternatively again, you may think that failing to see any implied meaning at all, beyond a face-value statement of charge (i.e. interpretation Ii), is merely naive about how news works, or even about how communication works in general.

Different meanings along these lines will collide in the course of any dispute about the utterance. The parties will each claim legitimacy for their own meaning, while impugning the other party's. So how can legal or regulatory procedures, or indeed any other approach to arbitration or mediation, find a way through? If courts or regulatory bodies are to tackle questions of meaning, they must establish an interpretive standard as a basis for deciding between the different contended alternatives (or for rejecting all of them). The credibility of that standard is what confers legitimacy on the judgment that one interpretation is warranted or acceptable, while another is not (or is less so). In addition to the question of whether any state of affairs A is or is not the case, therefore, courts and regulatory bodies must apply a standard that specifies what kind of interpretive strategy (such as those illustrated as Ii–iii) it is appropriate for an interpreter to adopt.

Let's say that an adjudicator (which could be a judge, or a combination of judge and jury in a libel action, or a tribunal body) reaches a decision in the Celebration Café dispute: that the meaning of the statement is neither that pleaded by the claimant (the 'guilt' meaning) nor that pleaded by the defendant (the 'charged and nothing more' meaning). Rather, by an inference from charge to suspicion but not to guilt, the meaning is given as that 'The owner of the Celebration Café is *suspected* of committing an offence…' (i.e. interpretation Iii). This 'suspicion meaning' is adopted as the definitive meaning for the case. It is this meaning which forms the basis for judging the publisher's behaviour in publishing or broadcasting the statement U. Both the claimant's and the defendant's petitions (viz. Ii and Iiii) will be rejected (though in some circumstances an action can continue on the basis of a more plausible, 'lesser' meaning).

Once a determination of meaning has been made, the selected meaning becomes the legally adopted – sometimes called the 'correct' – meaning. In the example above, it will be the 'suspicion' meaning (not the others) which is tested against the question of whether *suspecting* someone of committing an offence under the Food Act 1984 satisfies the legal test of being defamatory (by lowering the claimant in the estimation of right-thinking people). This second judgment, of whether the utterance is or is not in fact defamatory, no longer turns on what a reader may or may not read in (or read into) the publication. Now, things turn on how the legally adopted meaning relates to prevailing social attitudes. Those attitudes include readiness to respond in a certain way, or alternatively reluctance to respond in a certain way, or perhaps even indifference in the face of certain kinds of suggestion (e.g. it may be none of my business whether a person is or is not gay, garrulous or German, but of concern to me whether he is a conman, cheat or convicted arsonist). What is important here is that, whether the claimant is defamed by the 'suspicion' allegation, as we will see in Chapter 9, turns on the set of public beliefs against which whatever meaning that the court decides has been communicated is judged.

Usually, it is this second aspect of interpretation (how the decided meaning plays, in the field of public belief and attitude) that is of interest to a defendant and his or her lawyer. But this question depends on the first. If the meaning determined for the Celebration Café example allowed an extended inference to guilt, then the probability of the published comment being defamatory is greatly increased, because the second question becomes whether being claimed to be *guilty* of a crime, if you are not, is defamatory. On the other hand, if the legally defined meaning turned out to be only the face-value interpretation, then the prospect of the published comment being defamatory will be correspondingly less.

What about discourse consisting not of words but mainly or wholly of images and sounds? Surprisingly, as I suggested in Chapter 5, interpretation of such texts in formal, contested situations is less different than you might think. Claims about what is meant by a song, TV documentary, film or visually organised web page are formulated as verbal statements of, or commentaries on, what is sung or shown. Images, dialogue, music and sound effects are construed by being distilled into a verbal account that expresses the perceived meaning as precisely as possible, as if perception of the text has now been translated into a more abstract 'language of thought'. Once in verbal form, the meaning claims are then compared and evaluated as above, subject to variation in what might be submitted as evidence.

As regards interpretive standards, what is significant in my discussion of the Celebration Café example is that, however great the differences between the three competing readings, each is arrived at on the basis of a plausible inferential strategy. Whatever recommends the legally definitive meaning over the other two must be some principle (beyond the conventional meaning of the words or images themselves) that governs *which* interpretive strategy should be adopted. That principle is what I am calling an 'interpretive standard'.

## 8.5    Conceptual and procedural standards

We can now address the question of where a 'principle' of authoritative interpretation can come from. There are several main possibilities. The range includes the *ex officio* power of individuals I have mentioned above through to abstract concepts or values. If the approach is adopted of appealing to special kinds of 'person' or 'role', the standard is one of expertise embodied in a professional capacity; judges cultivate interpretive wisdom, for example, in order to be able to make fair and disinterested judgment. Alternatively, responsibility for meaning can be spread from any one individual onto a version of community or collective wisdom, reflecting 'contemporary community standards'. A jury or panel system offers interpretive commonsense created by a group of people functioning as a mini speech community, sufficiently familiar with how discourse works in a language and a culture to make judgments that command public confidence. Any one of us might fail to see what a text is getting at, but that risk is mitigated if we interpret as a group. Other sources of interpretive authority involve what might be called 'concept' authority; although implemented by judge and jury, this type of authority is based on a commitment to, say, truth or logic or reason, values held to be right or correct on general (e.g. moral or religious) grounds. Still other sources emphasise interpretive strategies as embodying norms of communicative behaviour that claim to reflect an acknowledged pattern of behaviour and in doing so extend or institutionalise it: the person making the judgment adopts a view on how some imagined *other* person would interpret in the given situation. Judgment along these lines is a matter of deciding what a particular kind of model reader (who may be different from the self, by being more credulous, better read or more media savvy, etc.) would have taken something to mean.

I have commented on *ex officio* individual judgment above. Such judgments are a distillation into decision-making of expertise derived from experience, legal precedent and authority, and established procedure. I propose now to consider the other categories, since they are what potentially make interpretive standards more generalisable and transparent. These other categories can be considered by retracing my list of possible kinds of interpretive standard above as a sort of continuum, from conceptual categories and values through concepts blended with models of interpretive process, to what are more obviously interpretive strategies or procedures. With this continuum of approaches in mind, I look first at the concept of 'truth' as an interpretive standard, then at ideas of 'validity', and finally at 'reasonable' interpretation and meaning arrived at by the 'ordinary reader'.

### 8.5.1     Truth

With some complaints (e.g. complaints over accuracy, bias or perjury, or that a publication was misleading or unfair), an obvious standard seems to recommend itself. The criterion of truth, along with related concepts of correctness, rightness, justification and degree of accuracy, presents itself as a suitable interpretive standard.

Truth is especially influential as a test of meaning for a number of reasons, not only in legal actions but more widely. The arguable primacy of truth/falsity judgments in deciding meaning is reinforced by several factors: by the evolutionary value to humans of accurate representations of the world around us; by ethical and religious prioritisation of honesty over lying and deceit; by the political value placed on truth-discovery as a justification for freedom of expression; by the centrality of factual truth or falsity in legal investigation and presentation of evidence; and, as regards meaning in particular, by the historical pre-eminence of truth-conditional semantics in linguistics – a field concerned with establishing what sentences mean by examining the conditions under which they are held to be true.

For all the cultural significance of these interlocking kinds of influence, truth-telling is problematic as a practical interpretive standard. 'Is it true?', as was suggested in Chapter 3, is rarely in practice an epistemological or narrowly semantic question. More often, it is a blend of issues to do with honesty and sincerity (in relation to motive or intention); to do with fairness (in relation to selection and some notionally balanced overall view of a topic); to do with relative priority (in relation to competing interests and demands); and to do with defensibility (in relation to prevailing expectations about communication and action). The question must then be asked: how can an interpretive standard of truth and falsity, or its cognate terms, reflect the cluster of values at stake in practical communicative judgments? 'Reliability' seems an outgrowth from truth, in that what is believed to be accurate can be relied on; but 'accuracy' itself cannot be relied on unthinkingly, in that it can represent a quite different relation from the relation between utterance and events or situations, functioning less as a close synonym for truthfulness than as the lower standard of merely faithful verbatim report. Even with these reservations, however, it is questionable whether this is what a senior MOD spokesman meant when he archly sidestepped the question of truth and falsity during his evidence to the Scott Inquiry in 1996 (concerned with the Matrix Churchill case about arms to Iraq discussed in the previous chapter) by means of the statement that 'truth is a difficult concept'.[2]

How is a standard of 'truth' applied in determining contested meaning? In deciding whether an utterance is true of a given set of circumstances, we typically decide what it refers to as a way into what it *conveys* (e.g. we establish who exactly the owner of the Celebration Café is, and which actual café is picked out by the name); we also judge whether the utterance is meant literally, figuratively or ironically, in each case perhaps implying something different

---

[2] Ian McDonald, Head of the Ministry of Defence's Defence Sales Secretariat, in evidence to the Scott committee, 'Q&A Scott Report', BBC News, 27 April 2004 (www.bbc.co.uk). The full report is *Report of the Inquiry into the Export of Defence Equipment and Dual-Use Goods to Iraq and Related Prosecutions*, 6 vols. (London: HMSO, 1996).

from what is said at face value. These acts of initial interpretation call for judgment, as we have seen. In principle, though, we might say that truth can be applied as a test if, having determined some proposition or propositions expressed, either explicitly or inferentially, we are able to ask whether what is expressed or implied fits the facts.

What is striking, however, is that by the time we are ready to ask this 'truth' question some key issues involved in establishing meaning have already had to be settled. Judging truth or falsity comes late in the chain of construal operations. It plays its part in establishing overall significance by checking for fit between meaning, once largely established (as Ii or Iii, etc.), and what is happening or has happened in the world (A).[3]

There is another difficulty with truth as a practical standard, too, besides this lateness in the chain of construal operations: that truth is an attribute of the meaning of only some utterances, or kinds of discourse, not all. As Jürgen Habermas and others have emphasised in exploring discourse validity claims, truth or falsity justifications apply only to assertions. You cannot judge promising, threatening, insulting or many other discourse acts that can become the objects of lawsuits or complaints as being true or false (an issue that will become central in discussing offensiveness in Chapter 11).[4] This is not only because such acts often employ specific speech act verbs or special grammatical constructions, since equivalent claims (and/or related effects) can be established indirectly, including visually and sometimes by depicted gestures. Rather, the validity claims in question involve communicative norms and expectations as to interpretive strategy, rather than truthfulness (e.g. whether, if in given circumstances you consider a promise or verbal threat from someone as likely to be kept, this is a perfectly reasonable interpretation, an excessive one, or a naive one).

For reasons such as these, the significance of utterances and texts is rarely reducible to true/false or accuracy/inaccuracy judgments, even where the relation of what is conveyed to a given situation or event is crucial. An 'inference to suspicion' meaning of the kind decided in the Celebration Café example is no more or less 'true' of the news statement than either of the two competing interpretations. Additional or different concepts and vocabulary are needed to

---

[3] Note that truth-conditional semantics and truth discovery in law work in opposite directions. In semantics, you start from a sense that you *know* what is true and what is false for a given scenario, then work backwards to what 'meaning' is. Semantics allows you to establish meaning by asking under what conditions something is true: 'The dog is eating the cat' is true if and only if the dog is eating the cat. If, on the other hand, you are just given the utterance 'the dog is eating the cat', you are in principle no wiser as to what is going on with the dog and the cat in the world.

[4] On speech-act validity claims, see Habermas, 'Social action, purposive activity, and communication', in *On the Pragmatics of Communication*, esp. pp. 140–54. Assertives are nevertheless probably the most important class of utterances in science and most branches of law, which may be why truth-conditional notions of meaning have commanded such interest in the history of semantics and philosophy of language.

determine meaning beyond truth and falsity. That vocabulary, I have suggested above, must still engage with the important relationship that holds between utterances and states of affairs (U/A) if communication is not to be detached from its information-exchange function. But it must also reflect the relationship that holds between interpretive strategies and the utterances they are applied to (I/U).

Common words for describing this second kind of meaning relation go far beyond 'true' and 'false'. The Café alternatives (Ii/U, Iii/U, etc.) might be described as an over-literal reading, a moderate or reasonable reading, and a precipitate or excessive reading. We might identify further scales (involving for instance relative persuasiveness, degree of rigour or thoroughness of thought, relative integrity of interpretive intent, attitude felt by the interpreter towards the speaker, likelihood of being useful, etc.).[5] Such scales broaden out from narrow judgments of factual accuracy, through predictable directions of inference, into more fanciful expressions of different attitudes towards how communicators relate to other people and the world around them.


### 8.5.2    Validity

Besides truth, perhaps the other most commonly invoked discourse attribute in determining correct meaning in conversation – already referred to in relation to Habermas above – is 'validity'. The everyday remark, 'That seems valid', is often offered as a standard of meaning that is broader, if somewhat more diffuse, than truth. So, is the concept of validity viable as an interpretive standard?

In the history of 'validity' as a word and concept, several different strands are traceable. One strand takes as its criterion of judgment fairness, relevance and usefulness; another, accuracy or logical derivation. There can be a legal dimension, too: the characteristic of bearing legal authority or force, or being legally binding (a sense which persists mostly in specialised combinations such as 'valid passport'). In the field of proof and assertion, 'valid' expresses the characteristic of being well founded or well reasoned, and applicable to a

---

[5] Common terms in commentary cluster into a small number of intersecting scales of evaluation, each representing a tacit interpretive criterion: *Degree of accuracy*: 'spot-on', 'wrong', 'accurate'; *Relative persuasiveness*: 'convincing', 'compelling', 'questionable', 'far-fetched'; *Rigour* (or thoroughness of thinking): 'careful', 'sensitive', 'detailed', 'faithful', 'precise', 'scrupulous'; *Integrity of intent*: 'mischievous', 'wilful', 'irresponsible', 'vexatious', 'reprehensible', 'self-serving'; *Attitude shown towards the speaker:* 'generous', 'malicious', 'suspicious', 'offensive'; *Taste* (or tact): 'vulgar', 'scurrilous'; *Originality* (or novelty): 'ingenious', 'insightful', 'original', 'routine', 'dogmatic', 'pedantic'; *Usefulness*: 'constructive', 'helpful'; *Interpretive excess*: 'mad', 'bonkers', 'zany'.

particular matter or set of circumstances; in this sense, something is 'valid' if it is considered to the point, or does not invite objection. Because of these different dimensions in the concept, appealing to a standard of 'validity' in interpretation brings in evaluative scales other than logical demonstration. Validity is attractive as a standard only at some cost in terms of precision (since, while verification may be possible in principle for truth claims, other validity claims – notwithstanding Habermas – are difficult to validate).

To see the difference between kinds of validity claim, consider what is meant by an on-package label for a cold or flu treatment, 'contains paracetomol'. Perhaps the basic meaning here is simply that of package *information*: 'this is what is in the pack, you decide what to use it for'. To someone in need of pain relief, though, the two-word sentence fragment also raises a promissory validity claim that has an extra dimension beyond straightforward information: 'if you need paracetomol to relieve pain, you'll find it here'. To a parent about to administer a painkiller to a child, on the other hand, the words raise a warning validity claim: 'remember, you should only administer this with care'. Judging meaning and effect (and, on that basis, responsibility for meaning and effect) calls for a complementary relation between the information claim and the further validity claim of whichever speech act is likely to be inferred. Even if you always read the label, understanding package information requires consumers to evaluate validity claims and expectations that go beyond truth claims. This may be why complaints about labelling are often about whether prominence and style of message are fit for purpose, rather than more narrowly about informational accuracy.

'Validity' faces a further difficulty as an interpretive standard, common to all regulatory benchmarks: that of contextual variation in the meaning of the term itself. A 'valid' passport, I have suggested, expresses a different notion of validity from a 'valid' opinion. Used in contextually varying ways, validity signifies slightly different standards of plausible interpretation depending on beliefs an interpreter brings to the text or situation. A subjective dimension enters into the concept of validity and shifts validity judgments away from conventions of the communicative code or the speaker's intention towards a relative standard based on reception. This is surprising, given that perhaps the most influential account of 'validity' in interpretation, E.D. Hirsch's treatment of literary value in *Validity in Interpretation*,[6] made a case for interpretive 'validity' as a measure of how far claimed meaning matches what was intended by an imagined speaker. In much contemporary usage, by contrast, validity is anchored in the receiver's perception, as subjective impact or *uptake*. It depends

[6]  E.D.Hirsch, *Validity in Interpretation* (New Haven, Conn.: Yale University Press, 1967). For discussion of intention in interpretation in literary study, see Gibbs, *Intentions in the Experience of Meaning*, pp. 249–52.

on a disposition to interpret in a given way rather than on a concept of intention. Validity is not only a subjective category but also a hybrid one: it combines what appears to be a stable conceptual standard with variable interpretive strategies likely to be brought to bear by the interpreter.

### 8.5.3    Being reasonable

Truth or falsity appears to be a stable attribute, however conceived, of the meaning of utterances. I have suggested, however, that in many cases practical judgments of truth and falsity involve many shades of grey and in other cases do not apply. Some ideas of interpretive standard address questions of what inferences are warranted, and under what circumstances, by moving closer to pragmatic capacities or dispositions employed in assigning meanings: *how* does someone judge meaning, and what can be said about how they should? Standards established on this basis require us to evaluate communicative practices, strategies and norms rather than abstract concepts or values. What is in question is a standard of interpretive behaviour rather than a supposed attribute of the utterance. The criterion of being 'reasonable', or judging something as a 'reasonable man' might do, is perhaps the most established standard of this kind.

At face value, the concept of 'reasonableness' seems predicated on proper use of reason: an Enlightenment value, rather as 'truth' appeared to be, according to which we apply general reason to the problem-solving task of constructing meaning. But the concept of 'the reasonable man' in English law is less a rational criterion of this kind than what the linguist Anna Wierzbicka (spelling out linguistic dimensions of long-standing legal critiques) has called a historically constructed 'key Anglo value', or cultural complex; the idea of 'the reasonable man' involves a cluster of socially constructed meanings that may not all be a matter of reason in an Enlightenment sense.[7]

Complex, culturally specific concepts of the kind that 'reasonable' is, Wierzbicka suggests, provide frames for orientation in daily life. They guide judgment and behaviour to an extent that becomes so ingrained that the concept is then taken for granted.[8] Wierzbicka describes 'the reasonable man' as an interpretive standard that consists of *social* values rather than the Enlightenment

---

[7] In *English: Meaning and Culture* (Oxford: Oxford University Press, 2006), Wierzbicka explores the cultural loading implicit in unreflective use of words such as 'reasonable'. Her analysis combines a historical account of philosophical and legal use with contemporary corpus analysis, mapping not just the word's range of senses but how those senses function together to create a field of cultural value. See chapter 4, 'Being reasonable: a key Anglo value and its cultural roots', pp. 103–40.

[8] Wierzbicka argues that such concepts serve as a 'basic kit of conceptual tools used for making judgments and evaluating actions and events', in *English*, p. 105.

concept of the power of reason. In the course of the eighteenth century, Wierzbicka suggests, 'reasonable' moved away from its pre-eighteenth-century general meaning of 'endowed with the ability to think' and took on a meaning something like 'compatible with reason but not requiring it'. Later, the word shifted again into a new, post-Enlightenment usage, influenced particularly (so Wierzbicka argues) by the thinking of Locke, signifying a cluster of cultural meanings including 'moderate', 'based in empirical thinking', 'commonsens-ical', 'practical' and 'tolerant'. It is these senses, Wierzbicka concludes, that lie behind 'reasonable' in its modern legal use (including use in the formula 'beyond reasonable doubt', which has become perhaps the most influential use).

If this account is right, then 'reasonable' means something like 'not wanting or demanding too much' and 'staying rooted in commonsense', rather than 'applying reason'. The 'reasonable man' is somebody whose judgment is reliable and can be trusted, perhaps more than that of a theoretician, philosopher or professional scholar.[9] As an interpretive standard, 'reasonableness' is associated with a belief that the thinking of the reasonable person is to be trusted not because such a person is always right but because that person has his or her feet firmly on the ground and can think well enough for practical purposes.[10]

How does this cluster of senses in 'reasonable' affect use of the concept as a standard in a given interpretive situation? The sense is of practical, common-sensical judgment rather than reason in an abstract sense or as something precise but pedantic. The 'reasonable man' standard is based on how people are assumed to interpret. It is a generalisation about social patterns in meaning-making, idealised as a norm: a commonsense, middle-ground approach to interpretive problems that is sometimes criticised as being socially loaded. Legitimacy for this standard of interpretation comes from how successfully it is grounded in popular feeling. This is what allows 'reasonableness' to shift easily between technical usage and whatever degree of wider popular assent judgments of 'reasonable interpretation' attain in English-speaking cultures, even while the notion carries historical and cultural baggage that may make the concept less than transparent in a multicultural society.[11] Because 'reasonable' reflects cultural values, rather than a precise philosophical concept, the term also

---

[9]  Wierzbicka, *English*, p. 107.
[10]  Speculating about the persistence of 'reasonableness', Wierzbicka argues that, in linking rationality and commonsense, the concept is able 'to guide communication between the legal profession and ordinary people'. The 'reasonable man' is modest and humble, echoing values famously attributed by Lord Bowen in 1903 to 'the man on the Clapham omnibus', who embodied sound judgment while not being an intellectual.
[11]  For possible connections between the ordinary or average reader and middle English values, see Digby C. Anderson, *All Oiks Now: The Unnoticed Surrender of Middle England* (London: Social Affairs Unit, 2004).

serves as a gloss for other formulations of essentially the same interpretive standard including the 'ordinary reader', who we should now meet.


### 8.5.4   Being ordinary

The standard for judging interpretations based on the 'ordinary reader', as set out in defamation law,[12] is perhaps the most detailed interpretive standard in English media law. The ordinary reader is, in effect, a cousin of the 'reasonable man'. If both were people rather than hypothetical constructs, they might look the same on their passports except for one distinguishing feature: while reasonableness consists of general commonsense and realism in making everyday judgments, the ordinary reader is discourse specific; he reads (generic 'he' is presumed) and what he gleans from what he reads is the 'natural and ordinary signification' of the discourse.

As well as being related to the 'reasonable man', the ordinary reader has other relatives, including the literary 'common reader' and 'average consumer' as well as 'the man on the Clapham omnibus'. What makes him distinctive within the family is that we know slightly more about how he interprets. It is accepted, for example, that the ordinary reader varies from period to period, reflecting social standards and knowledge of his day (so being called 'German' or 'homo-sexual' may be defamatory in one period but not in another). Where the situation demands, the ordinary reader is only ordinary for one particular newspaper or media format rather than for all, in recognition that ordinariness comes in specialised varieties in a society with niche audiences.[13] His attentive-ness may sometimes be in doubt, as we have seen, as regards whether he attends only to headlines or also to later paragraphs of news stories, to captions that accompany images, and to the small print. The ordinary reader also varies between different 'temperaments and outlooks', since some people are 'unusu-ally suspicious, while others are unusually naive'.[14] Variation of these kinds is irrelevant in the end, however, because the ordinary reader is not a socially situated individual but an embodiment of 'reasonableness' used by judges and juries as an interpretive heuristic, or legal benchmark.

To function effectively in legal actions involving a jury, the ordinary-reader standard must be simultaneously technical and yet accessible. The term there-fore calls for latitude in detailing the ordinary reader's features. It is unimpor-tant, accordingly, that both 'natural' and 'ordinary' (in the phrase 'natural and ordinary signification') are peculiarly difficult concepts in English;[15] or that 'natural' signification has almost an opposite meaning from 'natural meaning'

---

[12] On the 'ordinary reader' in defamation, see Robertson and Nicol, *Media Law*, pp. 49–53.

[13] Robertson and Nicol, *Media Law*, p. 52.    [14] Robertson and Nicol, *Media Law*, p. 49.

[15] See entries for 'natural' and 'ordinary' in Williams, *Keywords*, especially Williams's comments on the scale of difficulty presented by 'natural'.

in the sense used by linguists or philosophers. The standard must itself be interpreted in a 'reasonable' way.

Put most simply, the ordinary reader's reading is the spontaneous, most likely, accessible reading of a text considered credible for a given interpretive situation. Esoteric, abstruse and counter-intuitive readings are ruled out. Where required, however, the ordinary reader can still see beyond an immediate, literal meaning in order to recognise indirect rhetorical strategy, for instance with irony. The need to bring litigation to a close allows judgment on meaning to press ahead in the face of the paradox that, if a discourse is ironic, then its 'ordinary meaning' may well be the opposite of what it means ordinarily.

## 8.6     Interpretive standards and legal outcomes

Given the terminological complications and conceptual difficulties, it might be expected that legal and regulatory bodies should be exercised by the complexity of establishing standards for determining meaning authoritatively at meaning troublespots. This is not evidently the case, for reasons that go to the core of differences between linguistic and legal approaches to meaning. For regulatory bodies, the task of establishing meaning is mostly subsumed under the more pressing task of asking whether whatever meaning is established meets the legal threshold of a particular offence or cause of action. This second task may still *seem like* a meaning question in my terms, because of its dependence on knowing precisely what meaning is under consideration. But the detail of the meaning question is a subsidiary issue in the wider problem of meaning perceived as a matter of effect or significance in which the *process* of making meaning is largely taken for granted.

Law and media regulation work practically to settle cases, not to engage in abstract debates. So while meaning plays a part, it is not allowed to distract from the effort to move towards a legal outcome. To achieve such an outcome, legal procedures begin with a problem of alleged social effects that need to be remedied or limited, and engage with questions of meaning only to the extent that they are held to be causally relevant to those effects. The procedures adopted are helped towards that aim by people's willingness to offer intuitive, prescriptive judgments about meaning without questioning what supports those judgments beyond commonsense; normative judgment as to which meanings are warranted and which are not is as deep in the culture as 'reasonableness'.

In this respect, normative decisions about interpretation in law reflect popular judgment. Interpretation is for most situations not a field of differences or relative judgments. Commitment to subjective variability of meaning may be advocated as a value, but it is by no means an intuitive priority or default assumption about communication. Many of the commonest terms for describing interpretations serve less to celebrate diversity of ascribed meaning than to evaluate (and criticise) meanings being attributed ('outrageous', 'misguided', 'naive' or 'ridiculous', versus 'original', 'interesting', 'insightful', 'thoughtful', etc.). There is a strong, normative ordinary-language predisposition in attributing meaning, backed up by high degrees of confidence in the interpreter's own subjective standard. Interpretations are 'improbable', 'excessive' or 'crazy' with respect to the interpreter's own attributed meaning. If your interpretation is deemed 'original', that means 'original' from the interpreter's perspective; the same interpretation may seem completely banal to you or to others.

This subjective focus (sometimes called a 'personalised' framework of meaning,[16] based on the speaker's own opinion, feelings and subjective state) is not only central to frameworks for attributing meanings conversationally or in popular opinion. It also enters into conceptualisation of meaning in law and regulation in the form of understandings given to words like 'ordinary', 'average' and 'reasonable', which provide formal standards of adjudication. While a subjective dimension in interpretation is no surprise in relation to conversation, it may seem more puzzling as a feature of interpretive standards in media law and regulation, given that, as regards legal discourse itself, interpretation is subject to precise doctrines of construction. Establishing interpretive standards for contested public or media discourse, however, is not the same as construction of legal discourse. Contested utterances and texts consist not of technical terms of art but of a changing fabric of social styles of representation. Deciding between alternative meanings for such representations is a question of finding common ground, in order to achieve whatever social policy goals have been set. 'Legitimate inference' in interpretive judgments of contested discourse depends, accordingly, on successfully facing in two directions at once. Interpretive standards command popular support and credibility to the extent that they reflect a changing social reservoir of values and meaning judgments, including about what interpretive strategies are appropriate under given conditions.[17] But such interpretive standards must also be precise and consistent enough to meet social expectations of fairness and transparency.

---

[16] Hill, 'Crises of meaning', p. 73.

[17] In this respect, interpretive strategies are a normative counterpart to what Geoffrey Leech, in *Principles of Pragmatics* (London: Longman, 1983), investigates as 'pragmatic principles' (e.g. his 'tact principle', 'irony principle', 'politeness principle', etc.). Note, however, that Leech is interested in providing a systematic description of intuitions regarding *how* particular kinds of interpretation occur, and on that basis an exploratory hypothesis as to *why*. *Should* falls outside the descriptive and explanatory aims of his linguistic study.

## 8.7    Summary

In this chapter I have reviewed different possible grounds for deciding on an 'authoritative' or 'authorised' meaning for a contested utterance. Drawing on the work of writers including Wierzbicka and Habermas, I have drawn attention to complications in establishing such interpretive standards. I have also suggested that applying interpretive standards in practical cases of adjudication involves a balance between making principled judgments about interpretation and finding sufficient common ground to achieve social policy goals. How competing demands are addressed in any given instance must be appraised in relation to the provisions of particular areas of media law and regulation, such as those I now consider in Chapters 9–11.

*Part IV*

Analysing disputes in different fields
of law and regulation

# 9     Defamation: 'reasonably capable of bearing the meaning attributed'

## 9.1     Introduction

Chapters 9–11 examine meaning in three areas of media law and regulation in greater detail. In the first of these three chapters, I look at one specific legal cause of action, defamation. I relate arguments about meaning presented earlier in the book to the challenge of deciding what utterances or texts mean in this field of law. Publications or media coverage alleged to be damaging to reputation, I show, are considered in terms of whether they warrant the meaning or meanings pleaded by the complainant to an 'ordinary reader' standard of meaning. Where publication was to an audience likely to be split in terms of relevant knowledge available to it, a further notion, that of legal 'innuendo' meaning, is invoked. I focus on the boundary between these two notions of meaning: between the 'natural and ordinary meaning of the words' available to an ordinary reader and the specialised kind of meaning associated with particular knowledge available only to a given, segmented readership. This distinction between 'innuendo' meaning and 'ordinary-reader' meaning, I argue, shows up wider problems in how meanings are ascribed and evaluated in defamation.

## 9.2     Libel and the meaning of words

When people involved in a libel action discuss defamation, the '-ing' word they use most is not 'meaning' but 'winning'. Yet despite defamation's lustre of gladiatorial struggle and gold, the protection extended to reputation by this area of law depends crucially on attributions of meaning. As Lord Diplock succinctly put it in his influential judgment in *Slim v. Daily Telegraph* [1968], 'libel is concerned with the meaning of words'.[1]

---

[1] *Slim v. Daily Telegraph* [1968] 2 QB 157, at 171. The same point was compellingly made by the Faulks Committee on defamation in 1975: 'The meaning of the words at issue is probably the most important single factor in a defamation case, since it is of cardinal significance at a great many stages. Upon the meaning depends whether or not the words are defamatory and, therefore, whether or not the plaintiff has a claim at all. If they are defamatory, the nature of any defence which the defendant may plead depends on whether in their correct meaning they are statements of fact or expressions of opinion. If they are statements of fact, the defendant, in order to succeed on

Lord Diplock's judgment in *Slim* is justly celebrated, more than forty years on, for its close engagement with meaning questions in libel. His initial reaffirmation of what most readers would accept as obvious is developed into a balancing of procedural needs against the difficulty of arguing meaning in court. Neither 'meaning' nor 'words', it turns out, is straightforward. Even less straightforward is their 'capability', as my title suggests, to 'bear a meaning'.[2]

The topics to be discussed in this chapter can be usefully focused by considering Lord Diplock's judgment in *Slim* slightly further. Early on, Lord Diplock outlines what amounts to the 'interpretive triangle' view of meaning outlined in Chapter 7:

> Everyone outside a court of law recognises words are imprecise instruments for communicating the thoughts of one man [*sic*] to another. The same words may be understood by one man in a different meaning from that in which they are understood by another and both meanings may be different from that which the author of the words intended to convey. But the notion that the same words should bear different meanings to different men and that more than one meaning should be 'right' conflicts with the whole training of a lawyer. Words are the tools of his trade. He uses them to define legal rights and duties. They do not achieve that purpose unless there can be attributed to them a single meaning as the 'right' meaning. And so the argument between lawyers as to the meaning of words starts with the unexpressed major premise that any particular combination of words has one meaning which is not necessarily the same as that intended by him who published them or understood by any of those who read them but is capable of ascertainment as being the 'right' meaning by the adjudicator to whom the law confides the responsibility of determining it... That is what makes the meaning ascribed to words for the purposes of the tort of libel so artificial.[3]

The 'artificiality' alluded to here is seen not as a limitation, necessarily, but simply as a peculiarity of legal procedure. It is a consequence of recognising diversity of meaning while needing to reduce it in a court of law to a single meaning. In this context it doesn't matter how far-reaching interpretive discrepancy may actually be. Rather, Lord Diplock argues,

> justification, must prove that they are true in their meaning; if they consist essentially of expressions of opinions, the defence of fair comment can succeed only if the defendant proves that in their meaning they are fair comment on a matter of public interest. Even if the defence is that the words were published on a privileged occasion, a question may arise with regard to the meaning of the words. Finally, if the plaintiff succeeds at the end of the day, the assessment of damages will depend substantially on the gravity of the defamation, which also hinges on the meaning of the words.' Faulks Committee report (command 5909) Para 92. Quoted in Sir Brian Neill, Richard Rampton QC, Timothy Atkinson, Aidan Eardley and Heather Rogers QC, *Duncan and Neill on Defamation*, 3rd edition (London: LexisNexis, 2009), p. 8.

2   This phrase occurs in RSC 82, r3A(2), the 'rule on meaning' in the Supreme Court Practice rules for defamation.

3   This passage is sometimes called Lord Diplock's statement of the 'one meaning' rule. *Slim v. Daily Telegraph* [1968] 2 QB 157, at 171–2. See also Spilsbury, *Media Law*, pp. 64–73.

What does matter is what the adjudicator at the trial thinks is the one and only meaning that the readers as reasonable men should have collectively understood the words to bear. That is the natural and ordinary meaning of words in an action for libel.[4]

Historically, Lord Diplock points out, this 'natural and ordinary meaning' was decided by the trial judge, who determined meaning free from any requirement to be specific about precisely what that meaning was beyond the fact that it was defamatory. Over the last century or more of English law, however, responsibility has shifted to the jury, at least where a jury is involved in a case. Recent reforms have also strengthened the requirement for meanings to be specified at an early stage in proceedings. Changes of this kind have had the result that libel in English law now has two interwoven stages in relation to meaning, and an important distinction 'between defamatory meanings which words are capable of bearing and *the* particular defamatory meaning which, for the purposes of the tort of libel, they bear'. The judge determines 'capability', and, if called on by a separate application, he can rule out certain claimed meanings as not possible.[5] Which of the remaining meanings becomes what Lord Diplock calls '*the* meaning' (from among those accepted as meanings that the complained of utterance is capable of bearing) is decided by the jury, or by the judge if there is no jury in the particular case.

This approach is reflected in a series of procedural steps. After an initial letter before action, the meanings to be put forward at trial are outlined by the claimant in a statement of claim. If those meanings are accepted by the judge as meanings the complained of discourse is capable of bearing, then the parties will, if the action is not settled out of court, submit their respective contentions as to what the meaning of the words complained of should be. More than one meaning can be pleaded, with different meanings claimed to be injurious to different extents. The notion therefore emerges of a scale of claimed meanings, of different degrees of gravity; this introduces into libel proceedings an element of strategic calculation in construction of meaning alongside efforts to settle on the 'correct' meaning: a sort of 'meaning poker' to which I return below.

Because more than one interpretation is constructed for the contested discourse, a defamation action proliferates descriptions of meaning. The process of putting particular meanings forward therefore requires additional, interpretive language, or metalanguage. This introduces its own complications.

---

[4] *Slim v. Daily Telegraph* [1968] 2 QB 157, at 173.

[5] RSC 82, r3A provides that '(1) at any time after service of the statement of claim either party may apply to a judge in chambers for an order determining whether or not the words complained of are capable of bearing a particular meaning or meanings attributed to them in the pleadings. (2) If it appears to the judge on the hearing of an application under paragraph (1) that none of the words complained of are capable of bearing the meaning or meanings attributed to them in the pleadings, he may dismiss the claim or make such other order or give such judgment in the proceedings as may be just.'

The trial judge in *Slim*, for example, had paraphrased meanings in such a way that Lord Diplock, at appeal, is led to query how successful he had been, and whether the words complained of did in fact bear the particular defamatory meaning

which he [the trial judge] expresses in a number of different phrases, all of them less precise than those used in the statement of claim, but which he apparently regarded as paraphrases of the relevant paragraphs of the statement of claim. To do so introduces into the proceedings a new complication about the meaning of words – this time not about the meaning of the words used in the alleged libel but about the meaning of the words used in the paragraph of the statement of claim to plead the defamatory meaning which the plaintiffs alleged was the natural and ordinary meaning of the words used in the alleged libel. Any paraphrase of that paragraph which was less precise than the actual words used in the paragraph could not bear the same meaning as the words themselves.[6]

A risk of proliferating variant statements of meaning is evident here, and emphasises the importance in libel not only of fixing the meaning of the words complained of, but also of fixing the meaning of subsequent accounts of those meanings that crowd in with each paraphrase. Clarification and stabilisation of meaning accordingly become major themes of libel procedure. In his discussion of difficulties that persist in explicating different meanings, Lord Diplock expresses concern that anticipation of 'minute linguistic analysis' of all the various possible statements of meaning might have a damaging or 'chilling' effect[7] on anyone exercising their right to free speech if they looked into the future and saw how their words might be dissected. Concluding his argument, Lord Diplock recommends the 'meaning construction' aspect of defamation as a 'fit topic for the attention of the Law Commission', lamenting that it has 'passed beyond redemption by the courts'.

Since the 1960s, when a number of key judgments provided still influential landmarks on defamatory meaning,[8] English defamation law *has* received a lot of attention. Much of that attention, inevitably, has been journalistic discussion of features that give rise to the continuing stereotypes: the unavailability of legal aid (which makes libel a rich person's plaything); differences between English libel law and that of other jurisdictions; disparities in the amount of damages awarded; risks associated with costs; and the unpredictability of juries in convicting, to name but a few recurrent themes. There have also been reforms whose main effect as regards meaning (as I have suggested) has been to modify

---

[6]  *Slim v. Daily Telegraph* [1968] 2 QB 157, at 177.

[7]  *Slim v. Daily Telegraph* [1968] 2 QB 157, at 179. For discussion of the 'chilling effect' of a possible libel action, see Eric Barendt, Laurence Lustgarten, Kenneth Nornie and Hugh Stephenson, *Libel and the Media: The Chilling Effect* (Oxford: Clarendon, 1997).

[8]  The three landmark cases on meaning I have in mind here are: *Slim v. Daily Telegraph* (1968) 2 QB 157; [1968] 2 WLR 599; 112 SJ 97; [1968] 1 All ER 497, CA; *Lewis v. Daily Telegraph* [1964] AC 234; and *Grubb v. Bristol United Press* [1963] 1 QB 309; 3 WLR 25; 106 SJ 262; [1962] 2 All ER 380.

procedure in the direction of more precise specification of what meanings are being argued about. These reforms have all been introduced in parallel with, and latterly under the umbrella of, continuing adjustment to the requirements of ECHR Article 10. However, the crucial difficulties that Lord Diplock probed during the 1960s remain, as much for Internet libel as for print libel. They appear to be fundamental questions about meaning rather than narrower problems of a particular stage in the history of defamation.

## 9.3    Defamatory potential: an illustration

To explore how meanings are constructed from an allegedly defamatory utterance or publication, I propose first to highlight different dimensions of meaning attribution using a made-up example.[9] I will then set the various points I make about that example in the context of English libel law. Using an example in this way presents several difficulties, however, which need comment before I start.

Naturally occurring discourse does not come 'tagged' for defamation. Although media advisers read and watch texts ahead of publication and advise on whether they are likely to be considered libellous, that advice is a matter of risk assessment rather than of parsing a text for libel in the way a grammarian might parse it for different kinds of sentence structure. So whether my made-up example below can be fairly described as 'an example of defamation' needs some preliminary clarification.

'Defamatory' has two senses within the general meaning of damaging someone's reputation with a false statement. It can denote what might be called the meaning potential of the complained-of discourse (what meanings it lends itself to), or, more precisely, that the discourse has been held to be defamatory as a matter of legal adjudication. My example is the first of these: 'defamatory' as potential rather than 'defamatory' as fact. A made-up example cannot have been tested against either a legal judgment of capability or the decision of a jury.

It can still be useful to discuss defamatory potential in this way. Attention is drawn away from particular facts in a given case towards *how* meanings are attributed to particular arrangements of words in ways that allow them to bear a defamatory imputation. To a defamation lawyer, constructing a defamatory

---

[9] This approach contrasts with the linguist Roger Shuy's emphasis on real courtroom data rather than made-up examples in *Fighting over Words*, as in his earlier publications. Made-up examples in this field are not always pale echoes of reality, nevertheless. Perhaps the most moving and thought-provoking *fictional* exploration of a libel action is Leon Uris's novel *QB VII* (New York: Doubleday, 1970), whose title is taken from the name of the courtroom in which the fictional trial takes place. Uris provides a highly detailed account, from the different viewpoints of the legal protagonists, of a distressing case based on allegations made in a published account of the Holocaust regarding medical experimentation conducted by the fictional complainant, a Polish internee and later famous doctor, while a collaborator with Nazi jailers at Jadwiga Concentration Camp.

meaning becomes an automatic reading strategy. But tracing pejorative possibilities in a text is a specialised art, different from more general approaches to ascribing meaning.

With this proviso, imagine the following copy as a minor story in the 'people' or 'gossip' column of a regional newspaper or on a news website.

At an awards and fundraising ceremony held last night at County Exhibition Hall, Mr Ali Khan, director of the charity Better World Together, received this year's Outstanding Achievement Award for his sometimes unrecognised commitment and international leadership. In accepting the award, Mr Khan spoke of the inspiration and support of his wife, the ridiculous councillor and expenses queen Beth Khan, whose Imelda-like stature graces glitzy events up and down the country. Last night, however, Mrs Khan, who is known to like the company of wealthy men, was not in attendance to see her husband receive the plaudits of fellow charity organisers. She was glimpsed dining privately with a friend in another part of the city.

In several respects, this story (however improbably) reflects a genre of journalistic lampoon or satire. It jibes at people perceived to be in a position of power or eminence, and intimates sleaze in a way that contrives to be simultaneously censorious and envious. In other respects, the story reflects what might be called a tabloid 'unhappy couple' genre. Stories of this type dwell on the marriages or romantic lives of celebrities or notable figures, implying discord and appearing to sympathise with one side while vilifying the other. In this case, the writer has certainly taken a dislike to Mrs Khan, and she will understandably be irritated and possibly upset. But what, if anything, would make this story not just upsetting but defamatory? A number of principles of meaning attribution can be traced in how this story *might be* constructed.

### 9.3.1    Basics of a libel action

Mrs Khan wishes to issue a writ for defamation. She feels the story will (to bring different formulations of what defines defamation together) tend to lower her 'in the estimation of right-thinking members of society', or expose her to 'hatred, ridicule or contempt', or cause her to be 'shunned or avoided', or injure her 'in her office, profession or trade'.[10]

Defamation can be either libel, if in writing (or some other permanent, textual form such as film); or it can be slander, if spoken (and so less widely distributed and assumed to be in this respect less serious). So, in this case, Mrs Khan's writ will be for libel. Injury to Mrs Khan's reputation may be less tangible than bodily injury, but in addition to vindication in the form of an apology she will seek money by way of damages. If she pursues her action, she will be the claimant; the newspaper will be

---

[10] For a composite of judicial formulations of what constitutes a defamatory statement, see for example Scott-Bayfield, *Defamation*, p. 10.

the defendant. With legal roles in place, she will need to demonstrate a number of things about the article in order to succeed with her claim.

Firstly, Mrs Khan must show that the article's allegations were published and are about her. There shouldn't be much difficulty with this. Although 'Khan' is a common name, she is also identified by her first name, as well as by the name of her husband and by reference to the awards dinner. She needs to affirm these things formally in case they are queried, either genuinely or opportunistically. But there seems little prospect of the defendant successfully arguing that the article may be defamatory but wasn't about her.

Mrs Khan also needs to convert her general sense of irritation and injury into specific meanings she believes the article conveys. To be relevant, those meanings must be ones which have the effect of falsely attributing to her actions or characteristics that might be judged defamatory; other possible meanings or aspects of meaning are extraneous. The meanings she identifies must be capable of being clearly stated, and likely to be ascribed by an ordinary reader of the article.

### 9.3.2 How meanings are constructed

A process of construction – or formal attribution of meaning – will turn Mrs Khan's response to the disparate mix of epithets and slurs contained in the article into a full-blown defamatory allegation that can if necessary be tested in court. Local features of the text will be viewed in terms of the contribution they make to an overall effect created by the article, if read spontaneously against a background of relevant knowledge and likely beliefs. It is the impression conveyed by the whole story that matters, rather than the power of individual words or phrases (so that defamatory potential in one expression can be offset altogether by what is said elsewhere in a suitably 'emollient' context).[11] Particular emphasis will be placed on what is considered to be the 'sting', or particular point, of the story, even if that sting is an overall implication rather than something directly stated.

For Mrs Khan's lawyers, the process of construction is likely to be a matter of instant, expert impression, later formalised as the statement of claim and courtroom arguments. My aim, by contrast, is to consider how discourse comprehension strategies of the kind outlined in earlier chapters funnel into more specialised processes of libel construction. This is a different approach from an overall libel reading. I propose to begin not with general impression, in the manner of a top-down reading, but with specific expressions that open up

---

[11] Judges refer, for example, to the counterbalancing effect of 'bane and antidote': '[if] in one part of the publication something disreputable to the plaintiff is stated, but that is removed by the conclusion, the bane and the antidote must be taken together'. *Duncan and Neill on Defamation*, pp. 13–14.

interpretive possibilities by their interaction with one another. Defamation law is set firmly against the idea that individual words *contain* defamatory potential (e.g. that calling someone a 'thief', 'spy' or 'swindler' is automatically defamatory), since expressions can be used for example as metaphors, in an ironic way, or in quotation. Considering individual expressions will nevertheless show, I hope, how effects created by specific words and phrases work together to build up what is perceived as an overall impression.

*9.3.2.1  'Ridiculous'*    This is hardly a flattering description. But what contribution could it make to the story being defamatory? Like most words, 'ridiculous' conveys simultaneously more than one kind of meaning. It has both a conceptual (or ideational) dimension and a social or expressive meaning. If you consider the social or expressive meaning of 'ridiculous' to be primary, then calling someone 'ridiculous' (or describing them to others as 'ridiculous') amounts only to saying that you don't like them. The particular word might be substituted by many others of equivalent effect.

If 'ridiculous' does have a conceptual dimension, it is that the person referred to inspires the dislike or contempt of the speaker, who by saying so is encouraging others to recognise and perhaps share that perception. Such 'words of heat', or vulgar abuse, are not in themselves defamatory. Uttered or written of a person in a position of public prominence, a description containing the word 'ridiculous' could conceivably arouse suspicion that the person is unprofessional or unworthy of public respect; and indeed here 'ridiculous' modifies 'councillor', and so does appear to be a criticism of Mrs Khan's professional role rather than her personal manner . But there is no law against disliking people, and even use of 'ridiculous' as an assertion rather than for its expressive meaning might be argued to be a statement of opinion rather than an imputation of unworthiness for public office.

In defamation, the distinction between expression of opinion and allegation of fact is important, as it is in other areas of media law, because 'fair comment on a matter of public interest' is one line of defence, if whatever is asserted or implied is based on sound evidence and expressed without malice. It is also the case (although the situation is less clear in English law than in US law[12]) that public figures are more constrained than other people in taking legal action against denunciations or disapproval of their professional life; such criticism

[12]  In US defamation law, following *New York Times Co. v. Sullivan*, 376 U.S. 254 (1964), public figures have less latitude in suing for libel; as public figures, they are expected for First Amendment reasons to accept tougher public scrutiny and comment. See Greenawalt, *Speech, Crime and the Uses of Language*, pp. 135–8. For discussion of *Sullivan*, see Emerson, *The System of Freedom of Expression*, pp. 520–8; on US defamation more generally, Jerome Neu, *Sticks and Stones: The Philosophy of Insults* (Oxford: Oxford University Press, 2008), pp. 171–92.

may be held to be legitimate exercise of freedom of expression in public life. (In the United States Mrs Khan would almost certainly be unable to mount an action against the news provider.) In this context, 'ridiculous' looks as if it could lend support to defamatory potential inherent in other expressions but provides little or no basis for complaint on its own.

*9.3.2.2 'Expenses queen'*   As well as being called a 'ridiculous' councillor, Mrs Khan is also an 'expenses queen'. This is a further expression of dislike. But here the balance has shifted away from social or expressive meaning towards a more definable conceptual meaning.

Being 'queen' of something signifies pre-eminence or special prominence. Used in respect of professional expenses, the expression is likely to be construed to mean 'taking more', and so viewed as a claim about Mrs Khan's professional behaviour. It is unclear, nevertheless, whether that suggestion would be of fraud, or excessive but not illegal behaviour (if for instance the expenses in question were discretionary). Evidence elsewhere in the passage is not conclusive. The story does contain seemingly relevant phrases, such as that Mrs Khan 'graces many glitzy events' and that she has a liking for men described as 'wealthy'. The combined implication of such expressions may strengthen an interpretation that Mrs Khan has a preference for money over public service. But neither implication supports a view one way or the other on the question whether what is implied is injudicious behaviour or fraud.

The key difference between 'expenses queen' and 'ridiculous' is that 'expenses queen' allows a testable assertion to be extrapolated, along the lines 'Mrs Khan takes more money by way of expenses than other people in equivalent circumstances.' That proposition might be shown to be false, and so at least potentially defamatory. Or it might be justified as true, in which case it could form the basis of a defence against an alleged libel. An imputation must be false if it is to be defamatory.

*9.3.2.3 'Imelda-like stature'*   This expression links the word 'queen' in 'expenses queen' to a reference conveyed by the relatively unusual name (in a British context), 'Imelda'. Partly because of its rarity, the name Imelda is likely to be perceived as a reference to Imelda Marcos, widely (but not universally) recognised as the wife of the former Filipino president Ferdinand Marcos. If that cultural reference is accepted, then 'Imelda-like' communicates something like 'regal in manner', even if (in political structure) Imelda Marcos was the wife of a dictator rather than a queen. Interpretation of cultural references is not fixed, however: 'stature' opens up at least two lines of possible inference. One concerns physical size, and an interpreter might want to consider implications of this possibility in a 'people' or 'gossip' story. If no relevant inference results from that path, however, another line beckons. This is that, if Mrs Khan resembles Imelda Marcos, then she is some sort of power behind the throne, close to her husband's public work while being also (or more) concerned – to draw on 'common knowledge' regarding for instance Imelda Marcos's shoe collection – with her own material desires and indulgence.

How much emphasis, if any, Mrs Khan's advisers might feel should be placed on an allusion of this kind depends on what contribution it is believed to make to the overall impression or 'sting' left by the article. As a cultural reference, 'Imelda-like stature' presents different interpretive difficulties from 'ridiculous' or 'expenses queen'. The expression might be considered to convey a common or generally held perception of Imelda Marcos, now part of what 'Imelda-like' means in English. Or it might be judged that such an allusion requires special knowledge that pushes reliance on the reference beyond predictable, ordinary meaning into special procedures for elucidation associated with innuendo meanings, to be considered below.

*9.3.2.4   'Who is known to like the company of wealthy men'*   If there is a sting in this story, arguably it shows itself in this short relative clause. Mrs Khan's alleged liking creates two main difficulties: one a specialised feature of defamation law; the other a more general point about interpretation.

The specialised point about defamation concerns the way that the underlying proposition 'Mrs Khan likes the company of wealthy men' is embedded under a suggestion that this proposition is already 'known', rather than something the writer is putting forward in his or her own voice. The word 'known' here might initially appear to relate to the degree of confidence with which the writer can make the statement, contrasting with 'believed', or 'suspected', etc. Linguistically, degree of confidence in assertion is commonly reflected in markers of epistemic modality, ranging from modal verbs like 'may' or 'might' through to hedging devices for describing relative certainty or doubt such as 'maybe' or 'possibly'. In this context, however, 'known' serves a different function. In libel law, hedges and disclaimers are seen less as indicating degree of certainty than as efforts to deflect responsibility from the writer onto other people, rather like claiming that something is 'allegedly' the case, or is 'rumoured' to be the case. Such disclaimers fail in their hoped-for deflective force, however: repeating a libel is normally taken to be equivalent to asserting it.[13]

Mrs Khan's liking for the company of wealthy men, then, functions as if straightforwardly asserted by the journalist who wrote the article. The possibility that the statement is a defensible comment, rather than an assertion of fact, may also be limited. While attributing subjective states ('Mrs Khan likes…') involves no obviously verifiable assertion, and so (on the face of the words alone) presumably constitutes some kind of comment rather than a factual

---

[13]   *Stern v. Piper* [1997] QB 123; [1996] 3 All ER 385; [1996] 3 WLR 715.

assertion (compare, 'Mrs Khan is disqualified from driving', where the relevant state of affairs *is* something that can be verified), defensible comment in libel must meet further tests.[14] In any event, the meaning of the words, here as elsewhere, is not only their face meaning but also their implication. The description of Mrs Khan's taste seems likely, viewed in context, to be understood as implying a tendency or pattern of behaviour associated with the taste.

Implications from Mrs Khan's alleged liking for the company of wealthy men are central to wider interpretive difficulties. These concern the implied connection between what is otherwise a gratuitous comment and the article's overall thrust: *why* is this liking mentioned at all, unless it has something to do with the rest of the story?

A literal reading of the words (simply that 'Mrs Khan likes the company of wealthy men') differs from similar comments such as that she likes coffee, horse racing, or holidays in Tenerife. Some people hold a strong belief that it is not appropriate for a married woman to like the company of men other than her husband. Such a belief is recognisably of a different order from views about coffee or Tenerife. Interpreting the statement 'Mrs Khan likes the company of wealthy men' in context of a belief that it is inappropriate to like such company would legitimise a further inference: that Mrs Khan likes things which are inappropriate or morally wrong, an inference that might open up an imputation of disrepute.

A more specific interpretive possibility is also hinted at. Because the clause 'who is known to like the company of wealthy men' is embedded in the main clause ('Last night, however, Mrs Khan... was not in attendance [to see her husband receive the plaudits of fellow charity organisers]'), the 'wealthy men' point is processed in that immediate context. In a parallel example, 'Mrs Khan, who likes holidays in Tenerife, was not in attendance to see her husband... etc.', we are encouraged to believe, although it is not stated, that Mrs Khan is in Tenerife. In the story as published we are invited correspondingly to infer that Mrs Khan's liking for the company of wealthy men provides an explanation for her absence from the ceremony.[15] This inference prepares the ground for a possible further inference later in

---

[14] On fair comment as a defence, see Spilsbury, *Media Law*, pp. 91–7; Robertson and Nicol, *Media Law*, pp. 79–85; Scott-Bayfield, *Defamation*, pp. 59–67. Note that following *Reynolds v. Times* [2001] 2 AC 127; [1999] 3 WLR 1010, clearer criteria have been established as regards how comment may be justified in relation to chosen source, means of verification, degree of public concern, urgency, tone and other aspects of the published statement.

[15] Michel Pecheux makes a related point about restatement as a construction of new ideas, but in a very different context. Pecheux traces non-restrictive relative clauses and other parentheticals from Frege through modern philosophical discussion as devices which create ideological, often hidden meanings (by means of what he calls a 'tranverse-discourse effect'). See Michel Pecheux, *Language, Semantics and Ideology: Stating the Obvious*, trans. Harbans Nagpal (London: Macmillan, 1982), esp. pp. 110–29. A more recent reworking and development of many of Pecheux's arguments is Lecercle, *Interpretation as Pragmatics*. For connections between debates about ideology and law, see Paul Q. Hirst, *On Law and Ideology* (London: Macmillan, 1979).

the story: that, when she is 'glimpsed' having dinner with a friend, that friend –
though again it is not stated – is likely to be a man.

*9.3.2.5   'Not in attendance to see her husband receive the plaudits'*   The
statement that Mrs Khan was not present at the awards ceremony appears
straightforward by comparison with previous expressions. It presents a statement of fact that can be verified. If Mrs Khan *was* present at the awards, then the
underlying fact relied on in construction of any comment evaporates. This is no
doubt the main significance of the sentence. But there are other details, in the
margins, that contribute to the story's overall effect. Consider the implication
that follows from 'in attendance' rather than just 'was [not] there'; choice of this
more formal phrase strengthens the theme of expectations on a dutiful wife. Or
consider the link between not being present at the awards and the suggestion
that Mr Khan's achievements are 'in some circles unnoticed'; presumably this
comment narrows that lack of notice to lack of interest by Mrs Khan in her
husband's charitable work.

The theme of expectations on a dutiful wife also signals a further, possible
interpretive direction. Mrs Khan may wish to argue that inferences about her
behaviour as Mr Khan's wife are especially damaging to her because she is a
Muslim. She may believe, for instance, that readers will draw specific inferences about her attitude to religious custom, guided by whatever understanding or stereotype of British Muslim behaviour standards they hold (e.g. about
what it means for a married woman to prefer the company of other men to
accompanying her husband to a public function). After all, comparable inferences about the basis of reputation might be invoked regarding what might
lower a surgeon, a socialist or a Scotsman in the esteem of right-thinking
people.

Two interpretive issues need to be considered here. The first is that it is not
Mrs Khan's own idea of what her reputation is based on that matters. Inferences
entertained by the judge or jury are required to be those of an ordinary reader of
the publication, not a reader of any particular class or faith. Cultural difference
may therefore be an integral but will not be a decisive aspect of construction.
Out of all the various, including culturally specific, meanings that might be
presented, it is the meaning that the jury, suitably informed and guided, decides
that becomes what Lord Diplock called '*the* meaning': the one that the ordinary
reader would have drawn when reading the newspaper.

But who is that ordinary reader? It is only if the story is published in a
newspaper aimed at a predominantly Muslim readership that the ordinary reader
test would reflect any culturally specific sensitivity, by showing regard 'to the
sort of people to whom the words were or were likely to have been published'.
Only then would it be relevant that, for liberal Western readers (including many
Muslim readers), the possibility of an aspersion on Mrs Khan's character might

begin only with an inference that she is interested in men for their money (a lawyer's conventional 'gold-digger' meaning) or with imputation of an extra-marital affair (because of its assumed hypocrisy). For readers with more fixed gender-role expectations, on the other hand, the threshold of defamatory possibilities might be crossed much sooner, possibly with merely the inference that Mrs Khan likes the company of men or simply chose not to attend the awards ceremony.

*9.3.2.6 'Glimpsed dining privately with a friend in another part of the city'* The reported sighting of Mrs Khan having dinner with someone is another assertion, for which evidence may be required. If she is shown not to have been dining at all, or to have been with her husband at the awards ceremony on the evening in question, the defamatory potential increases substantially.

At the same time, details of this final sentence create meaning effects that go beyond bare assertion. The idea that Mrs Khan was 'glimpsed' rather than 'seen' implies an element of secrecy or subterfuge. Choice of the adverb 'privately' strengthens this impression and introduces a further contrast, between the cosiness of her meal and the public nature of the ceremony at which her husband spent the evening. Relatedly, choice of the phrase 'in another part of the city', rather than naming a particular place, highlights less where Mrs Khan was seen than where she wasn't seen.

Oddly, given the genuine distress felt by claimants when they read things about themselves, tuning in to effects of this kind is like reading fiction. Careful word choice and connotation make significant contributions to overall impression; and local description works metonymically, inviting inferences to general tendency or character. From specific, sometimes apparently minor details of behaviour or events, readers are expected to infer a character's role in the story, including especially whether he or she is a good character or a bad character.

The most significant detail in the final sentence is arguably 'with a friend'. Choice of 'friend' over 'someone else' or 'one other person' creates an implication of relationship, although the nature of that implied relationship is left vague by the choice also made not to comment further. Considered alongside cumulative other inferences, the expression seems likely to be interpreted as implying that the clandestine dining companion is a wealthy man, at a dinner chosen to coincide with Mr Khan's more appropriate presence somewhere else.

This is all conjecture. The features of the story I have picked out might alternatively be considered just par for the course in the genre of 'people' or 'gossip' stories, and so likely to be read sceptically or humorously. The point I want to make is a more general one: that libel litigation is a matter of arguments put forward to guide a jury towards a definitive meaning in the face of competing possibilities. Extrapolating from details to create a credible sense of the overall impression conveyed is a crucial part of that process. Commenting in another influential 1960s case largely concerned with problems of meaning, Lord Devlin summed up the challenge of possibly defamatory copy in the following words: 'A man who wants to talk at large about smoke may have to pick his words very carefully if he wants to exclude the suggestion that there is also a fire: but it can be done.'[16] Whether my Mrs Khan example conveys smoke or fire depends on interpretive strategies brought to bear on words that will have been carefully picked either in order to inflict or to avoid a defamatory imputation.

### 9.3.3    From paraphrase to imputation

For Mrs Khan, the particular meanings she wishes to allege must now be put forward. They must be formulated in the section of her statement of claim that pleads particular constructions of the words. As outlined above, though, the meanings do not yet indicate precisely what is alleged. They must be focused differently. In the statement of claim, the meanings laid out will be fixed (unless later amended) for the duration of the action. They will need where appropriate to be supported by evidence, and will be the meanings that the defendant must meet in mounting a defence.

The statement of claim reflects legal strategy and addresses procedural issues as well as describing meanings. To see how drafting is a process both of interpretation and of strategy, it is worth considering how the relevant section of the statement of claim might gloss meanings of the kind sketched out above. By means of such drafting, meanings are translated from an object language (the language of the text), through an enriched, inferential form in which they are mentally represented by the reader, into a specialised legal metalanguage (the language of the statement of claim). That metalanguage is distinctive in two respects. As far as possible it lists, as the meanings of the text complained of, a series of propositions which can be verified or at least linked to underlying facts; it also presents meanings as far as possible as imputations of actions or characteristics likely to lower the claimant in public esteem.

There is a conventional formula for laying out meanings in the statement of claim, along the following lines: 'The said words in their natural and ordinary meaning meant and were understood to mean that the claimant...' followed by a separate statement of each meaning alleged. Where alternative interpretations exist that the claimant wishes to contend simultaneously, some meanings may be pleaded 'in the alternative'. Possibilities for Mrs Khan to consider arising from the discussion above might include statements (with varying prospects of success) along the following lines:

---

[16]  Lord Devlin, in *Lewis v. Daily Telegraph* [1964] AC 234 at 285.

The said words in their natural and ordinary meaning meant and were understood to mean that the claimant,

1. conducted herself in such a way as to bring discredit on her public office as a councillor;
2. misappropriated money (or there is reasonable grounds to suspect that she misappropriated money) in the form of expenses related to her role as a councillor;
3. acted in a hypocritical manner, in neglecting her duties as a councillor in order to pursue personal relationships and gain public acclaim;
4. used an opportunity presented by a charity awards ceremony to conduct an extramarital affair;

[etc.]

At the end of a suitably chosen list, a correspondingly formulaic, concluding statement is added, framing the meanings alleged with emphasis on the damage they have inflicted on Mrs Khan's reputation. Such a statement takes something like the following form: 'By reason of the publication of the said words, the claimant has been gravely damaged in her reputation and suffered great distress and embarrassment.'

The precise nature of Mrs Khan's allegations depends on how the meanings constructed so far can be restated in this 'imputation form'. Each of the meanings suggested relates to a particular type of allegation: the first might be described as a 'professional disrepute' meaning; the second has a 'fraud' meaning (along with a 'reasonable grounds of suspicion of fraud' meaning); the third is a 'hypocrisy' meaning; and the fourth is an 'infidelity' meaning. If these meanings, as restated, are accepted as meanings that the discourse complained of is capable of bearing, then they form a kind of scale of gravity of imputation, or gradient of misconduct. The 'higher' and 'lower', or 'greater' and 'lesser', meanings can be matched to hopes on one side and fears on the other as regards damages.

No single scale of gravity of imputation can be consistently applied. Such scales change, including over time and to reflect social values and attitudes (e.g. whether being said to be German was defamatory in wartime, to whether being said to be homosexual could be considered defamatory now).[17] But while changing at the edges, the imputation scales include established types of defamatory meaning: ingratitude, uncharitableness, hypocrisy, conflict of interest, dishonourable motives, sexual impropriety, negligence, unethical behaviour, improper influence, mental incapacity or insanity, inability to pay debts or financial difficulty, cowardice, fraud, corruption, malice and criminal activity. Each type can be preceded by the hedging expression used in the second imputation above: 'reasonable grounds to suspect x or y'.

---

[17] The *gap* between the 'reasoned' sense and the 'ordinary person' sense of 'reasonable' is perhaps clearest in defamation in discussion of whether being raped or being homosexual can be considered a defamatory imputation.

The particular meanings and list of imputations I have suggested for the Mrs Khan example are not put forward as being strategically plausible. Technical considerations also need to be addressed for a statement of claim to be formulated realistically. My suggestions are intended only to give an idea of *how* meanings, reformulated as 'imputations', relate to an original discourse from which they have been derived. In the process of construction, each meaning undergoes a shift, from being an inference derived from a text read in ordinary circumstances into a re-reading aimed at accentuating a sting in the article considered likely to be damaging to the claimant's reputation.

## 9.4     Ordinary and extended meaning

At the beginning of this chapter I introduced a distinction made in libel law between two kinds of defamatory meaning. One kind, the 'natural and ordinary meaning of the words', has been outlined. What of the other kind? The possibility of an 'innuendo meaning' has in fact already been glimpsed, in the expression 'Imelda-like' in the Mrs Khan example. Doubt surrounded whether sufficient information about Imelda Marcos would exist as part of general knowledge to support the relevant inference from the allusion. We should now consider innuendo meanings more directly.

A 'true' or 'legal' innuendo is an extended meaning created if words of the discourse complained of are used in a sense, other than their ordinary meaning, that is considered to be defamatory even if the ordinary meaning is not. Innuendo meanings of this kind are created by expressions which are not defamatory at face value but which may carry discreditable implications to those with additional, specialised rather than general knowledge. The innuendo must be more than simply an indirect meaning based on inference from the words themselves. An innuendo meaning must be supported by what are called 'extrinsic facts', 'matters' or 'circumstances' that show the basis of the innuendo: these are its 'particulars', which must be pleaded and proved. The alleged innuendo constitutes a separate cause of action, in parallel with that created by any imputation associated with the same expression because of inferences that follow from the words alone. To accommodate innuendo, the ordinary-reader test is modified and becomes a test of meaning for the reader with knowledge of the relevant facts; and because an innuendo must be supported by evidence, witnesses and an explanation of those relevant facts are allowed in support of the particulars, though not of the inference drawn from them (which remains a matter for the jury).

To see why innuendo meanings are important in how libel treats meaning, it is necessary first to consider how far meaning is usually taken to be inherent in, or automatically associated with, the words of a text themselves. With ordinary meaning, what is understood as the meaning of the words is taken to include not only conventional, literal meaning but also inferences either reasonably prompted by their typical context of use or formed on the basis of general knowledge. Such inferences are considered 'intrinsic' and thought 'inescapable', as if they are straightforwardly aspects of word meaning. This is the sense in which the 'natural and ordinary' meaning is the meaning that the words convey to ordinary people who 'read between the lines in the light of their general knowledge and experience of worldly affairs'.[18]

Libel law takes a different view of inference than is usually adopted in linguistics or psychology. In those fields the idea of inferences other than entailments being 'intrinsic' to a word is problematic. But in defamation the approach to handling meaning is practical rather than theoretical. It is permissible to plead natural and ordinary meanings and innuendo meanings together, even if they must be kept procedurally separate in order to ensure that particulars are provided where needed but not allowed to exert artificial leverage over the jury's commonsense understanding. A practical rather than theoretical test is used to distinguish the two kinds of meaning. If the meaning is indirect but still an outcome of a way of reading, rather than of specialised knowledge, then it is ordinary. If, on the other hand, the meaning can only be grasped if the interpreter has access to specific, extra knowledge of some kind, then it is innuendo. One important consequence is that natural and ordinary meaning includes many effects that on the face of things seem to go beyond the words themselves: oblique or indirect expressions; use of rhetorical questions or conjectures; epithets; exclamations; and contrasts and other persuasive devices that depend on the reader's ability to read beyond the words but do not rely on knowledge of anything specific beyond the words and their context of use.[19]

There are problems, I want to suggest, with this way of drawing the distinction. In the history of libel, there has been an ongoing argument about precisely where the boundary is to be set between extended, inferential meaning and true legal innuendo. The underlying difference between ordinary inferential meaning and innuendo is therefore best seen if the two kinds of meaning are laid out slightly more formally. Ordinary, inferential meaning (including 'false' or 'popular' innuendo) might be formalised as follows:

> Meaning A, plus facts (known to everyone), triggers extended/inferred meaning B (available to the ordinary reader).

Legal innuendo, by contrast, is:

---

[18] Sir Brian Neill and Richard Rampton commenting on the George Washington innuendo in *Grubb v. Bristol United Press* [1963] 1 QB 309; 3 WLR 25; [1962] 2 All ER 380, in *Duncan and Neill on Defamation*, p. 10. Full discussion of this example follows in 9.4.1.

[19] *Halsbury's Laws of England*, ed. James Bowman and Land Herilsham of St Marylebone, 4th revised edition (London: Butterworth, 2005), p. 92 para 178.

> Meaning A, plus facts (known only to some people), triggers extended/inferred meaning B (available only to readers who know those facts).

Allowing for some imprecision in what constitutes the literal or face-value Meaning A in the first place, and in what constitutes the scope of facts or 'particulars' that are added, a description of this kind fits the canonical examples. The most commonly cited textbook case, for instance, is what is known as an 'identification innuendo'.[20] A man is described as having entered a particular, named house. No defamatory implication there, unless the reader happens to know that the address in question is a brothel. In this example, the innuendo arises as follows:

> Meaning A, plus facts (about what the expression refers to, known only to some people) triggers extended/inferred meaning B (available only to readers who know the facts about what the expression refers to).

Not all examples are so straightforward, of course. In the next section I discuss two borderline areas which illustrate how the framework for understanding meaning in defamation is caught up in more general problems of meaning and interpretation.

### 9.4.1   The problem of not being George Washington

One of the most influential authorities in English libel literature on how far ordinary meaning can extend before special pleading of innuendo is required is to be found in a robust appeal judgment handed down by Lord Justice Holroyd Pearce in *Grubb v. Bristol United Press Ltd* [1963]. Holroyd Pearce tackles head-on the need to reconcile the idea that the ordinary reader is capable of reading beyond literal sense to indirect implications with the contrasting need to limit proliferation of ingenious extensions or embellishments of meaning that he dismisses as kinds of 'quasi-innuendo'.[21] How can this be done? Holroyd Pearce lays out a detailed historical and theoretical argument and focuses on the following example to show why there is no need for so many, separately pleaded innuendoes:

> If the defendant published of John Smith: 'his name is certainly not George Washington', then, however much the defendant may argue that the words were a harmless truism concerned merely with nomenclature, the natural and ordinary implication of the words is that John Smith is untruthful; and presumably the jury would find that to be the ordinary meaning of the words.[22]

---

[20] *Duncan and Neill on Defamation*, p. 23; Scott-Bayfield, *Defamation*, pp. 21–33.
[21] Lord Justice Holroyd Pearce, quoted in *Grubb v. Bristol United Press* [1963], at 313.
[22] Lord Justice Holroyd Pearce, quoted in *Grubb v. Bristol United Press* [1963], at 327–8.

How can an obviously cultural reference be merely an ordinary meaning rather than an innuendo? 'George Washington' is not an ordinary expression of English but a proper name. Allusion can be made to that name, but any such allusion appears to depend on background, encyclopaedic information rather than on linguistic competence. But because the first US president is presumed to have become general knowledge, an allusion to his name is held to constitute an ordinary meaning rather than an innuendo meaning. To say of John Smith that he is not George Washington is therefore interpreted something like this:

The name 'George Washington' may be substituted by the meaning for that name, based on general knowledge; in this instance, 'George Washington' means 'someone who could never tell a lie'. If John Smith is not 'someone who could never tell a lie', then he is someone who *could* tell a lie. Such an observation is relevant only in circumstances where (and this is what makes the comment more than the 'harmless truism' that the name 'John Smith' is not the same name as the name 'George Washington') there is someone of whom it is relevant to say that they are capable of telling a lie. Hence, the person under discussion, John Smith, is considered capable of telling a lie in whatever circumstances are relevant.

The obviousness of this reading depends on whatever obviousness is associated with the equation that allows the name 'George Washington' to mean 'someone who could never tell a lie'. In choosing this example as his illustration of the inescapability of inferential meaning, Lord Justice Holroyd Pearce must have felt that the relevant, bridging information would be general knowledge among those he was addressing: lawyers and others present in court, as well as later readers of law reports. Whether he considered such an allusion would be self-evident to readers of the *Western Daily Press and Times and Mirror*, the publication in *Grubb*, or what proportion of members of contemporary British society he expected to recognise the allusion, is unclear. But it is not relevant either, because they were not the readers to whom his remark was published.

The general question, though, of what readers know and how they activate that knowledge is important. The question is not as straightforward as the example suggests. Undoubtedly in the early 1960s, as now, many people recognise the George Washington allusion. Equally, many others are unaware that George Washington cut down the little tree with his hatchet and had to own up. Who George Washington was is a preposterous question for one person but a necessary question for another. Different amounts and kinds of knowledge are available to people with different life experiences and different educational backgrounds. Whatever the empirical facts may be for any given readership, describing such an inferential meaning as 'intrinsic' or 'inescapable' seems questionable.

For some readers, interestingly, *more than* one piece of information about the subject of an allusion may be known. In such circumstances, it is the contextually salient information, rather than any single, best-known piece of information, that will be activated. If a 'George Washington' allusion is made not in relation to a truth-telling topic but instead in relation to a personal accomplishment topic, then the resulting inference about John Smith is likely to be different: John Smith is not George Washington; George Washington was a great man; John Smith is not a great man, etc. Even in a 'truth-telling' context, an inference about George Washington's achievements may be triggered first but rejected as not contextually relevant before the 'who could not tell a lie' inference is accessed in a continuing search for relevance.

The signifying potential of some allusions (e.g. to Hitler, Stalin or Mother Teresa, or to places like Copacabana, Guernica or the Sahara) may have become conventionalised over time. But it is risky to assume this of most cultural references, which depend on specific facets being brought into focus by context (e.g. where allusions occur in a list and so allow a 'common denominator' reading, referred to by lawyers as a 'rogues' gallery': compare, for instance, 'Machiavelli, Goebbels and the Prime Minister' and 'Nelson Mandela, the Dalai Lama and the Prime Minister'). Relevant meaning for any given allusion is narrowed down inferentially. In a libel action where an MP's wife had been likened to the character Sue Ellen in the TV serial *Dallas*, it was necessary to argue over alternative 'glamorous woman' and 'degenerate alcoholic' meanings.[23] As is the case with other words, names and cultural references have potential to be shaped into meanings when construed in combination and in context. They do not have 'intrinsic' meanings.

Little about the point I am making here has escaped notice in libel law. Legal authorities routinely caution that cultural references (the most discussed problematic instances in the literature include Man Friday and Casanova[24]) can move across from specialised into general use and so no longer constitute innuendo meanings (with the result that evidence as to meaning is no longer admissible about them). Others may never have been fully in general use, or may have moved in the other direction, away from innuendo into ordinary meaning.[25] Indeed, the passage in which Lord Justice Holroyd Pearce presents his example continues with discussion of how the Washington allusion might alternatively be pleaded as an innuendo. In more recent exposition of innuendo, modern authorities have sometimes queried Lord Justice Holroyd Pearce's

---

[23] For discussion of the libel action (unreported) in which Jonathan Aitken MP claimed another MP's wife resembled the character 'Sue Ellen', see Scott-Bayfield, *Defamation*, pp. 15 and 96–7. Cultural variation in how this TV series was interpreted has been investigated from a media studies perspective in T. Liebes and E. Katz, *The Export of Meaning: Cross-Cultural Readings of Dallas* (Oxford: Oxford University Press, 1991).

[24] See discussion of Casanova in *Grubb v. Bristol United Press* [1963], at 336–7.

[25] I argued this about the phrase 'economical with the truth' in Alan Durant, 'On the interpretation of allusions and other "innuendo" meanings in libel actions'.

suggestion that it would be 'probably unnecessary' to plead an innuendo in the Washington instance. Duncan and Neill, for example, advise instead that 'in any case where a comparison is made with a historical figure, it would be unwise to rely on a jury's assessment of the general knowledge of the ordinary man and that an innuendo should be pleaded, at any rate as an alternative'.[26]

### 9.4.2   Technical, slang and local meanings

The George Washington example is a borderline case between general and specialised factual knowledge. This is what makes it interesting as regards the boundary drawn in defamation between ordinary and innuendo meaning. In other circumstances, it is linguistic rather than factual knowledge which makes the innuendo threshold problematic. Such circumstances include where the meaning at issue is that of a regional or class dialect term, a term of professional jargon, or part of underworld slang (for instance to do with drugs, guns or prostitution).

In order to get the secondary meaning of innuendoes that are 'language based', particulars need to be presented in support of inferences related to patterns of language use rather than factual knowledge.[27] An innuendo meaning may be triggered by an expression which involves some kind of linguistic obscurity. This situation can arise where an expression has a technical, slang or local (dialect) meaning (e.g. as part of an underworld argot or anti-language), or where an expression has an idiomatic meaning for some other reason that is unlikely to be familiar to the ordinary language user. The particulars provided cannot, however, be 'linguistic' in a general sense, such as an interpretation of some other part of the text (as had been unsuccessfully contended in *Grubb* itself). The specialised information is, however, about how language is used rather than about brothels or trees-and-hatchets. With some expressions, it is even suggested that there may not even be an ordinary meaning, since the expression may only gain a meaning at all (as in the case of specialised or technical areas of vocabulary) where a language user has acquired a relevant

---

[26] *Duncan and Neill on Defamation*, p. 11.

[27] *Halsbury's Laws of England*, p. 24 para 46 and esp. p. 91 para 176. As regards admissibility of expert evidence on special facts about language (such as slang, dialect, technical terms, etc.), while there is forensic expertise in bloodstains and firearms the court normally sees itself as expert on language and vests authority in juries. Within linguistics, there is then an implicit scale of relative 'expert' authority: phonetics is usually considered to offer firmest or most scientific evidence; stylistic evidence (e.g. as regards authorship or the authenticity of disputed documents) is often viewed as more speculative; and meaning evidence is commonly regarded with scepticism. On linguistic evidence in courtrooms, see Lawrence Solan, 'Linguistic experts as semantic tour guides', *Forensic Linguistics*, 5 (2) (1998), 87–105. Clear and persuasive arguments *against* use of semantics (e.g. in helping judges ascertain the 'plain meaning' of words in statutory interpretation) are presented in Cliff Goddard, 'Can linguists help judges know what they mean? Linguistic semantics in the court-room', *Forensic Linguistics*, 3 (2) (1996), 250–72.

field of understanding, or (as with dialect or slang) for members of the relevant language community or sub-culture.

What is interesting about 'language-related' innuendo is that the particulars required to support the inference are linguistic facts rather than encyclopaedic facts. This opens up an area of exceptions to the principle adopted in defamation that linguistic understanding is a matter of ordinary usage, which should be treated as a question of fact for the jury to decide rather than something to be established by evidence.

Together, the two different kinds of borderline case I have outlined point to what seems an order of relative importance between two main attributes of innuendo meaning: additional facts, without which the relevant inference cannot be drawn; and restricted availability of those facts to an in-group of people within a wider readership. Innuendoes arising from technical language or slang suggest that the essential feature is less the nature of the additional 'matter' than its restricted availability.

Innuendo might accordingly be understood as functioning to create an 'insider meaning' for some while excluding others (as might be expected for something called 'innuendo', though the other common expectation, that of sexual *double entendre*, does not apply). If defamation law had no innuendo category, then speakers, writers and other text producers could get round the purpose of defamation law by using obscure linguistic forms or allusions as a sort of special code whose hidden meanings insiders would understand perfectly well. The category of innuendo meaning provides a way to break such codes. On the other hand, limiting the category of innuendo as far as possible ensures that claimants are not encouraged to embroider their pleadings with extravagant meanings that, 'with the aid of Roget's Thesaurus', unduly widen ordinary meaning.[28]

## 9.5     Capable of bearing the meaning attributed

Implicit in the framework of ordinary and innuendo meanings in defamation is the essential 'meaning question' for libel: whether, as my chapter title asks, an expression is 'reasonably capable of bearing the meaning attributed' to it. To link my discussion of defamation to more general points made earlier in the book, I want now to consider this formulation more directly. Each of its three central concepts deserves attention: 'the words'; 'bearing' a meaning; and 'capable of bearing' a meaning. Each, I suggest, is equivocal by comparison with the precision of procedural aspects of defamation law. Choice of the three expressions may play an important part in both the functioning of, and also the difficulties faced by, libel's framework for meaning construction.

---

[28]  *Grubb v. Bristol United Press* [1963] at 329.

Consider first the expression 'the words' (or just 'words'). Sometimes this expression is used to indicate the formal material of language, what might otherwise be called word forms or signifiers: groups of letters on a page or sounds in the air, on tape, or in a file. Such 'words' are resources out of which meaning is created. On other occasions, however, the same expression is used to denote words (or groups of words) that are already endowed with particular meanings (in this view, words are stable, conventional 'containers' of meaning, or signs made up of signifiers along with their signifieds). Picking out a 'word' in this second sense is not a matter of its material form prior to any attached meaning but already has a meaning linked to it. This second use of 'words' comes close to commitment to stable, literal meaning of words in a particular context. In libel, as we have seen, it may also include whatever is accepted as an 'intrinsic' inference from the word. On other occasions again, the expression 'the words' is used to refer to a whole published text, and so as a synonym for 'passage', 'discourse' or 'text'. This third, widespread use is in turn equivocal between the two senses already mentioned: whether meaning for those 'words' – i.e. for the whole text – is a question still to be asked (how those 'words' are linked to some particular meaning in a given context) or whether that question has already been answered (the 'words' are the words as anyone understands them, already replete with their established meaning).

In everyday discourse, of course, the term 'words' is used similarly ambig- uously, though conversationalists may not be as adept as lawyers in systemati- cally exploiting the different senses. In fields other than law that are also, in Lord Diplock's phrasing, 'concerned with the meaning of words', it is more usual, however (as I have done in earlier chapters) to draw distinctions between the different senses, in order to separate out the processes at work in how meaning is created. Why should this matter? When elaborated as the expression 'the natural and ordinary signification of the words', the notion of 'the words' offers a reassuring sense of meaning as something emanating from a discourse rather than something which has to be created out of multiple, perhaps divergent possibilities.

Whatever comfort people derive from this image of stable, conventional meaning, it sits uncomfortably with the interpretive challenges that libel actions face and will continue, perhaps increasingly, to face in future. This will be especially so if we go beyond the ambiguity of the phrase 'the words' to consider what the *relationship* is between words and their meaning in libel. On this, we are told that they 'bear' it. But 'bear', like 'words', turns out to be equivocal. 'Bear' has the sense of 'bring', as when people bear gifts; in this sense, 'bear' indicates a process by means of which 'words' bring their mean- ings with them, so that their meaning can be taken from them by an adjudicator. At the same time, 'bear' also has the sense of 'support', as when a bridge bears a weight. In this second sense, meaning is placed or built on a word, rather than part of it. The adjudicator must assess a meaning not in virtue of its 'intrinsic' or 'inescapable' properties but depending on how it is constructed and whether the word or words can carry it.

How can we know if the meaning that a word is thought to bear is a fair account of it? We ask if it is 'capable' of bearing that meaning. 'The acid test', Lord Justice Hirst affirms in the Court of Appeal in *Stern v. Piper*,[29] is 'whether the meaning sought to be justified is one which the words are reasonably capable of bearing'. In this context 'capable' can either indicate the potential of the signifying resources to create a particular meaning, because language creates a range of alternatives that need to be decided between in a given context, or it can report a decision: that a given expression has been judged to be capable, or not capable, of bearing some particular meaning. The first sense is consistent with judges striking out meanings at an early stage if they believe the particular meaning has no realistic prospect of success, because the words are not capable of bearing that meaning among a range of other meanings that are more likely. The second sense is more consistent with the authority of judge and jury to determine a definitive meaning for the purpose of the case, in the face of incompatible, alternative meanings demonstrably held by the opposing parties.

As in previous chapters, it is necessary to ask whether what is exposed here is anything more than wordplay. Do the different senses lead to practical consequences? Defamation is a field of law, not a topic for a semantics seminar. For libel protagonists, as I suggested at the beginning of this chapter, 'winning' is what is important, not 'meaning'. But meaning and winning in libel are inextricably tied together. My reason for calling the process of meaning attribution a kind of 'meaning poker', above, was that questions of meaning in defamation are both interpretive and adversarial, in several related respects. Firstly, to win a libel action it is essential to construct meanings that will be plausible in relation to a public 'belief bank', or body of social beliefs and attitudes that a jury brings into court. What will *they* think the utterance plausibly means? What will *they* accept as a suitably nuanced, but not too far-fetched, interpretation? Secondly, to win a libel action the plausible meanings that are chosen must be turned into imputations that a jury will accept as not only reflecting what was said but being sufficiently damaging to be worth taking seriously. Thirdly, to win a libel action each meaning put forward must be supported by evidence, in anticipation of possible defences equally based on evidence that may be available to the other side. And fourthly, to win a libel action it is essential for the jury to be guided towards the meaning being argued; while some meanings may be ordinary

---

[29]  Lord Justice Hirst, in *Stern v. Piper* [1996] 3 All ER 385 at 393.

enough to be common knowledge, there are others that may be essential to winning but which members of the jury would not think of unless suitably prompted. Where meanings are cards in your hand, in a game of high stakes, then precisely what the rules of the game are is crucial information.

## 9.6    Defamatory meaning and common knowledge

I want finally to bring together the question of different kinds of meaning with the larger purpose and future of defamation. So far I have argued that borderline cases between ordinary and secondary meanings are acknowledged as a matter of standard procedure in the established framework for determining defamatory meaning. An expression may shift over time from one category to another. Such changes reflect the living and changing nature of discourse and culture, as well as the responsiveness of libel law. An obscure allusion can become part of mainstream understanding; a recognised, topical allusion may become obscure or even opaque. Today's innuendo based on a slang term may be the ordinary meaning of a common vocabulary item tomorrow.

Difficulties with this framework are considered exceptional. Most areas of meaning are presumed to involve either the face meaning of the words or inferences based on common knowledge. My discussion, by contrast, suggests that exceptions may be less marginal than this, in ways that reflect not only courtroom procedure but how meaning works more generally.

How can I support that claim? Here is a brief account. Even in the period since the influential 1960s decisions on defamatory meaning that underlie much current thinking about meaning in defamation, British society has become much less homogeneous in religious, cultural and ethnic terms than in any previous period. Over the same period, the media environment in which secondary meanings are created has also diversified dramatically. In print, in audio-visual media and on the Internet, the range of material now published has massively increased the variety of language and sources for allusion or reference in circulation. Publication on this scale puts into the public domain a far wider range of different voices and cultural references than that confronting judges in the 1960s, and in doing so creates a greater likelihood that any given cultural reference or culturally specific idiom will be viewed differently, from often incompatible points of view.

Such shifts have ramifications. As regards cultural references (e.g. the already symptomatically dated question of whether, in the Aitken case, the *Dallas* character Sue Ellen signified female glamour or drunken prostitution[30]), determining meaning may be increasingly difficult in defamation actions. Lord

---

[30] Scott-Bayfield, *Defamation*, pp. 15 and 96–7.

Justice Holroyd Pearce cited with approval Lord Grey's eighteenth-century argument that an innuendo 'means nothing more than the words "id est" or "scilicet" or "meaning" or "aforesaid", as, explanatory of a subject-matter sufficiently expressed before' (i.e. simply a different way of saying the same thing). In doing so, he presumed agreed equations between the subject of a cultural reference and its meaning: 'George Washington', for example, means 'a person who could never tell a lie'. The social homogeneity embodied in an imagined ordinary reader who knows such meanings, however, obscures how far meaning for any given allusion involves not a ready-made equation but an interpretive act. That act alters the sense of an expression because of differences which may be fundamentally resistant to being distilled into a singular, 'ordinary-reader' perception.

To say of someone that he showed himself to be the 'Tony Blair' of his company's management team may seem to invite an equation of the George Washington type (though even the linking theme between these two cases may be viewed differently by different readers). Interpretation of a 'Tony Blair' allusion along the lines of 'leader', 'eloquent advocate' or 'statesman' is clearly available. But such a meaning will have to compete, for any given readership (including one that would be widely considered 'right-thinking'), with other available meanings such as 'deceiver', 'US puppet' or 'opportunist'; and these in context might constitute a defamatory imputation. Even between the writing of this example and when it is read, the relative salience between different possible meanings of such an allusion will change, in ways it is impossible to predict. The same point might be made about slang and dialect. Changes and reversals of word meaning require the jury, in a highly differentiated multimedia environment, to be far more fine-tuned to attitudes and language use than the ordinary-reader test can accommodate, if mistakes are to be avoided with even such common terms of mixed, pejorative and non-pejorative meaning as 'wicked' or 'gay'.

The problems I have drawn attention to are not problems limited to defamation. They are wider issues of contemporary media and culture. But they do present a particular challenge to contemporary libel law, as the idea is increasingly accepted beyond legal circles that a variety of legitimate inferences exist for many utterances or publications that are not easily reconciled with the idea of innuendo as an exception to the jury's presumable competence in matters of language and a culture's symbolic codes. The jury's 'ordinary usage' competence is a sustainable idea so long as members of the jury are thought only rarely to lack further particulars of esoteric allusions and obscure slang or argot. If, on the other hand, the category of innuendo reflects a routinely more differentiated field of modern public discourse, then the ability of any twelve language users to act as a common standard of linguistic competence and social knowledge may increasingly come into doubt.

## 9.7     Summary

In this chapter, I have described the standard of interpretation adopted in defamation law, and outlined how the parties in a defamation action set about establishing the meaning they wish to plead. I have suggested, however, that the distinction made between two standards of meaning applied in different circumstances – between the 'natural and ordinary meaning of the words' and specialised meanings associated with knowledge available only to a given readership – shows up problems in how meaning is judged in defamation. The role played in interpretation by inference, I argued, cannot be divided cleanly between processes that are an ordinary part of meaning-making and specialised activity triggered by localised kinds of cultural knowledge. I concluded by suggesting that difficulties presented by inferential interpretation in libel are exacerbated by the diversity of backgrounds, beliefs and expectations of segmented media audiences in multicultural societies.

# 10 Advertising: 'not only what is said, but what is reasonably implied'

## 10.1 Introduction

In this chapter, I consider the meanings conveyed by adverts and other marketing communications. I discuss how both explicit and implied product and service claims can be challenged in advertising law and complaint procedures. When a complaint is made, the meaning of an advert is typically tested against an interpretive standard based on the view of an 'average consumer' (supplemented in some jurisdictions by evidence from consumer surveys). Problems to do with meaning arise, however, in two main kinds of borderline case: with legitimate 'trade puffs', which sing the praise of a product or service in a genre of accepted marketplace exaggeration; and with face-value claims that are defended on the paradoxical basis that no one will believe them. Widening my account of advertising, I compare two established approaches to consumer meaning: a belief that product-related facts, which may or may not be known to the consumer, determine what a contested expression means in a given commercial use; and an approach based on inferences drawn by a consumer in a given sales context. These two approaches underlie two acknowledged axes of advertising content, 'information' and 'persuasion'. The claim is commonly made that a clear contrast is perceived between these two axes. I argue, by contrast, that the distinction between information and persuasion fails to provide a reliable classification of advertising 'meaning'.

## 10.2 Commercial information and persuasion

As I open a packet of 'washed and ready to serve' salad from my local supermarket in London, I notice that 'country of origin' is given as Kenya. In a period of global supply chains and distribution this is no surprise. My attention is drawn, however, to a small promotional bubble on the packet. This informs me that the salad has been 'washed in spring water'. I visualise African uplands where rocket flourishes alongside fresh streams. That romanticised image soon gives way, however, to lack of geographical information. Does rocket even grow in regions in which Kenyan springs rise? Perhaps the water originates in springs but the washing is done, or the water drawn, somewhere more convenient downstream? At what point downstream would the 'spring' water that links my salad to the economic value associated with branded bottled water cease to be spring water and become mere river water, hardly a feature worth publicising?

The back of the pack doesn't help much:

We are proud to work in partnership with our suppliers, who participate in an independent audit programme that ensures responsible pesticide usage and encourages environmental protection and wildlife conservation. Established over half a century ago this family run business specialises in growing high-quality, tender baby leaves... Every leaf is picked young and washed in natural spring water drawn from within the chalk beds of the Hampshire Downs before being packed. At certain times of the year produce is sourced from equally high-quality farms in the Iberian peninsula, Italy, Kenya and North America.

If I want to test whether my image of the produce has been stretched, not just from the chalk beds of the Hampshire Downs to Kenya but in other ways, where could I begin?

Partly, it would be a matter of establishing with the suppliers how the salad is in fact washed. This would be much like consumers questioning equivalent processes with 'organic' and 'guaranteed GM free' produce. But the promotional role of the packaging is rhetorical as well as factual. It is also about how 'spring water' is understood symbolically (e.g. as something pure and enriching, given that for example washing coins in spring water is mythically thought to increase their value). There are dictionary definitions of 'spring', of course. There are also technical specifications that 'spring water' must meet in the bottled water industry (e.g. Statutory Instrument No. 1540, 'The Natural Mineral Water, Spring Water and Bottled Drinking Water Regulations, 1999').[1] But even if the definitional aspects seem watertight, it is unlikely that a given distance from source will be specified before 'spring water' for washing salad, rather than bottling it for drinking, must be referred to as river water. Perhaps the world would be madly over-regulated if there *was* such an officially prescribed distance?[2] Failing some such definition, however, what ensures fairness of presentation, such that consumers don't need to worry – not only

---

[1] 'The Natural Mineral Water, Spring Water and Bottled Drinking Water Regulations 1999', published by HMSO (and online at www.uk-legislation.hmso.gov.uk).

[2] Not everyone takes this view. The European Food Information Resource (EUROFIR) Consortium (www.eurofir.net) undertakes detailed description of foodstuffs in order to strengthen consumer protection with more reliable statistics (e.g. on testing and trend-spotting). It has produced a report on difficulties of description, including difficulties presented by natural language. Food preparations at the border between liquid and semi-liquid, such as 'sauce' (an 'accompaniment or adjunct') and 'soup' ('liquid food, often containing pieces of solid food'), present typical definitional problems. The terms in question are defined and linked to supplementary guidance notes: SYN = synonym; RT = related terms; SN = scope note; and AI = additional information. In efforts

about their freshly washed salad but about dozens of commercial products and services every day?

## 10.3     Advertising and promotional discourse

Although a salad wrapper is a kind of advertisement, it isn't the sort of advert typically subjected to analysis.[3] It is on-pack labelling, and so what is sometimes called a 'silent salesman'. Typically an advert is a separate text drawing attention to the product or service when the potential consumer is not in front of the product, but somewhere else. To this extent, the salad wrapper is not prototypical of the kinds of advertising discussed from an interpretive point of view. The marginality of the example nevertheless helps draw attention to how promotional discourse works, a term which I take here in its broad sense of representations that promote products and services for sale: what is generally understood by the expression (not as widely used in British English as in American English) 'commercial speech'.[4]

The wider notion of commercial speech is introduced here for both practical and theoretical reasons. The practical interest is that, as well as traditional magazine, broadcast and online 'big' adverts, there are many other kinds of sales-related discourse in the modern, more targeted media mix. That mix includes packaging and other point-of-sale language and design; display ads and classifieds; postcards in shop windows; posters and billboards in public places; websites and pop-ups; search engine listings and spam; messages to mobiles; signs painted on vehicles, buildings and clothing; puff pieces in magazines over which the subject has copy approval and which are made to resemble features or stories; sponsors' logos at events such as sports events; direct mail and interactive marketing; blogs, discussion threads and other online content that is not genuinely user-generated but planted by marketers; and adverts dissembling as other text-types, prizes and events. All these different forms of marketing communication share a defining characteristic: they seek, at some level of explicitness or indirectness, to manipulate preference formation and future buying patterns.

One theoretical interest of 'commercial speech' is that it is unclear precisely where the boundaries of the category lie. It is also unclear what a reader or viewer is to make of promotional discourse in which commercial speech

to establish a coherent and consistent nomenclature, one person's Swiftian excess is another person's prudent administrative measure. Consider, for instance, the currently problematic distinction between what is a biscuit and what is a cake, which has implications as regards VAT.

[3] The fact that my salad example is insignificant is what makes it significant. In everyday communication, a salad wrapper is unlikely to become an issue (though in fact as I write some consignments of imported spinach 'pre-washed in spring water' are being recalled because of bromate levels above specification in the spring water).

[4] See Barendt, *Freedom of Speech*, pp. 54–63.

features are intertwined with other discourse functions. This is not an obscure theoretical interest, but an important resource in marketing as an industry. One explanation for the diversity of modern marketing communication, for example, is that advertising piggybacks on whatever communicative forms and opportunities present themselves. If advertising is to be regulated, accordingly, characteristics other than form need to be taken into account. But what other characteristics? Possibilities include overall social effect, conceived as a balance between the perceived benefit of a wide circulation of commercial information and countervailing risks of confusion in the marketplace, deception, and offensiveness. Other characteristics that might distinguish legitimate from excessive or harmful advertising include the meanings that adverts convey. But if advert 'meaning' is to be a significant category, then we need to be confident we know what advert meaning is, within the many ways that discourse communicates about goods and services.

## 10.4    How discourse represents products and services

Marketers have a rich vocabulary for describing formal elements within commercial communication. They talk of imagery, taglines, straplines, slogans, theme lines, positioning statements, signatures, catchphrases, and many other kinds of product-linked or service-linked creative content. It is worth recasting this terminology of specialised devices within a more general vocabulary for describing how meanings are produced.

Ten main ways are worth listing in which an advert or marketing communication can 'talk about' or 'depict' a product or service:

1. It can simply **show** a photo (or other graphic) of the product, making the product recognisable visually. For physical goods, the prototypical visual identifier is a standard 'pack-shot'.

2. This identifying function of an image can be extended to designate the product linguistically, by **naming** it (e.g. by means of a distinctive trade name or logo). Such a name or logo serves the general function of a trademark, even if the particular name or mark is not registered. The name acts as a sign of origin, reducing search costs for the consumer among a range of similar products of variable quality that are available, and supports a perception of reliability of origin within a changing marketplace. The mark may also help to secure rights in the product's value for its producer or owner.

3. An advert or marketing communication may also – with or without an accompanying visual image, though usually alongside a name – present a **description** of the product. Such description elaborates on the naming function (though the two may sometimes get confused, if the chosen name is itself descriptive). Description makes more detailed claims than just a claim of existence. It may give information about product quantity,

size or method of production; or about its composition, fitness for purpose, performance or accuracy; or about conformity with a type or approved standard. Such descriptions commonly involve a geographical indicator, or marker of place of origin.

4. Supplementing such description, **further information** may be added. The advert might present technical information (e.g. nutrition information for food, or about power supply for electrical goods); or it might contain a product warning (describing hazards, especially in relation to use by children) or instructions (e.g. about assembly, use and safe disposal).

5. Description may be coloured by the way an advert **connotes** qualities and values. Such connotations weave associative meanings into description of the product's features (e.g. pastoral designs may be used for food produce; conventionally exotic styles chosen for Asian goods; children's toys shown in comfortable play rooms). Connotations can be associated with any of an advert's design features, including its music, costume or choice of actors, as well as any accompanying language. The impact of the connotations is a suggestion of the product's desirability: by a figurative process, qualities of design, packaging and advert scenario transfer to the product.

6. Not always easily distinguishable from such associative meanings is a related displacement of favourable connotation onto the consumer. An advert can **evoke** lifestyle, cultural identity and aspiration (e.g. by association with fashion, style of music, or endorsement by a particular celebrity); the products that consumers choose in this way appear to make statements about how they view themselves or wish to be viewed by others. By a similar figurative process to the one described above, qualities of the advert scenario transfer onto the product's user.

7. Description and evocation are mostly not neutral or dispassionate. They contribute to the sales patter that serves to **puff** favourable characteristics of the product or service, incorporating praise by the vendor into what otherwise appears to be description. This type of positive impression, sometimes with its seriousness minimised by marketers as 'flights of fancy', is typically conveyed by evaluative words, including exaggerated praise. In such puffing, the descriptive or informational function of an advert gives way to a persuasive function.

8. All the preceding ways that discourse relates to a product depict what the seller wishes to promote, either directly or indirectly. But products and services exist in a competitive marketplace. So an advert can also **compare** the product favourably in some respect with a competitor's equivalent product (e.g. in terms of pricing, quality or reliability). The result is comparative advertising.

9. Because of competition between them, advertisers will not always wish to (or be able to) say positive things about their own product by comparison

with those offered by rivals. In such cases, an advert may go beyond comparative advertising to denigrate or **disparage a competitor** (or, where such 'knocking copy' goes on to create a claim that is inaccurate or maliciously intended, it may constitute a trade libel against a rival or malicious falsehood about that rival's product).

10. Finally, advertising may not depict the advertised product at all. Instead it may convey a style or create an atmosphere that merely **attracts attention** to the product. Such advertising may use media experimentation or a break from established genre expectations, or shock in order to prompt extra, secondary publicity. Such adverts must still be recognised as in some way associated with the product, for instance by allusion or indirect reference. But more than any other kind, such adverts displace the detailed work of selling onto supplementary small print, an accompanying website, in-store information, general reputation, or all of these.

Suitably qualified and filled out with detail, these general relations between sign and product are the main ways in which advertising copy represents products or services in discourse in whatever medium it occurs. The different relations are not alternatives but combine and overlap. Adverts show, name, describe, inform, connote/evoke, puff, compare, disparage and/or just attract attention in a complex and changing mix of discourse styles.

Note that the categories are not formal styles or techniques. They are relations between form and product. Different resources, in many different media, can be used to achieve each kind of relation. The overall trend in marketing communication may be towards more oblique, evocative advertising, at least if magazine and broadcast adverts are taken as the benchmark. But there continue to be major differences of style and approach across genres. Distinguishing the various functions of advertising discourse alongside stylistic differences is essential in understanding how advertising communicates in a rapidly changing commercial environment. This requires as much clarity as possible as regards what adverts mean when they say something, if we are to relate the expressive capability of marketing communications to consumers' expectations of them, and to frameworks developed for regulating them.

## 10.5    Advertising law and regulation

In Britain (with parallels in some other European countries), the social policy goal of controlling advertising is achieved through a complementary system of law and self-regulation. The legal measures are not all of a kind. They range across fields including a right of action for misrepresentation, unfair competition and consumer protection law, trademark law, trade descriptions enforcement by trading standards officers, and EU directives and regulations on unfair commercial practices and misleading advertising.[5] The voluntary measures are overseen by the Advertising Standards Authority (ASA), which administers the British Code of Advertising Practice (BCAP) and adjudicates complaints alleging breaches of the code. The ASA also gives guidance in advance to advertisers on whether a proposed advertisement would be regarded as acceptable. Under the banner of its four keywords – 'legal, decent, honest, truthful' – the ASA pursues a broad agenda of public acceptability. Only where voluntary means for dealing with advertising complaints fail are legal measures invoked. Part of the ASA's public acceptability agenda is commitment to maintaining the spirit, not only the letter, of the advertising code.[6] Although many features of this joint legal and extrajudicial system differ between European countries and between Europe and the US legal system, the main distinctions apply closely enough for the purposes of my discussion. Rather than describing the detailed workings of UK arrangements, I want to focus on issues of advert interpretation that go beyond any one jurisdiction.

## 10.6     Product and service claims

Legal and regulatory measures relate to particular functions served by any given piece of advertising discourse (e.g. whether it is a puff or a description) and to alleged effects (e.g. whether it unfairly discredits a competitor's wares). It is not always easy, however, to map aspects of the form of an advert satisfactorily onto either their specific function or effects.

Such interpretive doubt can create problems. Where adverts are disputed, this can arise because of genuine confusion, especially given the range of different kinds of function we have seen adverts can serve. In some circumstances, however, it can arise because of the adversarial dynamic associated with meaning troublespots outlined in earlier chapters. It can be in the commercial interest of an advertiser to edge as close as possible to restricted areas of what can be

---

[5] 'Misleading advertising' [in accordance with 1988 regulations implementing Council Directive 84/450/EEC, September 1984] means advertising 'which in any way, including its presentation, deceives or is likely to deceive the persons to whom it is addressed or whom it reaches and which, by reason of its deceptive nature, is likely to affect their economic behaviour or which, for those reasons, injures or is likely to injure a competitor'. In the ASA's code, the idea is drawn more widely: 'No marketing communication should mislead, or be likely to mislead, by inaccuracy, ambiguity, exaggeration, omission or otherwise' (there are then further specified restrictions). The complementary UK Trade Descriptions Act 1968 was replaced (April 2008) by an EU directive on Unfair Commercial Practices aimed at controlling misleading and aggressive sales practices, pressure selling, closing-down sales, fake prizes, and other uses of false or untruthful information likely to deceive and lead to sales that wouldn't otherwise have taken place. See also Barendt and Hitchens, *Media Law*, pp. 198–241.

[6] The first principle of the ASA's code (2.1) is that 'all advertisements should be legal, decent, honest and truthful'. Less well known is principle 2.8: that 'the Codes are applied in the spirit as well as in the letter'. See codes at www.asa.org.uk.

said or shown, and then reinterpret what they claim their advert promises if it is complained about. Significantly in this context, marketers often prefer to substitute for the idea that adverts communicate 'claims' the alternative notion that adverts express different kinds of 'appeal'. This reformulation maintains an ambiguity between how far the message is created by the advert and how far it is an attraction inherent in, or already actively sought out by, the interpreter.

### 10.6.1   Prototypical product and service claims

When does something said about a product or service become a claim? The meanings created by adverts are, as we have seen, of many different kinds, even if a lot of advertising discourse does not make claims at all. Despite the centrality of the concept of a 'claim', too, there is no fixed definition; and borderline cases are frequent. But claims and promises of different kinds are made. In this section, I illustrate the idea of product or service claims by describing a number of unexceptional, recently contested UK examples.[7]

A prototypical claim involves an assertion made (either explicitly or as a clear implication) about the features, properties, manufacture or cost of a product or service. In this respect, advertising claims might be considered an extension of trade descriptions into the discourse styles typical of adverts. To advertise a car wash as taking less than five minutes, or to indicate that a toy requires two AA batteries, or a ticket costs £19.99, or that there are no hidden charges for a particular service, is to make a product or service claim. What makes such a statement specific enough to be a claim, rather than merely a suggestive enticement, is that it could in principle be verified (by substantiation with supporting evidence) or alternatively falsified. In this sense, the claim is a matter of testable fact rather than persuasion or opinion. The source and form of evidence will differ from case to case, and will also differ in degree of precision. But a prototypical claim is one that in principle allows substantiation.

With a view to testing claims where necessary, the ASA's procedures include a stipulation that, before distributing or submitting a marketing communication for publication, advertisers must hold documentary evidence (that can be made available in the event of a complaint) to prove any claims they make, whether direct or implied. The adequacy of that evidence is judged on whether it supports both the detailed claims and the overall impression conveyed by the advert.

What is primarily at stake in relation to an advertising *claim*, then, is whether it is true or false. But while truth and falsity appear to be clear-cut standards, they are applied in advertising to claims that may not always allow decisive evidence; and for this reason, adverts in Britain tend to be referred to less often

[7] See the weekly online ASA decisions 'profile' for recent adjudications at www.asa.org.uk.

as being false than as being 'misleading'. 'Misleading', of an advert, encompasses many of the styles of deception outlined in earlier chapters. Most complaints about misleading advertising information or promises are straightforward. Cases become difficult, however, where the meaning or implication of a particular word or words, or some feature of an accompanying image, lends itself to conflicting interpretations, with the result that it is not clear what has to be substantiated.

In an early test case of the 1988 European measures on advertising, a clear judgment on what constitutes 'misleading' was given by Lord Hoffmann in the case of *Director General of Fair Trading v. Tobyward* [1989]. This case concerned a motion for an injunction to restrain publication, by the manufacturer of a slimming aid, of adverts that the advertiser had continued to publish after the ASA had ruled they were misleading. Among six claims alleged to be misleading was a claim of 'permanence' (to which we will return below): 'Speedslim is an awesome discovery that will enable you to lose weight easily and, most importantly, permanently.' Ordering the injunction, Lord Hoffmann offered the following clarification:

'Misleading', as I have said, is defined in the regulations as involving two elements: first, that the advertisement deceives or is likely to deceive the persons to whom it is addressed and, second, that it is likely to affect their economic behaviour. In my judgment in this context there is little difficulty about applying the concept of deception. An advertisement must be likely to deceive the persons to whom it is addressed if it makes false claims on behalf of the product ... The other element, namely that the advertisement is likely to affect the economic behaviour of the persons to whom it is addressed, means in this context no more than that it must make it likely that they will buy the product. As that was no doubt the intention of the advertisement, it is reasonable to draw the inference that it would have such a result.[8]

Each of the two essential elements involved here, that of deceiving an addressed audience and that of affecting a purchasing decision, is explained by the judge. But if Lord Hoffmann's judgment makes 'misleading' much clearer, it gives less guidance on what precisely constitutes a 'claim' that can turn out to be false. So it is worth drawing out slightly further what features may make something a 'claim'.

Product claims cannot always be read off directly from an advert's written copy or scenario. In another influential formulation, a claim is 'not only what is stated but what is reasonably implied'.[9] To become a claim, what is stated or implied is interpreted either as a definite proposition or as a scattergun effect of

---

[8] Lord Hoffmann, in *Director General of Fair Trading v. Tobyward Ltd and Another* [1989] 2 All ER 266, at 270. For discussion of this case, see Barendt and Hitchens, *Media Law*, pp. 211–12.
[9] Iain Ramsay, *Advertising, Culture, and the Law* (London: Sweet and Maxwell, 1996); most but not all of Ramsay's cases are Canadian.

weakly implied or ambiguous impressions. Some of those impressions may seem only indirectly related to what was said or shown. At least three types of claim are then normally acknowledged: claims directly expressed as assertions, which can turn out to be literally false, as a factual matter; claims recognised as not being literally false but still considered to be false by necessary implication (an audience will recognise such claims as readily as if they had been explicitly stated); and claims that may be literally true or ambiguous, but which nevertheless implicitly convey a false impression and so in context are likely to deceive consumers.[10]

To establish whether a product or service claim is false, accordingly, it is necessary to show *how* that claim is conveyed, including whether it distorts by being selective or incomplete as a representation of the product or service. Only once the meaning of the claim has been established can a decision be made whether it is true or misleading, or infringes the advertising code in some other way such as by being offensive (e.g. whether, as in one complaint, the word 'poncey' used of excessively flamboyant or theatrical diving by footballers during matches derogates homosexuals).

In an overall framework largely of self-regulation, step-by-step 'construction' of advertising claims is rarely undertaken. Instead an impressionistic approach, coupled with advice and recommendations as regards good practice, is adopted as the way to reflect the wider 'public acceptability' agenda. In cases where attempts *are* made to construct claims more carefully, three main areas of interpretive difficulty arise. Firstly, some inferred claims are vague or indeterminate, and it is difficult to decide precisely what is being claimed even though it is clear that *something* is. Secondly, boundary problems arise in relation to where permissible 'puffery' starts. Thirdly, ironic or humorous claims that are defended on the paradoxical basis that no one will believe them may in some cases not be easy to differentiate from seriously asserted ones. Each of these areas of interpretive difficulty is now discussed.

### 10.6.2   Vague and implied claims

Claims can be vague rather than precise, and implied rather than stated. Earlier chapters have considered how far communicators are responsible in general for interpretive inferences that follow from what they say. In advertising, what is notable is that, while some implied meanings create claims for which an advertiser will need to provide substantiation, others do not. The precise borderline is unclear. Claims come in different degrees of strength, depending on

---

[10] Classification taken from US law: Graeme Dinwoodie and Mark Janis, *Trademarks and Unfair Competition: Law and Policy* (Boulder, Colo.: Aspen Publishers, 2004), pp. 766–71. For finer classification of claims, see also Preston, *The Tangled Web They Weave*.

where they are on a scale that ranges from being directly stated, being necessary implications of what is said, being presuppositions of what is said, and being weak implicatures of what is said. The extent to which implied meanings can be plausibly denied varies correspondingly, in ways that are at least to some extent regular and predictable.[11]

In a pioneering account of US TV advertising in the 1970s, the linguist Michael Geis showed how the effects created by traditional advertising techniques that depend on implied meanings to do with quantity are not randomly the responsibility of each reader or listener but follow predictable inferential patterns.[12] Because of general principles that underpin conversational inference, implied meanings associated with words like 'most', 'several' or 'many' become strained if they go beyond broadly agreed boundaries (e.g. if 'many' is used to mean two, or 'several' is used to mean more than about four). Inferences from approximate numbers are also limited by context, so that while 'over 30 pieces' could in principle mean 31 to infinity it usually means 31–35 because speakers round off numbers to tens (hence, not 'over 34 pieces'). Thirty years on from Geis's pioneering analyses of the TV advertising of that period, advertising claims of this kind seem stylistically dated. It is possible that consumers have become too familiar with and too cynical about techniques such as use of hedges (e.g. 'up to' before a number, or 'roughly'). Adverts now tend to present factual claims directly, as consumer information separated from the advert's persuasive pitch, or to embed claims in some form of stylisation, pastiche or irony, in order to foster ambiguity regarding the intended message. Stylisation, rather than separation, makes an advert more susceptible to competing, plausible interpretations and obscures the precise claim that would need to be defended if the advert is challenged. Detailed research on how adverts project claims that are not clearly differentiated as in effect contractual information, and how determinate those claims are, continues to be published.[13]

In some areas even vaguely implied claims are subject to specific provisions. This is the case with health and medical advertising, which has remained an area of special sensitivity since nineteenth-century campaigns against quack doctors and patent medicines. A recent ASA survey on compliance in the field of health,[14] for instance, criticised an advert for a magnotherapy product which

---

[11] Relevant topics in pragmatics include presupposition and implicature; for explanation, see Levinson, *Pragmatics*; for media-related examples, Thomas, *Meaning in Interaction*. For a Relevance Theory approach, Blakemore, *Understanding Utterances*.

[12] Michael Geis, *The Language of Television Advertising* (New York: Academic Press, 1982).

[13] A good example is David Green, 'Inferring health claims: a case study', *Forensic Linguistics*, 3 (2) (1996), 299–321.

[14] 'Advertisements for magnotherapy: the compliance team is concerned about marketing communications for magnotherapy products', at www.asa.org.uk. See also 'ASA Compliance Report – Health and Beauty 2006'.

claimed that the product offered 'drug free pain relief' and that consumers would 'feel the difference the new magnetic mattress underlay can make to your wellbeing'. By way of endorsement, the advert stated that 'an estimated 120 million people worldwide have experienced the positive therapeutic effects of magnetic therapy'. Arguably no precise, measurable claim is made here but a perceptible amount of relief is implied. In criticising the advert, the ASA stated that it had not seen enough evidence to support 'efficacy claims' for magnotherapy products. The ASA also made a more general point. They emphasised that although some people believe in the power of magnets, the advertising code states that testimonials alone do not amount to substantiation. The code requires advertisers making anything that resembles a medical or scientific claim about health-related products or services to hold evidence in the form of clinical trials conducted on human subjects.

One persistent difficulty in relation to health advertising (and in the field of beauty treatments, which are classed along with health) has been claims that use the word 'permanent'. Like 'safe', 'open' and other complex, common words I have drawn attention to, 'permanent' is surrounded by difficulties of contextualised interpretation. In the same way that it can be argued that nothing is completely 'safe', nothing is completely 'permanent' either. Notwithstanding the apparent counter-example of death – even that example is viewed differently by religious and non-religious people – 'permanent' requires some kind of situationally adjusted meaning. An often-cited American advertising case from the 1940s turned on whether it could really be misleading for a shampoo to be claimed to colour hair 'permanently', since it is obvious that hair colouring only affects newly grown hair. The 1940s court ruled that the advert *was* misleading. That judgment, however, is now sometimes ridiculed for having taken 'comparatively stern measures against this type of particularly crude, if not cruel, appeal to the human vanities'.[15]

In the 1940s case, it was felt important to protect consumers who would now be regarded as gullible. That approach gave way to a different approach to problems such as 'permanent'. A complaint brought by the British Association of Electrolysists Ltd objected to a magazine advertisement for hair removal that stated that treatment 'has never been so easy' and that the product in question offered 'permanent hair removal'.[16] The complaint, which was upheld, challenged whether hair removal was permanent. What distinguishes the modern ASA response to this complaint from the 1940s case is that it addressed the interpretive difficulty raised by 'permanent' not with guidance as to what

---

[15] *Gelb et al. v. Federal Trade Commission* 144 F.2d 580 [1944]. See Ramsay, *Advertising, Culture, and the Law*, p. 78.

[16] Complaint by British Association of Electrolysists against Babyliss, reported November 2002 at www.asa.org.uk.

'permanent' *means*, or how different interpreters might be susceptible to different implications of the word, but with a classification (as part of its good practice
guidelines) of modern means of hair removal. The implication is that the
difficulty is to do with hair removal rather than with the notion of permanence.
Different methods of hair removal (including needle electrolysis, tweezer
electrolysis and laser treatments) are given ticks and crosses in a chart to
indicate whether they are permanent, painless and versatile – and also, incidentally, whether they are 'safe'. At the end of the ASA list, a cautionary note is
added: 'Check "permanent" claims for Epilight or laser with the Copy Advice
team.'[17] In light of the always contextually variable meaning of 'permanent',
this would be good advice in relation to almost any claim involving the word.

In examples of this kind, the two different approaches to meaning in advertising outlined at the beginning of this chapter go off in alternative directions. In
one direction, there is the possibility that any process described as 'permanent'
must meet a factual standard of 'duration without change', since 'permanent'
should have a reliable meaning of that kind; what the consumer needs is clear
and stable information. The other approach prefers a contextualised view. It
allows for modulation of word meaning according to circumstances of use, and
is prepared to ask what 'permanent' is likely to mean when applied in each
particular context; what the consumer needs, in this approach, is a set of more
finely tuned interpretive strategies.

There are attractions but also risks in each direction. The 'definition'
approach, in which advertising claims are believed to convey information that
can be relied on without contextualised interpretation, opens the door to a battle
of the experts, and a battle of the dictionaries in cases where qualities, attributes
and judgments rather than measurable facts are at stake. The 'contextually
relevant meaning' approach offers greater latitude to both advertiser and consumer. But it may loosen the regulator's hold on meaning too far, allowing
'permanent' to become little more than an advertiser's way of saying 'especially
long-lasting'. Recognising such difficulties, regulators and courts decide individual cases on their merits, while understandably avoiding putting any pressure on the wedge that might be driven between these two overall interpretive
frameworks.

### 10.6.3   Trade puffs

A second area of complication with advertising claims arises because some
product claims are either so vague or beyond substantiation that, when uttered
by the seller, they appear no more than blustering or boasting that no reasonable

---

[17] See 'Health and Beauty Checklist (substantiation)' and Committee for Advertising Practice
(CAP) 'good practice' guidelines at www.cap.org.uk.

buyer would rely on in making a purchase. A distinction is accordingly drawn between a mere 'trade puff', for which there is no liability, and statements making specific claims that give rise to liability if shown to be misleading.[18] Non-actionable puffery expresses opinion. It typically involves assertions of quality or superiority in a persuasive rather than informational context, where hyperbole might be expected. The modern legal rationale for immunity extended to puffing presumes that the consumer will make a rational choice about factual attributes while appreciating, or possibly actively enjoying, the rhetorical characteristics of puffing within what is overall a free flow of opinion, including in shopping.

Prototypical trade puffs take the form of superlatives. The product or service is outstanding, or the best in some respect. The following examples are typical: 'The best Christmas album ever'; 'Keenest, competitive prices'; 'Expert product advice, unrivalled service, top value'; 'Unbeatable prices'. In each case, the claim is one of generalised comparison with commercial rivals, about whom the seller would not be expected to take an unbiased view. In some cases, the element of boasting is underscored by obvious exaggeration or falsity of the claim, as with 'unbeatable prices' (a claim that must however be precisely defined if extended, as it sometimes is, into a more specific marketing promise). When the treatment 'Speedslim', described above, was characterised as 'an awesome discovery', this was held to be misleading because the therapeutic approach turned out to have been around for some time and was not a 'discovery'. But the evaluation 'awesome' was acceptable as a legitimate statement of advertiser opinion.

Some puffs edge closer to description. Their implied value judgment and vagueness in context nevertheless still allow that no specific claim is being made. Examples include 'Home-cooked food' signs in restaurants or pubs; the description 'fully interactive' of a computer game; or 'contains latest updates' of many technological gadgets. In each of these cases, unless the language is linked to or qualified by other information, the phrase reads as enthusiastic endorsement rather than claim. This is still the case with advertising copy like 'insurance you can trust' or 'friendly service', as well as 'exclusive' of a newspaper story, or 'official' or 'authentic' of a product.

With similarly approving slogans like 'A quick way to cook rice', however, the trade puff reading begins to weaken by comparison with something more measurable: the time typically taken to cook rice by different methods. With a statement like 'Spicy tomato sauce', the expression 'spicy' as general praise

---

[18] See Ivan Preston, *The Great America Blow-up: Puffery in Advertising and Selling* (Madison: University of Wisconsin Press, 1975). The name 'trade puff' for such exaggerated claims is sometimes traced to the character Puff in Richard Brinsley Sheridan's play *The Critic* (1779) though it seems more likely that Sheridan's satirical characterisation drew on an already current term.

blends into the more specific notion of what ingredients conventionally make a sauce spicy. Part of the art of copy writing is to make a puff sound as much like a description as possible, while retaining a form of expression that remains defensible as a puff. This tension is evident, for example, in the toothpaste strapline 'complete oral care with unique cleaning': 'unique' may be argued to mean 'very good' rather than singular or 'distinctive' in a testable way, and 'completeness' of oral care that can be achieved without any intervention by a dentist is likely to be considered exaggerated. But overall something more than this seems to be asserted.

Puffery can be implied. In a TV advert, a man is depicted at home enthusiastically preparing his clubs for a round of golf. He notices a breakfast cereal on the kitchen table, hesitates, then is shown phoning a friend to postpone the game before sitting down to eat with an enthusiasm matching his earlier preparation of the golf bag. In this advert, the puff activates an assumption available to viewers that '[some] men/people are obsessed with their enjoyment of golf'. That assumption combines with the choice the man is shown making in order to imply that pleasure associated with the brand of breakfast cereal takes precedence over golf if it comes to a play-off. The entire effect is achieved without any audible words, as if in mime.

Like specific factual claims, trade puffs are often viewed as occupying a rather worn-out middle ground in contemporary magazine and broadcast advertising.[19] Mainstream contemporary advertising has to some extent, I have suggested, vacated that middle ground in favour of more polarised alternatives: evocative suggestion of brand values and separately stated consumer information. But there is still a difficult boundary between the two kinds of statement. At the borderline, expressions such as 'famous', 'original', 'genuine' and 'real' all vary in meaning in different contexts of use and can signal either a specific claim or a puff. Adverts can be contrived to exploit the border zone as far as possible, for instance where it is unclear whether an endorsement is simply exaggerated, subjective opinion, or whether it is based on survey information. Like many useful copy words already mentioned, 'favourite', 'most popular' and other similar expressions can do different kinds of work. The words of the British Airways 'world's favourite airline' adverts, for example, were ambiguous between specific information (consumer data that can be counted and compared) and subjective ratings that, because they are not amenable to substantiation, remain permissible advertising rhetoric.

---

[19] Advertising language has evolved. See e.g. Geoffrey Leech on vagueness and other effects in advertising language in the 1960s, in *English in Advertising: A Linguistic Study of Advertising in Great Britain* (London: Longman, 1966); on more contemporary verbal styles, see Greg Myers, *Words in Ads* (London: Edward Arnold, 1994), and Guy Cook, *The Discourse of Advertising*, 2nd edition (London: Routledge, 2001).

## 10.6.4   Ironic and humorous claims

A third area of complication with advertising claims arises in relation to state-ments that remain exempt from liability because they are considered obviously not serious, and so unlikely to deceive. Such techniques seem increasingly widespread. Irony, other forms of humour and pastiche all convey product and service claims in ways that acknowledge how old-fashioned the more conventional styles can seem to modern consumers. In the advertising code, exemption for adverts that wink knowingly at the consumer in making their statements is presented as follows:

> Obvious untruths or exaggerations that are unlikely to mislead and incidental minor errors and unorthodox spellings are all allowed provided they do not affect the accuracy or perception of the marketing communication in any material way.[20]

It is easy to see why such exemption is necessary. If the aim of advertising regulation is the practical one of avoiding consumer confusion while imposing as little restriction as possible on commercial speech, then allowing complaints about ironic or fantastical details would show advertising regulation to be out of touch with people's commonsense or wish to be entertained. There would also be a more serious difficulty. Since many complaints about adverts come from commercial rivals rather than from consumers, leaving exaggerations and obvious untruths open to complaint would invite competitors to torpedo each other's campaigns still more than they can do already. Exemption of ironic and humorous claims nevertheless creates a problem of its own. Borderline cases arise where it is unclear whether a serious claim will be attributed or not, and if so by what proportion of potential customers.

Consider a prototypical example of the claim that is not a claim. An advert shows a beach at sunset, accompanied by the caption 'No-one goes to Cyprus only once.' Read literally, this statement is a verifiable (or at least falsifiable) claim. Equally clearly, that claim is false. Read inferentially, however, the consumer appreciates that the literal meaning is not something the speaker is likely to have intended; instead, the interpreter infers a different meaning along the lines 'Cyprus is somewhere everyone wants to go back to' (i.e. a trade puff rather than a claim). Appealing to literal truth in such circumstances – to facts conveyed by the claim – would miss the rhetorical point. Similarly with a magazine advert for a 4×4 SUV, the Toyota RAV4: 'Warning! Mundane use of the new RAV4 is a crime. Warning.' In this case, the advertising copy is not a warning; and 'mundane use' of the vehicle is not a crime. In this advert, even a false product warning inaccurately indicating that something is illegal is

---

[20]   Section 3 ('Substantiation'), Code of Advertising Practice (CAP, non-broadcast), para 4, www.
asa.org.uk.

allowable, because it is possible to be confident that the advert will not be taken literally.

Not all cases are so clear-cut. Control over advertising is needed not only to guide advertisers in avoiding confusion where their copy is poorly drafted or designed, but also to discourage stylised and non-literal advertising in a competitive marketplace that is really a ploy to avoid liability for false or misleading truth-claims while benefiting from the enticement they convey.

An advert in the (free, giveaway) *Take Sport* magazine on behalf of an online betting company stated in large text 'The lazy man's way to get rich', and was accompanied by a photo of a man reclining on a sofa while looking at a laptop computer. A complainant objected[21] that the slogan 'The lazy man's way to get rich' was misleading because most gamblers lose money as a result of their betting. The advertiser responded that the slogan and image were intended to convey the advantages of Internet betting by comparison with the traditional channels of a betting office or racetrack. Alongside the appeal to consumer benefits, the advertiser claimed that the slogan 'The lazy man's way to get rich' was an idiomatic advertising slogan that would be familiar to readers as such, rather than as the basis of a specific claim. The complaint was upheld. The ASA noted the advertiser's assertion that, in the context of the advert, the slogan would not be taken literally and accepted the arguments made about consumer benefits. But the regulator considered that an overall impression was still given that gamblers who bet online win frequently, and that it is easy to win. The ASA therefore concluded that the claim was likely to mislead and was irresponsible.

### 10.6.5    Comparative claims

My final category of complications with advertising claims concerns comparative claims. Most claims are made about an advertiser's own product or service. But complaints can also be made about false or misleading statements that an advertiser makes about a rival's goods or services (e.g. 'our product X is 10 per cent cheaper and 20 per cent more efficient than Y's equivalent product Z'). Given competitive pressure for market advantage, complaints are most likely to come from commercial rivals, who use complaint opportunities either to contest the positive dimension of an advertiser's claims about its own product or its negative claims about the complainant. Disputes still focus on advert meanings; but they are also weapons in wider commercial competition. Complaining about a competitor's advertising is a strategic decision, because of the risk that controversy about contested adverts can give valuable free publicity to the advertiser complained about. At the same time, fear of a complaint initiated

---

[21] One complaint against a magazine advert placed by Global Betting Exchange Ltd in the giveaway *Take Sport*, reported December 2006 (www.asa.org.uk).

by a rival (or of more serious legal action for misrepresentation, malicious falsehood, product disparagement or trade libel) limits what a competitor is likely to try to say in its advertising.

A particularly interesting example of a struggle between competitors is the legal action for trademark infringement and malicious falsehood initiated by BA (British Airways) against a competitor airline, Ryanair, following comparative press advertising by Ryanair. The most well-known of the adverts that were complained about carried a headline 'EXPENSIVE BA...DS!' The ASA upheld an initial complaint from members of the public against this 'bastards' advert, judging that the headline was likely to cause serious or widespread offence. The wider dispute went to court, however, reportedly as a matter of principle on both sides. In deciding for the defendant, the judge lamented BA's persistence with its claim that price comparisons contained in the adverts were misleading. He summarised BA's claim as being that Ryanair 'exaggerate in suggesting BA is five times more expensive because BA is only three times more expensive'.[22]

## 10.7    Beyond product and service claims

Each area of interpretive uncertainty I have outlined points to a general difficulty with frameworks for regulating advertising based on the idea of reliable and determinate textual meanings. Vague, ambiguous and ironic or humorous claims are all part of a shift that has taken place from advertising that presents specific product or service claims towards promoting the reputation of commercial brands by stylised evocation. Contemporary marketing commonly seeks to gain the attention of, and to engage, consumers in a new relationship: not so much by presenting information as by more oblique advocacy based on image and style. For advertising regulation, this shift (which is often linked to claims of increased sophistication on the part of the consumer) results in a new fragility – some would argue futility – in regulating by trying to fix a single advert meaning.[23]

Consider a TV advert for a train company in which a spread of weakly implied meanings and associations is suggested. The advert showed a white man sitting in a first class train carriage, writing in a notebook. The train was

---

[22] *British Airways plc v. Ryanair Ltd* [2001] ETMR 24; [2001] FSR 32.

[23] In his wide-ranging discussion of 'adworlds' (the overall consumption environment of contemporary advertising), Greg Myers argues that two tendencies dominate contemporary TV advertising: disruption of conventions of direct address to the audience, to sidestep the sense of speaker authority that attracts liability to anything that might be construed as a product claim; and address to the audience less as consumers who need to be persuaded than as viewers who are already too aware to be taken in by advertising techniques. The two tendencies work together to create new styles, in which values and meanings are still implied but which switch unstably between the product, the self-perception of the consumer, and how advertisers have treated similar themes in the past. Greg Myers, *Ad Worlds* (London: Edward Arnold, 1998).

'attacked' by a group of Native Americans on horseback, though their attack on the train failed. At the end of the advert, one Native American is shown serving drinks on the train. Text at the end of the advert stated 'MAN WHO GO ON BIG TRAIN HAVE BIG IDEA.' The complainants, some of whom were Native Americans, found the advert offensive. They said it was racist and used an outdated cultural stereotype of Native American people.[24]

The advertisers said the advert was a humorous and affectionate homage to the 'Cowboy and Indian' film genre. In this way, it was in keeping with the rail company's theme of making adverts in the style of classic films. This particular advert was intended to show, in a tongue-in-cheek, humorous and fantastical way, that a valuable idea could be conceived while working on a train, and that the idea conceived on the train might be so good that it had commercial worth and someone might want to steal it.

The complaint was not upheld. The ASA considered that, because the advert was set in a fictional and imitative context, it was likely to be viewed as a parody of Western films rather than as a comment on Native American history or contemporary Native Americans. The regulator concluded that, although some viewers might find the advert in poor taste, it was unlikely to be seen as racist or as trivialising Native Americans. It was therefore unlikely to cause serious or widespread offence. In dealing with the complaint, the ASA's approach was to consider overall impression rather than undertaking a close reading. As his Honour Judge Jacob put it in the case of *BA v. Ryanair* referred to above, 'A minute textual examination is not something upon which the reasonable reader of an advertisement would embark.' To simulate the effect of an advert on a reader, media regulation urges a similarly impressionistic interpretive process. Arguing that thoughts or thematic contrasts were put forward coherently and seriously in the train advert, the ASA reasoned, would fail to recognise how far any meaning asserted is deflected by the prevailing irony and stylistic imitation. Whether an advert represents an outdated cultural stereotype, in such circumstances, is a judgment to be made less by interpreting what it may seem to say than by judging the general climate of what is considered entertaining.

## 10.8    Deciding what an advert is telling you

Given these different ways that claims, promises and evocation of products and services are communicated, how does a consumer go about making sense of an advert when faced with one? In this section, I begin to discuss what 'interpretive standard' is expected of the consumer and how that relates to specific processes

---

[24] A total of eighty-three complaints against Virgin Trains, reported November 2006 (www.asa.org.uk).

of understanding. This is not the same as the general question of consumer behaviour. Rather, it is a question of how meaning is constructed for promotional discourse when alternative strategies seem to point towards different interpretive risks.

So far, I have outlined three main discourse types within advertising. They may even coexist within a single advert. The first consists of technical description or information, which should be factually accurate; the second is a matter of ordinary persuasion, which may involve exaggeration typical of the marketplace; the third is ironic or stylised discourse that openly tells you it does not convey much meaning, even if it may seem to say something. We need to consider how consumers, faced with some combination of the three styles, know what kind of interpretive strategy will be consistent with expectations raised by the regulatory standard of the 'average consumer'. The issue is one not of an overall type of consumer – rational, capricious, avaricious, risk averse or gullible – but of how shifts between interpretive strategies are to be made where appropriate. What is in question is a consumer who only becomes 'average' as an idealisation by being trusting in one situation but suspicious in another, and who varies between the two because of cues that are as much about communication in a commercial context as about the type of product or service they are buying.

Faced with compound, mixed styles of promotional discourse, I suggest that consumers inevitably respond with situationally variable interpretive strategies, combining four main strands.

1. The consumer relies where appropriate on technical specifications known to producers and regulators but that for many products are unlikely to be known by the consumer herself or himself. Trust that the regulatory regime ensures the accuracy of the meaning of such expressions obviates the need for suspicion. This might be called a 'trusting' interpretive strategy; but it is open to question how far the strategy depends on confidence in an efficient marketplace or gullibility (e.g. where regulation has not kept up with promotional techniques, where an advert is in breach but has not been complained of or withdrawn, etc.).

2. The consumer spontaneously applies an 'ordinary meaning' approach to copy that doesn't seem technical at face value. Meaning for these statements can be relied on to be whatever those statements would usually be taken to mean. Consumers infer that if they don't understand something, that failure to understand may be part of the calculated effect, since the material will have been shaped to appeal to and not confuse or cheat, if approached with this interpretive strategy. This strategy nevertheless runs the risk of consumers inferring meanings based on background or amount of product-related knowledge that put them at risk.

3. The consumer shows interpretive scepticism, as typically with trade puffs, but sees most or all advertising discourse as exaggerated in the same way.

The consumer believes some or none of what they hear, and discounts all promotional content at a substantial percentage because of the seller's persuasive intent and self-interest in the message.

4. The consumer responds to the entertainment value of the advertising but insists on looking to some other, independent source for any information they may need to rely on in making a purchase. The consumer may note the name of the advertiser and respond to the brand values conveyed, but won't trust anything that comes closer to a specific claim or promise.

The four strategies vary between situations, for reasons that are a mix of type of purchase (pet food, phone contract, timeshare property); reputation of provider (local shop, nationally known brand, googled online source); and other reasons. It is never completely clear, however, how an interpreter knows when to shift between one strategy and another within the overall experience of responding to an advertisement or marketing promotion. If we are to see how strategies are not just attributes of types of consumer, but interact in making sense of each advert, then we need to consider how any 'interpretive strategy' is activated in a given instance.

Consider an example from one of the more tightly regulated areas of advertising, food advertising: in this case, for a brand of yoghurt that carries a label 'low fat'. Some consumers will construe 'low fat' as a technical specification. Consumers are unlikely to know the technical definition of 'low fat' (no more than 3 per cent), but if they follow the first interpretive strategy outlined above, that should not trouble them unduly.[25] Such consumers can look for further details, even if such detail will only make sense if they *do* know what the significance of the technical information is. More important than the information is that, beyond personal checking, a consumer reading this way trusts a system of externally applied trading standards: the information on the pack wouldn't be there unless it gives an accurate impression because someone will have already checked it.

Alternatively, 'low fat' might be interpreted (in line with the second interpretive strategy above) as informal comparison with other available products. 'Low fat' then means something like 'less fat in this brand than in the others on the shelf that don't carry an equivalent label'. Consumers who construe 'low fat' in this way no longer rely on official assurances about a claim's technical content. Instead, they exercise more limited trust: that the advert won't be

---

[25] In case some readers are among consumers who don't rely on precise definitions in buying yoghurt, the Food Labelling Regulations 1996 (HMSO) require that a 'low fat' claim should only be used for foods that contain no more than 3 per cent fat; 'fat free' should only be used for foods that contain no more than 0.15 per cent fat. Further Dairy Industry Federation guidelines (the Code of Practice for the Composition and Labelling of Yoghurt, compiled in consultation with the Local Authorities Coordinating Body on Food and Trading Standards) provide an additional, voluntary code (www.dairyuk.org).

misleading in a general sense. Following this strategy calls for more responsibility than the first strategy. But consumers who do so take more risk: they rely on their own wits in deciding what 'low fat' ordinarily means in the context of choosing a yoghurt.

Alternatively again, 'low fat' may be construed as effectively a trade puff (following the third interpretive strategy). The expression echoes others like 'low maintenance' or 'low emissions' that might be interpreted similarly, as well as 'low prices' (and also contrasting expressions like 'high quality', 'high speed' or 'high energy'). On this reading, the meaning of 'low fat' is bleached into something like 'special' or 'good for you'. Rather than showing interpretive generosity, the consumer who adopts this approach exercises guardedness and suspicion.

Finally, if the consumer follows my fourth strategy above, he or she might think that a yoghurt pot has to have a marketing highlight or angle of some kind, and that a 'low fat' label is as good as any. Almost whatever it says on the pot is not to be taken seriously except as overall design that any product needs if it is to stand out on the shelf.

## 10.9    The average consumer

Each of these interpretive approaches, which blend into and overlap with each other in complicated ways, relies on its own kind of commonsense. For advertising law, however, as with other areas of media law and regulation, a single standard governing interpretive inferences cuts across the different strategies. As with the ordinary reader, the interpretive standard adopted is personified, in this case as the 'average consumer'.

The average consumer, in general terms, is the ordinary reader gone shopping (in that ordinary interpretation is combined with the commonsense needed in buying things in a marketplace[26]). Earliest conceptions, it has been argued, were a matter of the consumer's assumed class and education.[27] More recent notions take the interpretive standard less from class of person than class of product or service. Overall, however, the average consumer is neither over-suspicious nor unduly influenced. He or she uses commonsense and sound inference to find a path through advertising rhetorics and product descriptions, and is, according to recent EU definitions, 'reasonably well informed and reasonably observant and circumspect'.[28] In niche markets (such as philately, DJ equipment or tending

---

[26] 'Market' is not a technical term (as 'low fat' may be) and its meaning is commonly presumed. Variability in the idea of what a 'market' is nevertheless needs to be taken into account. On historical development and complexity of the concept, as well as difficulties in current operation of markets, see Alan Aldridge, *The Market* (Cambridge: Polity, 2005).

[27] Jennifer Davis, 'Locating the average consumer: his judicial origins, intellectual influences and current role in European trade mark law', *Intellectual Property Quarterly*, 2 (2005), 183–203.

[28] Davis, 'Locating the average consumer', p. 183.

herbaceous borders), 'reasonably well informed' will mean a higher standard of knowledge and specialist interest than in wider markets such as kitchen cleaners or toothpaste, where a lower expectation of attention and product familiarity is foreseen.

In policy terms, appealing to the average consumer's understanding steers between the easily influenced, gullible (or credulous) consumer, who in the past was held to need paternalistic protection, and the contemporary customer who is believed to see through advertiser manipulation. Set the bar too low and implied meaning, irony, humour or other kinds of indirectness trigger complaints that the credulous consumer has been deceived. Set the bar too high and the consumer's interpretive acuity is an easy alibi for manipulative or even fraudulent advertising. Set the bar differently for too many different classes of advertising (pet food, private health care, toys and timeshares) and consumers lose their grasp of what degree of protection they can rely on.

Having a public, regulated standard that determines which adverts are permissible still leaves the difficulty of how any particular advert is interpreted in the shop or online, especially if commonsense can be activated in incompatible ways by the same advertising copy. If you are concerned whether 'low fat' is an accurate statement, you may feel encouraged to trust that the words are informational and have reliable, tested meanings; assured in this way, you draw the appropriate sound inference and feel confident in buying the product. On the other hand, if you think the words 'low fat' sound promotional, as if they may be puffing the product with exaggerated praise, then you may feel cautious and act warily, resisting any appeal that the expression means something over and above the advertiser's wish to sell you the yoghurt; warned in this way, you draw the appropriate sound inference and do not proceed. In such ways, your interpretive strategy depends on how you react to meaning as much as on how you react to yoghurt or shopping.

The interpretive difficulty for consumers is how they decide which interpretive approach should apply to *which aspect* of the advert in front of them. How does the consumer decide which aspect of the discourse should be treated in which way? This problem is upstream of the practical regulation of particular markets. It concerns the premise that advertising discourse divides in a stable and recognisable way between informative and persuasive kinds that consumers will know how to respond to, despite the clear benefit to advertisers of taking advantage of uncertainty between the two.

## 10.10    Generalised interpretive strategies

How do actual rather than hypothetical, average consumers reconcile the different requirements of interpreting when they go shopping? Because it is not always possible to tell which interpretive strategy to bring to an individual advert – or part of an advert – generalisation of a preferred or previously tested interpretive strategy on the part of any given consumer is likely. In forming a sense of how to read adverts, consumers react to their accumulated perceptions of their marketing environment. The degree of interpretive generosity or scepticism they show is partly a matter of their readiness, based on an assessment of risk involved in communication, to interpret many or even all adverts along the same lines. This is partly what justifies the insight that consumers have different dispositions: gullible, average, suspicious, devil-may-care, risk averse, etc.

Interpretive generalisation can have serious consequences, nevertheless. Ambiguous, ironic, vague or in some other way obscure advertising may lead some consumers to activate a cynical 'all advertising is hype' strategy. If such an interpreter reads a technical specification or piece of product information cynically, as if potentially a trade puff or piece of deception, then she or he mistrusts unnecessarily. Cynical interpreters who over-generalise scepticism in relation to commercial speech may view advertising as universally a pernicious social force, and resist not only taking adverts seriously but also taking labelling seriously, including product and health warnings. The informative function of advertising in such circumstances has broken down because of the corrosive effect of rhetorical excesses. Another consumer may generalise a more trusting, 'trading standards assured' interpretive strategy. Such trusting interpreters will be more likely to view advertising as helpful, even essential public information. But if they construe trade puffs as reliable information, guaranteed by external authority, they may be misled into unwarranted beliefs. Such consumers may always read the label but they are prey to unscrupulous advertisers and rogue traders.

Is acknowledging problems at the interpretive extremes simply a roundabout way of reaffirming the case for the average consumer standard? Not, I believe, if that average consumer is considered to be someone who makes informed, rational choices about shopping but is not considered in terms of how he or she makes choices and manages risk in relation to meaning. The challenge of attributing meaning when faced with an advert is not only about product attributes or commonsense understanding of markets. Neither is it only a question of being already a kind of person who makes choices on the basis of disposition or character. It is just as importantly a question of making choices about what something means in a given case. As such, what is involved is interpretive strategy and risk, taking into account the conflicting interests of the parties, the regulation in place and its assumed enforcement, and a surrounding culture of communicative interaction and reasonable trust.

At the beginning of this chapter, I suggested that problems of interpretation are often thought to be taken care of if advertisers maintain a clear distinction between 'informational' and 'persuasive' content. I have put a case for not overstating the rigour and effectiveness of that distinction. Occasionally what can only be called a clash of information and persuasion reaches even into the core of communicating a commercial offering. As a measure of our contemporary 'commercial speech' environment, therefore, consider finally the practice of so-called 'vanity sizing' of clothing.[29] In this marketing practice, persuasion is dressed as information. The labelled size of garments, in centimetres, inches or conventional clothing sizes is not an actual measurement, as the numerical presentation suggests. Instead, size comes up differently for different garments, adjusted in the direction of whatever size the supplier thinks is likely to appeal to the customer's self-image.

## 10.11     Summary

In this chapter, I have explored interconnections between the informative value and persuasive effect of advertising and other marketing communications. Drawing especially on work in pragmatics, I have highlighted difficulties in deciding which implied meanings are authorised by an advert (and so should be considered the responsibility of the advertiser) and which are wilful reading, fuelled by desire or aspiration on the part of the consumer. I concluded that uncertainty as regards how best to establish boundaries to what is assumed to be the consumer's legitimate inference allows considerable scope for potentially unfair commercial practices. Such interpretive latitude is nevertheless often obscured by appeals to the notion of commercial 'information'.

---

[29]  See Melanie Rickey, 'Vanity sizing', *The Times*, 22 September 2007, p. 27. A detailed survey of clothing sizes (no date) has been conducted by Size UK (www.sizeuk.org). Among other things, the survey shows that more expensive brands tend to come up bigger.

# 11 Offensiveness: 'If there *is* a meaning, it is doubtless objectionable'

## 11.1 Introduction

In this chapter I consider some underlying communicative distinctions that seem essential in shaping debate over offensiveness. My aim in doing so is to clarify the role played in the 'offensiveness' of a discourse by that elusive attribute, its 'meaning'. Discourse ranging from local, abusive comment through to sustained hate speech is felt to be offensive by different groups of people on a number of grounds. Adjudication in such circumstances, I show, typically involves assessing how far an allegedly offensive discourse expresses a viewpoint or alternatively how far it carries out an action (such as encouraging a crime or inflicting a violent verbal or symbolic assault). Arriving at a judgment in such situations depends on deciding – however that decision is actually formulated – as to the speech-act force, or 'performativity', of the material in question. Such decisions are arrived at despite the force of an utterance or text being not so much a settled convention as a matter of context-specific implication.

## 11.2 Meaning and boundaries of acceptability

Legend has it that when the artist Antonin Artaud, who had written the screen-play, attended the premier of the silent film *The Seashell and the Clergyman* (1928), directed by Germain Dulac, he was so angry with what she had done to his script that he got up and shouted at the screen, calling her a 'cow'.[1] Artaud was reputedly unhappy with Dulac's realisation of his scenario. The anti-clericalism he was aiming for, in a priest developing a lustful passion that plunges him into bizarre fantasies, had been undermined, he felt, by the film's lyricism. It is unclear how far Dulac was offended by being called something as prosaic as a 'cow'. An intention to insult is unmistakable. But the chosen vehicle for its expression, a dead metaphor (she is not literally a cow so the hearer infers cow-resemblances, but any analogical force has deadened over

---

[1] *La coquille et le clergyman* (1928, dir. Germain Dulac). Dulac was an almost lone woman film maker in her generation; the film is often viewed now as an important predecessor to Bunuel and Dali's *Un chien andalou* (1929).

time into conventional epithet), seems almost comical by comparison with the open-ended, symbolic expression of the film she had made.

The offensiveness of Artaud's use of 'cow' is not to be found only in his choice of epithet, of course. As has been shown in previous chapters, words are modulated in meaning according to contexts in which they are used. Dulac may have felt more wounded because Artaud chose the occasion of the film's premier, a ceremonial event with its own speech conventions, to insult her. There is also something in his reported choice to direct his outburst at the screen, even with the director present, bypassing her and acting as if his comment formed a fitting soundtrack to her silent film. Whatever Dulac felt at the premier, though, the problem of the film's own offensiveness was only just beginning. The more widely known story about the reception of *The Seashell and the Clergyman* concerns the decision made by the British censor of the time to ban it, with now famous words that vividly reinforce the contrast between the worn-out meaning potential of Artaud's epithet 'cow' and the film's unsettling creativity: 'If this film has a meaning, it is doubtless objectionable.'

The film censor's sentiment would be unexceptional if uttered by a member of an audience. Its significance lies in what it suggests about public adjudication in the area of offensiveness. The statement encapsulates a sense that being offended trumps, or in some way cuts through, perception of meaning. In this respect the censor's words are part of a tradition of viewing outrage and emotional distress as something visceral, cutting or burning through interpretation to the body. In the lead-up to the UK Obscene Publications Act of 1857, for example, the Lord Chief Justice Lord Campbell described what he called 'Holywell Street traffic' (a euphemism for the pornography trade, at that time conventionally located in London at Aldwych rather than in Soho) as the sale of 'poison more deadly than prussic acid, strychnine or arsenic'.[2] Similar statements run through the history of other areas of law and regulation concerned with offensiveness, including blasphemy and more recently incitement to racial and religious hatred. On the analogy that you don't need to try prussic acid or arsenic to know it isn't good for you, some people consider it irrelevant to engage with what a discourse is about in order to know it should be banned.

It is easy to dismiss such restrictive views and enthuse about a work like *The Seashell and the Clergyman*. It must be recognised, on the other hand, that the film's experimental character contrasts strongly with the relentless formula and repetition of most allegedly pornographic texts or hate speech utterances. Comfort in the established liberal view also depends on the fact that *The Seashell and the Clergyman* is a story from another era. What people report they find offensive now is less easily dismissed. Being offended is still generally

---

[2] Lord Campbell made the analogy during the House of Lords debate leading up to the Act of 1857 (Hansard, weekly index 145:102).

recognised as something in principle to be balanced against benefits of freedom of expression. But any general principle of freedom of expression must be implemented in changing, practical circumstances, not only exalted in ideal terms. What is significant in this light is that, in the period since 1928, two quite fundamental social changes have taken place: massive expansion of media access, in terms of different media and as regards the range of providers within any given medium; and migration and globalisation leading to more diverse audience tastes, expectations and sensitivities. Together, these social transformations pose unprecedented difficulties for any approach to judging offensiveness, as has traditionally been done, on the basis of community standards.

Given the range of beliefs and values to which easily accessible expression is now given (in print and niche broadcasting and on the Internet), it is unlikely anyone can look into publicly available discourse and not see anything they consider not just uncomfortable but potentially harmful.[3] A suitable regulatory response in such circumstances is less likely to be the absolutist one of 'never', as – however reluctantly – whether, in what cases, if so how, on what basis?

## 11.3    Cause for complaint

Offensiveness in the media involves a *reaction* which is attributed to the power of a discourse to prompt that reaction. The reaction of being offended comes in many different forms, commonly associated with the topics that prompt it (e.g. treatments of religion, sex and sexuality, race, violence, drug use, etc.). Complaints are often not considered to be about meaning at all (as the example of *The Seashell and the Clergyman* illustrates). Rather, they are typically couched – to follow distinctions used in previous chapters – in terms either of discourse *use* (whether people should or should not be allowed to say or show something, or to see or read it) or of *effect* (whether a text or discourse causes a specific harm).

The variety of legal offences concerned with people feeling offended is considerable, with the result that offensiveness is sometimes characterised as a cluster of 'diffuse harms'.[4] Arrangements for controlling the social harms created in this area differ between jurisdictions and in different periods, and involve measures created often in highly specific circumstances to address

---

[3] If in doubt, consider some of the following: graphic pornography involving children, animals and torture, both real and simulated; a video montage of actual killings, suicides and fatal accidents; hate speech encouraging attacks on all major ethnic and religious communities; manuals on building bombs and weapons, and manufacturing drugs and poisons; vitriolic abuse in many chat rooms and on bulletin boards, etc.

[4] The phrase 'diffuse harms' is used as part of chapter titles 8 and 17 in Greenawalt, *Speech, Crime and the Uses of Language*.

particular social problems, outcries or alarms. It is also worth remembering that much of the day-to-day arbitration of alleged 'offensiveness' does not rely on formal regulation or law at all. Instead it is a matter of adaptation by individuals and groups to tacit conventions governing communicative behaviour. At varying degrees of formality beyond such communal self-regulation, nevertheless, an array of specific measures exists.

Working outwards from arguably the least punitive, there are informal – as well as increasingly formalised – speech codes adopted by organisations and institutions. These are often a matter of general principles, fulfilling a duty to implement legislation (e.g. in relation to equality of opportunity in employment, or race relations, etc.). The policies are then available to be given practical grounding when needed. Moving up a level, public behaviour involving speech, display or spectacle of different kinds is governed by public order, nuisance and licensing offences. Some of these offences overlap with, or have been extended to, broadcasting and institutions at a border between what is thought of as public exhibition and media, such as art galleries. Beyond these measures, extrajudicial systems of regulation concerned with taste, standards and decency play a part in governing media content, having been developed in Britain from the 1950s onwards. Underpinning such regulation, there are specific but infrequently used criminal statutes: the Obscene Publications Act (1959), for example, and the common law offence of blasphemy. Other measures, not much used but arguably likely to be invoked more frequently, include laws controlling incitement to religious and racial hatred. Overarching the various provisions, general principles in protecting communication of ideas and values are codified in ECHR Article 10, which provides a framework within which the other measures must fit.

The various arrangements are constantly changing. In a period of rapid media innovation, those changes may obscure, but are unlikely to contradict, the points about contested meaning and interpretation I want to make. I propose to focus less on provisions related to any particular, identified harm than on communicative issues about meaning reflected in the various different fields of offensiveness considered together. For each area, I describe in general terms 'what is being communicated' in order to show why it is important to see a 'meaning' dimension of offensive utterances and texts if arbitration of disputes is to do justice to the many different kinds of discourse that represent socially sensitive topics.

### 11.3.1    Bad language

Many complaints to regulatory authorities are about what is called 'bad language'. They express outrage at, for instance, 'a torrent of four-letter filth' on the television or radio.[5] Mostly, such 'bad language' means swearing.[6] Often offensiveness is attributed to words that do not appear to be *about* anything in particular, but are simply routine fillers in a way of speaking. Even the most taboo words are well known, from playgrounds to presidential offices, so their offensive power is hardly created by the shock of the new. Rather, swearing in this unfocused, 'texture of discourse' way is an issue of appropriateness and taboo governing different social situations. What is in question is speakers' management of (or socialisation into) a continuum of socially available options: not swearing at all, swearing selectively in some situations but not others, swearing continuously. The choices involve meaning, but mostly the issues are about what I have called expressive rather than conceptual meaning.

Swearwords transgress conventions governing situations. They typically combine transgression of taboo content (in areas including religion, sexuality and bodily functions) with slang or low register. Equivalent terms for each word exist in other (middle or technical) registers; and there are slang terms for non-taboo referents. It is the combination of slang and taboo that produces the stylistic distinctiveness of swearing.[7] The combination of elements that constitutes swearing allows speakers to choose to use some but not all swearwords, depending on underlying topic or focus of the taboo, and results in the scales of verbal offensiveness commonly reported in media regulator surveys.[8] Whatever the local interest of such scales, nevertheless, they all make an assumption that must be questioned: they presume fixed values, as if words carry their offensive meaning straightforwardly from context to context. While taboo words *do* originate in particular semantic fields and have denotative meanings that are culturally symptomatic, their significance in any given instance of use is mostly unrelated to conceptual dimensions of their meaning. Instead, their significance

---

[5] This particular phrase (among many like it) comes from a *Daily Mail* article under the headline 'Four-letter TV poem fury' reproduced in Tony Harrison, *V,* 2nd edition, with press articles (Newcastle upon Tyne: Bloodaxe Books, 1989), pp. 40–1.

[6] Geoffrey Hughes, *Swearing: A Social History of Foul Language, Oaths and Profanity in English*, 2nd edition (Harmondsworth: Penguin, 1998); Lars-Gunnar Andersson and Peter Trudgill, *Bad Language* (Harmondsworth: Penguin, 1990), pp. 53–66. For a detailed critique of approaches to controlling language use, see Deborah Cameron, *Verbal Hygiene* (London: Routledge, 1995). For recent discussion, see Steven Pinker, *The Seven Words You Can't Say on Television* (Harmondsworth: Penguin, 2008).

[7] Compare the pairs 'prostitute' and 'whore', 'faeces' and 'shit', 'masturbate' and 'wank' (adapted from Andersson and Trudgill, *Bad Language*).

[8] For analysis of audience reaction to broadcast swearing, see research undertaken in 2000 jointly by the Advertising Standards Authority, the British Broadcasting Corporation, the Broadcasting Standards Commission and the Independent Television Commission, published as 'Delete expletives?' (author: Andrea Millwood-Hargrave). The four top, most offensive swear words, as rated by this sample, remain the same as an earlier 1997 study conducted by the Broadcasting Standards Commission: 'cunt', 'motherfucker', 'fuck', then 'wanker'. Seeming to track wider social changes, however, and almost certainly interesting in relation to US data, the word 'nigger' rises from only 11 in 1997 to 5 in the table, and 'Paki' rises from 17 to 10; 'shag' drops from 8 to 11. See 'Delete expletives?' at www.ofcom.org.uk.

depends on expressive force, as a marker of speaker attitude towards a particular event, experience, group of people, or addressee.

What about swearing in media discourse in particular? Given these basic distinctions, three main functions of swearing in broadcast programmes or online can be identified.

Sometimes swearwords convey their 'dictionary meanings'. In such cases, discussion *is* about sex, or religion, or body functions. The relevant editorial (or regulatory) issue is what styles are appropriate for public discussion of the topic in question. Judgments must be made about what range of actually occurring discourse is permissible about a given topic in a public, 'media domain'.

In other cases, media swearing is simply a stylistic marker. Swearwords are used irrespective of underlying semantic field. In these circumstances, the expressions reflect speech habits of the speaker being depicted. Swearwords in this case are markers of social dialect. Similar editorial issues arise to those raised by allegedly inappropriate vocabulary in discussing taboo topics. But now the issues are focused on whether the speakers being depicted should be required to switch codes, within their available linguistic repertoire, to respect audience expectations related to a media format unrelated to any taboo topic. For this purpose the media format becomes a kind of social situation, with its own etiquette or rules for appropriate language use.

With fictional media texts, swearing is better understood as register rather than dialect. It is how scriptwriters signal a character's attitude or feeling in a given situation, by giving prominence to choices between different ways of saying effectively the same thing. In dramatised contexts, it is the overall text that 'speaks', rather than the character. Swearing is a stylistic resource, and debates about swearing of this type are commonly part of more general arguments about a text's need for 'realism'.

While there is clearly *some* consistency across contexts in the impact of particular words, the offensiveness of swearwords varies significantly according to situations of use and reception, in media as elsewhere. Understanding the 'meaning' of media swearing is accordingly a matter less of fixed meanings than of communicative relevance. Being first to say 'fuck' on television[9] was significant for a media generation that saw media as a forum for affirming public identity, national standards and taste, and for whom the power of verbal taboo outweighed the variability with which such words are used. Current issues surrounding media 'bad language'– which the pervasiveness of complaint

---

[9] When theatre critic and writer Kenneth Tynan said 'fuck' on TV in 1965, four motions were tabled in Parliament. In 1976, Steve Jones, guitarist of the Sex Pistols, used the same word on a teatime show and was banned from further appearances. In 2004, an audience of more than 10 million watched John Lydon, alias Johnny Rotten also of the Sex Pistols, say 'cunt' on TV and fewer than 100 people complained. 'Fuck' is now commonly permitted in evening viewing in Britain in a number of different genres.

suggests still has power to offend and embarrass – are more about the grounds *why* a text should or should not include swearing, rather than whether it can. Beyond specific scheduling issues (e.g. in relation to children's TV), it is the meaning of the text, rather than the meaning of the swearing, that is the main issue.

### 11.3.2    Insults and hate speech

Within people's varied use of swearing, one particular area needs closer attention: insults and 'vulgar abuse'. Insulting language ranges from conventional personal insults (often formulaic, and with meanings that have become generalised and bleached until they seem comparatively 'mild') through to deeply wounding and provocative hate speech, focusing on group membership in terms of ethnicity, gender, sexual preference, religion or disability. Such insults cause shock and a feeling of being hated. In doing so, they give expression to structures of social domination and subordination.

In form, insults of this more aggressive kind draw on epithets that, like swearing generally, shift in relative strength from period to period and situation to situation, depending on many factors including the nature of the relationship between communicator and addressee. Sometimes such insults are supplemented by reference to stereotypical aspects of group membership that are gratuitous in the sense of not being related to the topic or situation. As regards their degree of seriousness, insults are often also judged according to the mode of address adopted. Different degrees of gravity are typically assigned to insults addressed, as a sort of targeted vilification, to specific individuals (or used about them in their presence), and to insults used about others who are not present, a practice which is seen as confirming the prejudices of the dominant, co-present group.

Media discourse events do not divide neatly between people present and people not present. So responses to insulting media discourse can often seem inconsistent or equivocal. An offensive expression presents some kind of core, offensive potential. But that expression may be part of the voice of a specific media character or persona within a text, and so must be contextualised as a significant attribute of the character selected for presentation. The construction of the programme has the effect of positioning that person or character in the programme discourse as a whole (e.g. as serious or comic, triumphant or victimised, etc.). As a result, the insulting material resists simple editorial guidelines on what can be said on air. The offensive language may nevertheless still provide an *indirect* vehicle for programme makers to express socially offensive attitudes if they wish. Between characters in the situation or drama depicted, the language may be shocking and offensive; but as overall communication between programme maker and audience it cannot be treated as being simply that. Texts containing such language nevertheless have a capacity to upset or provoke members of an audience while appearing only to reflect an editorial decision to represent a world in which inflammatory discourse exists.

### 11.3.3   Hate speech that is simultaneously expressive

Insults and hate speech can be difficult to respond to in media discourse without shifting backwards and forwards between interpretive levels. I have suggested that this is largely because of the different voices at work in the polyphony of media discourse. Such multi-voiced discourse is also problematic in relation to other categories appealed to in making editorial judgments as to acceptability. Perhaps the most acute problems arise, paradoxically, when rather than being restricted to isolated, local insults, media discourse presents a more sustained representation of prejudice and stereotype.

When combined into a sustained treatment, insults and expressions of disrespect may, while continuing to be offensive in the ways indicated above, be claimed to belong to a category of discourse that is often considered very differently: as expression of ideas and opinion that (however insulting their effect) are permissible as legitimate exercise of freedom of expression. A judgment then has to be made: whether there is enough 'message', 'exposition of ideas' or 'content' in what is otherwise a provocative insult for the discourse overall to be justified as expression of opinion (e.g. as perhaps an excessively vigorous, ideological statement that still expresses ideas even if it seems more like intemperate shouting); or alternatively whether the main 'meaning' of the discourse is just a kind of verbal fist-shaking. On this second view, the discourse will be regarded as a threatening social act dressed in 'communicative' form, rather like gesticulating at the beginning of a physical assault. The overall message conveyed would be one of intimidating, or encouraging physical violence; such messages are referred to, in US legal traditions (which have a richer vocabulary in this area than English law), as 'fighting words'.[10]

With texts whose overall genre – and therefore the expectations surrounding them – can be thought of as an expression of viewpoint or argument (e.g. a sermon or newspaper editorial, and by extension most broadcast programmes including a great deal of fiction), the same question is asked the other way round: how far do the derogatory or insulting implications go needlessly beyond mere choice of style in which to convey ideas or opinion?

Difficulty in deciding between an 'expressive' interpretation and an 'insulting conduct' interpretation is increased by the uncomfortable premise of freedom of expression as a value: that no interpreter should expect to like all the ideas that have a legitimate claim on being expressed. Ideas do not cease to be

---

[10] Comprehensive treatment can be found in Kent Greenawalt, *Fighting Words: Individuals, Communities, and Liberties of Speech* (Princeton: Princeton University Press, 1995).

ideas because they are rebarbative. But the affront some ideas may give can make them distasteful or disgusting to a degree that *feels* more like an insult than communication of an idea. With some media texts (think particularly of contemporary art exhibits or controversial books and films), expressive potential is closely interwoven with calculated provocation.

### 11.3.4   Incitement

Incitement overlaps with hate speech. It may even be a different aspect of the same act of communication. With incitement, however, the communicative action performed is viewed less as expression of hatred or vilification than as a way of inflaming feelings and urging an audience to illegal action. Incitement goes beyond emotive discourse and constitutes a crime – sometimes called an 'inchoate' crime, as I have said, in that it is the preliminary element of some further action which the law seeks to control – because it stimulates or solicits the ensuing action and so abets or assists it.

Incitement is easy to understand as a public order offence when it is associated with public speaking and meetings at which discourse addressed to specific people and about other specific people creates a threat of violence.[11] Measures to prevent communication inciting violent action are also embedded in broadcasting regulation, however. Responsibility is placed on programme makers to exclude or critically contextualise possible verbal incitement, for which they will be liable unless an actor or programme contributor can be shown to have improvised off-script during a live broadcast.

Not all instances are clear-cut between the categories of hate speech and incitement. A provocative communication may prompt two contrasting – in some cases, complementary – reactions from different groups within the 'same' media audience. One group experiences the communication as degrading or intimidating ('fighting words', if they feel confident in fighting back). The other group experiences the communication as exhortation to inflict violence on the first group. Consider, for example, an inflammatory, homophobic 'fire and brimstone' sermon by a TV evangelist. The sermon consists of a combination of general statements that homosexuality is sinful, claims of biblical authority for this belief, personal comment and expressions of disgust, along with statements of unwillingness to acquiesce in a contemporary secular order. For one section of the audience, such a sermon is likely to be construed as insult or

---

[11] In circumstances where expression and action are closely interwoven, discourse is sometimes referred to as 'speech plus'. The 'plus' is self-evident in cases such as marching, picketing, provocative costume, or accompaniment by drums. Focus on face-to-face interaction between interlocutors can make an 'action effect' seem more warranted than reaction based on communication of ideas or opinion, because of what in the US system has evolved, since *Schenck v. United States*, as the 'clear and present danger' test. See Greenawalt, *Fighting Words*, pp.17–20.

intimidation. For a different section of the same potential audience, the same words of the same sermon may be taken as active encouragement to violent action against gay people.

In form, the kinds of utterance or text most likely to be viewed as incitement will be explicitly signalled speech acts (e.g. imperatives, or utterances containing performative verbs of imploring, urging, requesting, promising, etc.). But they may alternatively be utterances easily inferred as having equivalent force in a given context. Inference to an 'incitement' meaning is not something that happens automatically, though. An alleged incitement may consist of quite indirect rhetorical manipulation, through exaggeration, overstatement, barbed jokes or made-up stories. If so, it may begin to seem defensible as a kind of 'ideological' mix of ideas and exhortation. Views vary on where the boundary between incitement and expression should be drawn. Drawing such boundaries is especially complicated where the offensive potential must be weighed up in complex media genres and formats.

### 11.3.5    Unspeakable ideas

Expression of ideas is not always considered acceptable or legitimate, even without any incitement dimension. Sometimes offensiveness is understood as a matter of content: it is considered to be the result of *any* kind of expression of particularly obnoxious, unspeakable ideas.

Consider the complex example of Holocaust denial. One line of argument about the offensiveness of this view focuses on insult and incitement. It is felt that expressing such views labels Jewish survivors of the Holocaust as liars, denying them due respect and dignity, and vilifies other members of the Jewish faith, at the same time inciting neo-Nazi aggression. A contrasting argument is that Holocaust denial is so intrinsically abhorrent that putting the idea forward in *any* form – regardless of incitement – is unacceptable. On this view, Holocaust denial is offensive because the opinion expressed is not only untrue (after all, it can be part of freedom of expression to protect even ideas that are considered untrue) but beyond the bounds of discourse that should be tolerated. Debates about regulating Holocaust denial reflect both lines of argument, as well as combinations of the two.

How can condemning 'unspeakable ideas' be reconciled with toleration of repugnant ideas that must be permitted in order to uphold freedom of expression, and with restrictions imposed on hate speech and incitement? This issue came to the fore in a British context in disputes about university Student Union branches refusing to grant recognition to campus Christian unions if those Christian unions make statements that homosexuality is sinful.

Reflecting on such disputes,[12] the Archbishop of Canterbury, Rowan Williams, argued that some ways of talking are inherently humiliating and deny people's human dignity. Williams includes Holocaust denial alongside abusive or threatening discourse and racist abuse in this category, and urges that such discourse should be restricted. At the same time, he distinguishes such insulting, 'hate' statements from what he considers only superficially similar forms of expression that include statements of traditional religious values hostile to homosexuality, both in Christianity and in Islam. The force of such statements, Williams suggests, is not that of hateful or offensive speech but that of moral judgment made concerning the life-options and acts of members of the same society. Such statements are therefore to be valued as communal dialogue. Hostile 'action speech', Williams argues, is close enough to hateful action to merit sanctions against it. But claiming that homosexuality is sinful, he suggests, can be a defensible exercise of freedom of expression.

Using the Student Union dispute as his example, Williams develops a more general argument. He laments the emergence of what he considers a new kind of 'personalised offensiveness' often to be found where an idea is felt as deeply unwelcome to someone. Ideas *may* be genuinely offensive in a personal sense, he recognises. But the wish to prevent such offensiveness by silencing the ideas that cause it, on grounds that they are hateful, is he suggests inspired by a misguided impulse: that disagreement itself is disturbing and that people holding different convictions is in principle disruptive. Silencing disagreement on important moral themes, because the particular views are offensive in this 'personalised' sense, Williams argues, 'psychologises' conflict over ideas: it denies the possibility of achieving the degree of detachment from ideas that is needed in debating moral or social issues. 'Personalised offensiveness', he argues, differs from the kind of offensiveness that is an attack on human dignity and puts people materially at risk. The Archbishop of Canterbury offers instead a religious foundation for freedom of expression, which he warns would need to be combined with moderation of potentially hurtful excess in moral debate. A moral challenge to someone on grounds of the life choices they are making, the Archbishop concludes, is in fact a tribute to human dignity in demonstrating that the speaker takes that person seriously as a moral agent and free person, whose choices matter.

## 11.3.6   Blasphemy

In insisting on a close link between freedom of expression and moderation of inflammatory rhetoric, Rowan Williams identifies an important aspect of how

---

[12] Rowan Williams, 'It is not a crime to hold traditional values', *The Higher*, 8 December 2006.

offensiveness is created: that even where a topic is considered a legitimate object of serious public discussion, some treatments of it go beyond fair debate into aggressive disparagement, especially in satire and other kinds of calculated ridicule or contempt. What constitutes offensiveness in such cases (in a way reminiscent of swearing consisting of 'oaths') is the cocktail of topic and dismissive treatment.

Complaints about depictions of particular topics, which include disability, violence, drug taking, death, and cruelty to animals, are often couched in terms of bad taste. Media content along such lines is widely described simply as 'sick'. As with all discourse, treatments of such topics are communicative *action* as well as expression of content: attempts to thrill, titillate, scare and shock (or alternatively, as might be contended by their producers, to inform, educate, warn or simply amuse). Where a topic holds a recognised, central and even defining place in a culture, however (for instance religious belief), the issue of bad taste escalates into one of cultural insult, arguably attacking people's fundamental beliefs, identity and self-esteem. This is the framework within which most modern defences of blasphemy are argued.

Historically, the crime of blasphemy provided majority-religious societies with an important means of limiting religious offensiveness. At the same time, the Archbishop of Canterbury's point above about criticisms of people's moral choices showing respect for human dignity sits slightly oddly with the church's historical record on dealing with challenges to the beliefs it promotes itself. Perhaps as significant now, however, is how far the offensiveness at stake in blasphemy has adapted to changing attitudes towards the Christian churches in Western societies.[13] Insofar as blasphemy continues to exist as a crime, the standard of offensiveness it requires is one of ridicule of the religious beliefs of others rather than anything about the blasphemer's own beliefs, salvation or the security of the state.

Critical attacks on Christian faith are only blasphemous now if disparaging comments are made about God, Bible characters or articles of the Christian faith in an outrageously indecent or scurrilous manner. Such comments must mock religion – rather than criticise it – and must arouse disgust and shock, wounding the feelings of religious adherents. In these respects, blasphemy combines derogatory treatment of articles or symbols of religious faith with offensiveness to people in a particular social group (in England, Anglicans and fellow Christians whose beliefs overlap with Anglicanism, though not Muslims or

---

[13] See Spilsbury, *Media Law*, pp. 416–30; Robertson and Nicol stress the requirement of 'indecent descriptions applied to sacred subjects' rather than vigorous criticism or denial of belief, *Media Law*, pp.160–5. For relevant history, see Joss Marsh, *Word Crimes: Blasphemy, Culture and Literature in Nineteenth-Century England* (Chicago: University of Chicago Press, 1998), and for contemporary discussion, Neu, *Sticks and Stones*, pp.193–213.

members of other religions – hence why no action for blasphemy was available to Muslims in the Salman Rushdie affair[14]). Strangely, blasphemy seems to be mutating towards precisely what Rowan Williams criticises as 'personalised offensiveness'. In Britain the offence increasingly means insulting people rather than their beliefs, with which other people are completely at liberty to disagree.

### 11.3.7   Obscenity

It is striking how many texts alleged to be blasphemous involve an element of scurrilous sexual innuendo in relation to religious figures.[15] If 'blasphemous text' were a genre, then sexual implication would be one of its prototypical features. Whereas seditious and blasphemous libel have been largely overtaken by other ways of dealing with the sensitivities they were created to address, however, the challenge of dealing with sexual representations, as obscene libel, has continued, albeit (as with blasphemy) subject to historical changes reflecting changing social attitudes.[16]

As with blasphemy (and also with swearing), the offensiveness of alleged obscene material combines topic and treatment. Sex, for instance, is viewed as perhaps the prime case of a private and intimate realm despite being everywhere publicly depicted and alluded to; but to be obscene, sexual representations must be held to go beyond general complaint about where society 'draws the line' in matters of taste and decency into treatments that are considered either unlawful (rape, paedophile depictions of children); or seriously demeaning, manipulative or exploitative; or in some relevant way incitements to predatory sexual behaviour that may or may not itself be illegal. In the exercise of line drawing, meaning issues arise where, alongside the text's heightening of emotional or physical states, differently represented mental constructs determine what the text seems to be saying about whatever it shows.[17]

From an interpretive point of view, sexual obscenity is complicated not only by complexity of its subject matter – as literally where the symbolic order meets

---

[14] The personal offence felt by many Muslims on publication in 1988 of Salman Rushdie's *The Satanic Verses* could not be addressed legally as blasphemy under English law. See also the unsuccessful application by a member of a Christian organisation to bring a private prosecution for blasphemous libel against the theatrical work *Jerry Springer: The Opera*. See *R. (on the application of Green) v. City of Westminster Magistrates' Court* [2007] EWHC 2785 (Admin); [2008] HRLR 12; (2007) 157 NLJ *1767*.

[15] *Last Testament of Christ, Life of Brian, The Satanic Verses*, Jame Kirkup's poem 'The love that dares to speak its name' in *Gay News* – or *The Seashell and the Clergyman* itself.

[16] For a history of obscenity as an offence, see Geoffrey Robertson, *Obscenity* (London: Weidenfeld and Nicolson, 1979).

[17] Except, on some views, in extreme cases where obscene material is believed to have a directly physical effect, like a sex toy. See Frederick Schauer, *Free Speech: A Philosophical Enquiry* (Cambridge: Cambridge University Press, 1982). For discussion, Greenawalt, *Speech, Crime and the Uses of Language*, pp. 149–50.

the body – but by various factors in a text's production, circulation and reception. Most obviously, the text's topic is relevant: its representation of 'sexual relations', sometimes in combination with violence, drug taking, and/ or various forms of violence or horror. Intention may or may not be relevant to whether an offence has been committed, depending on the particular offence or infringement being alleged; but the producer's intention is typically taken into account: whether, as is assumed of hard-core pornography, the motive is simply commercial or whether a redeeming, creative (artistic or sociological) intent is ascribed. Formal aspects of treatment are also relevant: not only how long or graphic any particular sexually explicit representation is, but whose point of view it represents, what role in the narrative or argument it serves, and which character or characters the text shows sympathy towards. There is also likely to be discussion of probable use of the text (e.g. for the purpose of sexual arousal, including as a masturbatory aid, or for advocacy of a particular sexual lifestyle, as in so-called 'thematic' or 'ideological' pornography).[18] Beyond these factors, anticipated effect is of prime importance: whether the text can be shown to 'cause public outrage' or 'offend against the taste and decency of reasonable people', or whether it has the widely quoted 'tendency to deprave and corrupt'.[19]

Two of the above factors (topic and harm) define obscenity as an offence. The other three – intention, formal attributes, and use or response – are relevant in deciding whether a particular text meets the threshold standard. Unsurprisingly, intention, form and response are the three main dimensions of interpretation discussed elsewhere in this book, suggesting that even if offensiveness is thought to trump or cut through meaning, meaning still has to be ascertained in deciding how it does this.

Linking meaning to harm is complicated, nevertheless, by the different sorts of harm thought to result from obscene material. Several main strands, each involving claims more specific than merely being 'poisonous', 'polluting', 'indecent' or 'immodest', are usually distinguished: firstly, there is a sense of shock, disgust or trauma felt by unwilling or unsuspecting readers or viewers. Evidence of such effects is easy to gather but inevitably subjective; although useful in practical regulation, such evidence may seem too impressionistic to form a solid basis for liability. Beyond this, causal relations are often argued between reading or viewing and some ensuing action, usually a 'copycat' form of imitation of what the text depicts (including sexual violence, rape or murder). Decisive causal links to underpin arguments along these lines, however, have proved difficult to demonstrate convincingly. Longer-range effects are also

---

[18] For the legal significance of 'ideological' pornography as something worth protecting as expression, see Emerson, *The System of Freedom of Expression*, p. 475.

[19] Robertson and Nicol, *Media Law*, pp. 107–8.

postulated, including weakening of the bonds of civil society and morality, eroding standards of acceptability, and affecting people's ideas of what is sexually possible, expected, or likely to be demanded of them by others (especially in relation to young people). Sexually obscene material is held in such thinking to contribute to long-term social changes by presenting a systematically unbalanced account of sexual behaviour and attitudes (e.g. giving disproportionate attention to easy seduction and sexually willing figures while ignoring pregnancy, sexually transmitted diseases, and the social and emotional consequences of sexual activity). These effects seem easier to show but are not easily attributed to individual texts.

Insofar as the effects identified in these frameworks can be linked to particular texts, rather than following from a broader and changing cultural climate, they depend on a notion of meaning that brings together textual interpretation with personal significance: not only what a text says or shows, or what you might legitimately infer from it, but how a given reader or viewer gives significance to and acts on what they take to be the text's meaning within their own and other people's lives. As with other kinds of allegedly offensive material, spontaneous shock or trauma cuts unpredictably even through indirectness, irony and narrative contextualisation, including explicit condemnation by other discourses within the same text. The challenge presented to interpretation, in such circumstances, is to hold different aspects and levels of the circulation of meaning and likely or possible effect together in debating them.

## 11.4    Meaning in action

Having briefly outlined the main, interlocking sources of media offensiveness as categories of behaviour and alleged effects, I want now to look more closely at two *interpretive* questions about offensive discourse that cut across those categories. The first concerns whether the 'meaning' of an offensive utterance or text can be explicated or paraphrased in anything like the way that the meaning of a libellous statement or most adverts can. The second issue concerns what audience standard is invoked in attributing meaning as a basis for adjudication, in circumstances where the effects in question are important because they can be traumatic and humiliating but are inevitably largely subjective and often beyond conceptual or propositional meaning.

### 11.4.1    Constructing the sense of being offended

In matters of offensiveness, as is clear from my preceding descriptions, meaning closely resembles a kind of social action. It is relevant to ask, therefore, how far the 'force' of a text or utterance – its functioning as communicative action rather than as a sort of expressive content – is amenable to analysis. In this respect, there may be an important difference between what constitutes meaning for offensive utterances or texts and the meaning of potentially defamatory imputations. For a defamatory imputation to exist, the meaning of an utterance must be expressible in a propositional form which can be supported by evidence and/or falsified, because falsity is part of what makes the meaning defamatory (hence why so-called 'vulgar abuse' and insults are upsetting but, unless constructed into specific propositional claims, not libellous).[20] Hateful utterances and other kinds of discourse 'action', having little or no propositional content, require a different approach to interpretation or construction: interpretation that characterises the force of the communicated act that sponsors the alleged injurious effect.

### 11.4.2   Performatives and speech acts

The general idea of utterances exerting forces of different kinds, as well as or instead of conveying information, is usually associated with the Oxford philosopher J. L. Austin discussed in earlier chapters. In *How To Do Things with Words* (1961), Austin proposed a class of utterances that he called performatives.[21] Such performative utterances are the verbal equivalent of actions, in that they carry out, or perform, the acts they designate, such as promising, betting, declaring war and apologising. Such performatives, as was suggested in Chapter 8, cannot be judged in terms of whether they are true or false, only in terms of whether they succeed or fail (in Austin's terms, whether they are 'felicitous' or 'misfire') in relation to conventions governing relevant kinds of social ceremony or ritual that take place within language itself. Such performatives Austin distinguished from statements, or 'constative' utterances, which convey information. In a celebrated reversal of the argument in *How To Do Things with Words*, however, Austin puts forward a second important insight that reverses the thrust of the first: he generalises from the specific case of performatives to claim that all utterances perform speech acts. Constative or informative utterances are also speech acts, in their case ones of asserting.

Analysis of utterances based on Austin's insights distinguishes between three different perspectives on what linguistic 'act' is performed. Utterances are locutionary acts (in being formed as intelligible utterances within a given language or code, and having an intended structure, meaning and reference); they are illocutionary acts (or conventional vehicles that embody the intention to carry out the

---

[20]  An interesting borderline case is the defamation action *Berkoff v. Burchill* [1996] 4 All ER 1008. A newspaper review stated that an actor/director was 'hideously ugly'. At the Court of Appeal, which held that the words were in fact defamatory, alternative views were expressed on how to draw a line between mere mockery and defamatory imputation: whether an impression was conveyed that the complainant was not merely physically unattractive but also repulsive in a way that might lower his standing as someone who makes a living in the public eye in the estimation of the public. For the alternative views, see quotations in Barendt and Hitchens, *Media Law*, p. 356.

[21]  Austin, *How To Do Things with Words*.

particular act by means of the utterance, subject to necessary conditions being in place); and they are perlocutionary acts (or achievements of particular effects brought about by performing the utterance).[22] Exactly which illocutionary act an utterance performs can be signalled explicitly, by a performative expression ('I hereby declare you man and wife'); by a particular construction such as an imperative ('Keep off the grass'); or alternatively, indirectly and sometimes ambiguously, by implied meaning and inference ('That dog looks menacing' might in different circumstances be an assertion, a compliment or a warning).

Discussion of different acts carried out in communication had a long history before Austin, of course, especially in rhetoric. But *How To Do Things with Words* prompted an important shift in linguistics towards investigating how speech acts work. In a later classification of speech acts modifying Austin's categories, John Searle, as described in Chapter 7, symbolised Austin's central insight as the general formula, F(p), in which a communicated proposition (p) is embedded under a function indicating device, F. For Searle and others in the 1970s, the crucial task seemed to be to classify different kinds of F.[23] What has subsequently been viewed as more significant in Searle's work on speech acts, however (and in accounts that follow from it), is that Searle inverted Austin's suggestion that illocutionary acts are subject to occasional 'misfires' or failures.[24] Instead, Searle showed how the conditions for success of a speech act are constitutive of that act, rather than merely determining whether it is successful or not on a given occasion. One implication of Searle's approach is that analysing constitutive rules for speech acts can be extended into accounts of many other aspects of the construction of social reality, something Searle himself has more recently explored.[25]

## 11.4.3   Situation-altering utterances

The development of speech act theory in linguistics outlined here is relevant to offensiveness because insights it contains have been drawn on, in different

---

[22] Some verbs perform all three types of act simultaneously. Others perform one but not another (e.g. 'urge' is illocutionary while 'offend' is perlocutionary); others again, such as 'persuade', do not fit the three-way distinction between acts so neatly. Habermas points to important but neglected difficulties in the nature of illocutionary and perlocutionary acts and effects, *On the Pragmatics of Communication*, pp. 123–9.

[23] John Searle, *Speech Acts: Essays in the Philosophy of Language* (Cambridge: Cambridge University Press, 1969).

[24] Speech acts that fail to meet their conditions of satisfaction may fail on a number of counts. There may for instance be no conventional procedure in place associated with the particular speech act. Alternatively, an existing, conventional procedure may not have been followed properly. In either case, Austin calls such failure 'misfiring'. The other main possibility is that the speaker's necessary intention is not present. Violation of this condition Austin considers an abuse of the speech act rather than a 'misfire': a failure to observe the sincerity condition essential for communication to succeed.

[25] John Searle, *The Construction of Social Reality* (Harmondsworth: Penguin, 1995).

ways, to clarify the conduct–expression distinction that runs through the types of offensiveness outlined above. That distinction often defines what constitutes 'expression' in legal arrangements for 'freedom of expression'.

Also in the 1970s, the legal scholar Kent Greenawalt studied how the conduct–expression distinction maps onto the many different kinds of verbal expression that the law seeks to control, and compiled a useful list of criminal offences and causes of action that can be achieved simply by using language.[26] Greenawalt's list includes threatening harm to someone unless they commit a crime; agreeing with, ordering or inducing someone to commit a crime; putting someone in fear of injury; warning a criminal how to escape from the police; offering a bribe; using insulting language; engaging in speech likely to lead people to commit crimes; perjuring oneself; falsely pretending to hold a public position; using language or other representations in a way that is offensive, and many other categories. Most of these offences and causes of action, he points out, are not a matter of statements or assertions of 'meaning' (though utterances in any given category may contain assertions). They tend instead to be different sorts of communicative *act*: what Greenawalt calls 'situation-altering acts'. Such acts are performed in speech or other forms of representation but could be (and often are) performed by other kinds of action. It is the action carried out by the words or other signs, rather than any content they convey, that is the offence.

Greenawalt's study draws particular attention to verbs in defining criminal and actionable communicative behaviour: 'solicit', 'disclose', 'threaten', 'promise', 'incite', 'exhort', 'offend', 'blaspheme', 'defame', 'mislead', 'misrepresent', etc. Some of these verbs are illocutionary but not explicitly performative in Austin's sense (e.g. you can certainly blaspheme, but not by saying 'I hereby blaspheme …'); many of the verbs *describe* types of communication that are typically performed indirectly. Because of close links between the verbs themselves, however, as legal descriptors of crimes, and kinds of action that speech acts involving such verbs commonly perform, Greenawalt is led to consider how far it may be possible to define kinds of communication that, as specialised kinds of action or 'conduct', should on these grounds be considered beyond the reach of 'freedom of expression' defences.

### 11.4.4    Performativity

A number of US writers, including Catharine MacKinnon, Judith Butler and others, have drawn an analogy between the special case of performative verbs and the more general category of representational acts and effects, and extended the concept of performative discourse much further. In doing so, they have

---

[26]  Greenawalt, *Speech, Crime, and the Uses of Language*, pp. 6–7.

sought to explain why certain kinds of discourse (for instance ethnic and religious epithets and pornography) are not simply insulting and upsetting but have an enduring, deeply wounding power. For MacKinnon, the main implication of such analysis is that it might be used to challenge defences of pornography as 'expression of ideas';[27] for Butler, analysis of 'performativity' not only serves this purpose but opens up critical reflection on how communicative acts give shape to people's formation as subjects, including how people are positioned by how they are addressed (hence how they can be dominated and subjugated by hate speech).[28]

What follows from viewing offensive utterances and texts as being performative in this way is a sense wider than Greenawalt's that communicative acts are situation-altering: they don't only alter situations but alter people. Both hate speech and pornography, accordingly, should be regulated as conduct rather than being exempt from such regulation as expression of ideas or opinion. The attractiveness of this idea of performativity, to those who advocate it as a basis for regulation, is clear: as a model of how discourse works, the notion of performativity offers a determinate link between offensive discourse and harmful effect of a kind missing from earlier communication 'effects' approaches. If offensive discourse can be shown to be performative in the sense of *achieving* the act it performs directly, in and by the act of performing, then pornography or hate speech is not only conduct but conduct linked causally to perlocutionary effects that follow from it. The act of utterance or representation would have to be considered as tied to its effects, rather than those effects being derived indirectly by interpretation of what was said or shown.

In established legal frameworks, the status of a text *as* obscene has to be established by interpretation rather than presumed. In a performativity framework, by contrast, a presumption of perlocutionary effect might be made that would limit free speech arguments in pornography cases so that they would hardly impinge, as is the case with charges of bribery, perjury or conspiracy.[29] In this sense, the idea of performativity offers a mechanism by means of which

---

[27] For example, MacKinnon argues that women are compelled to act or be treated as shown because the act of representation creates a psychological or social reality to which women are subject: sexual abuse and 'speech' are effectively in the same category. Catharine MacKinnon, *Only Words* (Cambridge, Mass.: Harvard University Press, 1993).

[28] Judith Butler, *Excitable Speech: A Politics of the Performative* (London: Routledge, 1997). Among the cases Butler discusses is the influential US case *R.A.V v. St Paul*, 505 U.S. 377 (1992), in which a white juvenile was charged with burning a cross inside the fenced yard of a black family's house (see esp. pp. 52–60). For discussion of that case from a different perspective, see Greenawalt, *Fighting Words*, pp. 55–8.

[29] Discourse judged to be obscene has been considered outside First Amendment protection explicitly since *Roth v. United States* 354 U.S. 476 (1957) and implicitly before. But on a performativity view a 'free speech' defence of pornography would be still more remote. Greenawalt, *Fighting Words*, pp. 50 and 99–123.

offensiveness bypasses attribution of meaning and, linking up to the perception of offensiveness with which I began, cuts or burns through to the body and subjectivity directly.

### 11.4.5    Force and inference

Future efforts to regulate insults, hate speech, workplace harassment and media obscenity are all likely to be dominated by arguments about the difference between *saying* something with words, sounds and pictures and *doing* something with words, sounds and pictures.[30] How compelling are interpretive arguments that rely on this distinction?

A link between the calculated force of an utterance or representation and injurious effects which follow, for which a communicator should therefore be held responsible, undoubtedly exists in the case of pornography and hate speech, as it does for all discourse. It seems too much, however, to depend on a speech act model to supply any more determinate account of meaning production than this.

The speech act model has increasingly been shown to be a simplification of how meaning is produced in verbal communication. Communicators typically have more than a single intention in mind at any given moment, often express more than one speech act in any given utterance, and use a great deal of indirectness in achieving communicative goals. Perlocutionary effects are not determinate.[31] Illocutionary force (the general category within which explicit performatives operate) is not linked to perlocutionary effect like the two aspects of the linguistic sign in Saussure.[32] The code-and-meaning view criticised elsewhere in this book understates the role played by listeners or readers in *inferring* illocutionary force, either by assigning complex utterances to illocutionary categories, as with indirect speech acts, or, on some more recent accounts, inferring to a relevant interpretation without any reference to speech act categories at all.[33] These are not only theoretical quibbles. The underlying

---

[30] Cf. *Fighting Words*, p. 152

[31] Austin's most famous example of a perlocutionary act – symptomatic in this context – is the slightly oddly chosen, 'shoot her!' The illocutionary force of this imperative may be that of ordering, urging or advising the addressee to shoot her; its perlocutionary effect may be that of persuading, forcing, cajoling or frightening the addressee into shooting her. Levinson points out (in *Pragmatics*) that the utterance might also have a perlocutionary effect not only on the addressee but also of frightening *her*. Perlocutionary effects are not much researched by linguists because they do not offer insights into the working of the language system; but they are often of crucial significance in social and legal discussion.

[32] 'The linguistic sign is, then, a two-sided psychological entity', Ferdinand de Saussure, *Course in General Linguistics*, trans. and annotated Roy Harris (London: Duckworth, 1983), p. 66.

[33] For a critique of speech acts from a Relevance Theory perspective, see Sperber and Wilson, *Relevance*, pp. 243–54; Blakemore, *Understanding Utterances*, pp. 91–120.

analogy relied on in regulatory arguments from performativity, for instance between performative verbs and pornographic films, is strained. If that analogy were to be tied more closely back to illocutionary force in linguistics, then the evidence surrounding illocutionary-force indicators in language would suggest that perlocutionary effects are a result of inference working in combination with signs' conventional and calculated meanings. Such effects form part of a more complex appropriation of discourse meaning into the social experience and identity of the reader or viewer. This is not to reject the overall political account of hate speech, pornography and other kinds of alleged offensiveness as having a communicative force that may outweigh any claims on expression; but it is to question how far the model of meaning-making on which the notion of 'performativity' depends should be thought to apply.

## 11.5    Interpretive variation and standards

My second question concerns the interpretive standard, or threshold of judgment conferring legal or regulatory authority on a meaning or interpretation, that is relied on in arriving at the meaning or force of an alleged offensive utterance or text. In some areas of law, as we have seen, the interpretive standard is conceived as a model reader (e.g. the 'ordinary reader' or 'average consumer'). With insults, the equivalent model interpreter would perhaps have to be an average or ordinary *addressee* (subject to complications I have outlined in how media speech events address audiences in different ways and at several levels). Reacting to offensive discourse, as we have seen, involves inferences about context and intention as well as a subjective sense of being offended or traumatised. Whose pattern of inference, we should therefore ask, provides the benchmark for an interpretive standard where a sense of being hurt, outraged or humiliated is in question?

Deciding on an interpretive benchmark in areas of offensiveness involves different difficulties from those presented by my other two case studies. In libel, trust was placed in an 'ordinary reader'; in advertising, appeal was made to the judgment of a suitably contextualised 'average consumer'. Both embodied ideas of reasonable interpretation. Offensiveness, by contrast, involves affective response, often to non-propositional aspects of the discourse in question. It also affects members of the specific, insulted social group differently from others. Responses will reflect social factors that vary still more than ways of reading brought to bear on propositional discourse. Offensiveness is dependent not only on personal belief but on self-perception, including people's complex sense of ethnic identity, religious faith and/or political belief, as well as personal affiliations. It is also shaped by radically varying levels of sensitivity and cultural vulnerability. The result is that offensiveness seems far less amenable to a singular, idealised interpretive standard. Some of the difficulties likely to be encountered in attempting to create an idealised standard or norm can be seen in the two following brief examples, both taken from obscenity law.

No attempt has been made in English obscenity law to characterise the appropriate interpretive standard in terms of 'average'. During the overhaul of US obscenity law that took place in the 1950s and 60s, however, a constitutional standard for obscenity was temporarily formulated as 'whether to the average person, applying contemporary community standards, the dominant theme of the material taken as a whole appeals to prurient interest'.[34] While 'prurient' and mainstream values were retained, however, later formulations moved away from the idea of 'average'. One possible explanation for moving away from ideas of average or ordinary adopted in other legal fields is this. As has been suggested in relation to marketing, an 'average' person is a more difficult concept to sustain when what is in question may be not rational but desiring behaviour. The difference between rational and desiring behaviour is well reflected by an American judge (in the 1933 obscenity trial of James Joyce's *Ulysses*) prefiguring the 1957 'average' wording with his own formulation of a 'person with average sexual instincts – what the French would call "l'homme moyen sensuel"'. That 1933 formulation, never taken further, exposes something of what is in question with 'average' in this field: not only diversity of human sexual behaviour but assumed gender symmetry (partly obscured in this wording by generic 'person' and French 'homme'). 'Average' begs interpretive questions in even imagining the range from which 'average' sexual appetites might be estimated. Yet without scale and range, intuitions as to norms or 'average' can only fall back on the sorts of prejudice and moral judgment that First Amendment aspects of *Roth*, and wider arguments about obscenity, sought to disentangle.

Consider an English case that raises related difficulties in formulating an interpretive standard. In *DPP v. Whyte* [1972], the Hicklin standard in obscenity law of a 'tendency to deprave and corrupt' needed to be clarified between two readings: that of mental and moral corruption of a publication's readers; and that of instigation of anti-social acts, especially sexual crimes. Attempts to clarify that question, however, opened up an underlying problem: exactly *who* is thought subject to a text's 'tendency'. In *Whyte*, the main consumers of the hard-core pornographic magazines on sale in a shop were acknowledged by the magistrate to be older men already regular consumers of the same type of material, unlikely to be depraved or corrupted further by the particular purchase. A verdict of not guilty followed. On appeal, however, the Lords concluded that the magistrate's decision (that the magazines could not be interpreted in the circumstances as having the necessary 'tendency') contradicted the purpose of

---

[34] For discussion of judging 'average' in *Chaplinsky v. New Hampshire*, see Greenawalt, *Fighting Words*, p. 52.

the 1959 Act. To achieve its purpose, the legislation appeared to require a compound of *two* idealised readers, neither of them average: a vulnerable reader, in need of protection from a fall into depravity and corruption; and an already depraved reader whose depravity might nevertheless be, if not extended, at least reinforced.[35]

Difficulties with 'average' in these two cases point to a more general challenge in finding a basis on which to adjudicate between competing interpretations in the area of offensiveness: that several interrelated, but not equivalent concerns play a part in any proposed standard of interpretation or sensibility used to define 'contemporary community standards'.

Historically, the implied reader of an alleged obscene text was considered paternalistically. Chief Justice Lord Cockburn's decision in *R v. Hicklin* [1868] not only stated the now famous 'tendency' test for obscene libel invoked in *DPP v. Whyte*, but addressed the impure thoughts of young or vulnerable people rather than the audience more generally. Similarly paternalistic statements can be found elsewhere in the history of English obscenity law, for instance regarding 'vulnerable members of society', 'the impressionable', a 'callow youth, or a girl just budding into womanhood', the famous 'wives or servants' at risk if they read *Lady Chatterley*, or in the *Oz* trial not 'your own children' but 'your neighbour's children'.[36]

Over the last century-and-a-half, however, community standards of acceptability have relaxed, reflecting weakening taboos in many areas of representation. This seems not to be a case of interpretive standards following a general narrative of liberalisation. As regards representations of ethnicity, gender and disability, for example, community standards of interpretation reflect less a narrative of abstract moral or communicative values than responses to specific political shifts (including decolonisation, globalisation, gender politics and the formation of modern multicultural societies). Such social changes are reflected in sometimes rapidly changing styles of expression, as is seen in complications surrounding historically inherited epithets. Construing alleged offensiveness inevitably faces the problem on some occasions of distinguishing offensive intent from unreflective, continuing use of older forms and styles, as commonly with older people or institutions whose usage has not altered in response to the changing symbolic field around them. Regulation also faces the challenge of dealing with ironic new styles and pastiche that challenge whatever is conventionally thought appropriate with representations calculated to shock.

---

[35] *DPP v. Whyte* [1972] AC 849; [1972] 3 WLR 410; [1972] 3 All ER 12; [1973] 57 Cr. App. R. 74; [1972] Crim. L.R. 556; [1972] 116 S.J. 583. For discussion, see Robertson, *Obscenity*; Robertson and Nicol, *Media Law*, pp. 110–12; Spilsbury, *Media Law*, pp. 401–4.

[36] For extensive discussion of these variable tests, see Robertson, *Obscenity*; Robertson and Nicol, *Media Law*.

'Contemporary community standards' provide a basis for public offensiveness judgments. But personal judgments of offensiveness involve deeply held, individual beliefs and different thresholds of emotional sensitivity. Evaluating meanings ascribed by some proportion of an audience satisfies social policy goals of regulation but cannot hope to reflect the diversity of media audiences in which small, sometimes specialised interpretive communities can have – or in some cases may need to be given – a disproportionate influence. The greater the variety of media content available, especially online, the more audience interpretive standards will need to be finely tuned to different media formats. The slightly paradoxical result, in terms of the history of regulation in this area, is that the values appealed to may end up reflecting how genres command audiences, rather than the permitted genres reflecting social values.

## 11.6    Symbolic shock effects

During the second half of the nineteenth century, paternalistic approaches to regulating the possible offensiveness of publications were largely concerned with protecting suggestible, newly literate readers in a period of expansion of literacy among the lower social classes. Contemporary regulation of offensiveness, by contrast, works largely by 'holding the ring' between rival opinions and values in far more media literate populations. In these circumstances, media regulatory bodies are less equipped to tackle the question of what constitutes a contemporary standard of offensiveness head-on. Instead they work to head off complaint and controversy by other means: by licensing agreements with broadcasters, classification of videos and DVDs, pre-publication or pre-screening guidance to text producers, scheduling policies including a content watershed, on-screen warnings, and encouragement to vendors to advise customers appropriately and to parents to monitor what their children watch and do online.

Is it possible, in such circumstances, to say what 'interpretation' of an allegedly offensive utterance or text should be? Notwithstanding the notion of performativity, deciding whether a media utterance or text is offensive involves constructing an interpretation of it. That interpretation, as the historical development of regulation shows, is obliged to go beyond reading-off fixed values for signs (a proscribed word, a forty-feet-of-film kiss, or a rule against showing specific body parts) into more contextualised discourse interpretation. Attributing meaning needs to make links between levels: between contested individual scenes or passages and their context in a whole text or discourse, reflecting how local meaning is shaped by preceding and following discourse; and between material contested and the genre in which it occurs, as well as its context of distribution, likely audience and the likely use that will be made of it. To achieve such multilevel accounts of meaning, interpretation must move between levels, acknowledging that voices, statements and viewpoints are embedded in other levels of discourse that frame or comment on them. At the same time offensiveness adjudications need to keep in view the culturally shaped power of individual words and symbols, where unwanted by an addressee, to shock or inflict some kind of crash on the symbolic order, *despite* any rational account of context or significance. Meaning is not purely self-contained or merely socially relative but has personal and social consequences.

Offensiveness judgments, like decisions at other meaning troublespots, are only partly about 'meaning'. They are matters of social policy concerned with balancing relative harmony between different interests and social groups against a competing value of freedom to express ideas and opinions. Interpretation is one aspect of a wider debate about meaning as 'significance'. This is why overall judgments need to take into account historical and present cultural struggles over available, public representations of social identities, lifestyles and beliefs that compete for public attention. The 'meaning' dimension of competing arguments has to be seen within larger, cultural and political debates over cultural identity and aspiration.

Analysing contested meanings at such pressure points can provide no ready-made answers or easy solutions. But it may help in building institutions and frameworks of discussion that draw the sting from communications whose effects are often strongest when least interrogated. By comparison with idealisation of a model reader or silent pursuit of consensus, active engagement with media discourse reception is less a way of ascertaining '*the* meaning' than of establishing provisional, practical kinds of interpretive legitimacy relative to the social policy objectives or cause of action in question.

## 11.7    Summary

In this chapter, I have outlined the main sources of verbal offensiveness. I have shown how legal and regulatory responses to the distress caused by such verbal behaviour often depend on deciding what act or function the allegedly offensive utterance or text serves in a particular context of reception. The general concept of 'situation-altering utterances' in legal thinking, I have suggested, has both the strengths and the weaknesses of ideas of performatives and speech acts in linguistics. Drawing on the work of Austin, Searle and others, I related the concept of situation-altering utterances to the claimed performativity of cultural discourse and artefacts argued by writers including Butler and MacKinnon. I suggested that deciding on the force of utterances or texts typically relies on inferential work rather than on stable, conventional speech act categories. I nevertheless concluded that understanding the meaning-making, including inferential, dimensions of offensive discourse is only part of understanding the symbolic shock that such discourse can inflict.

*Part V*

# Conclusion

# 12    Trust in interpretation

## 12.1    Introduction

In this final chapter, I link challenges presented by discourse meaning in the media with wider debates about representation, misrepresentation and unresolved questions to do with 'information'. I close by asking how much trust or suspicion we should feel towards contemporary media communicators.

## 12.2    Meaning and speculation

To illustrate how the continuous, daily flow of meaning disputes is both an immediate, local problem and also a longer-term social question of representation and information, I begin by drawing out some wider social issues from a news story extensively covered as I write this morning.[1]

Today's newspapers, radio and TV news, and online news sites all report an unexpected fluctuation in the share price of HBOS, the UK's biggest mortgage lender.[2] What makes the fluctuation newsworthy – after all, share values fluctuate continuously – is that it is thought to have been triggered by speculators spreading false rumours about an alleged funding crisis at the bank, in order to cash in on the resulting fall in share price by short-selling (that is, by borrowing shares and selling them, then spreading a rumour that causes their value to fall and buying the shares back at a profit when the rumour is not substantiated and the price recovers, then returning the original shares and keeping the profit). To counter the damaging effect of such rumours (and in this case following temporary suspension of trading after shares in the bank had

---

[1]  20 March 2008.

[2]  E.g. Julia Kollewe, 'How the HBOS attack unfolded', *Guardian*, 20 March 2008 published online at www.guardian.co.uk; Jill Treanor, 'Authorities avert run on HBOS caused by false rumours', *Guardian*, 20 March 2008; Jane Croft, 'Funding jitters annoy HBOS', *Financial Times*, 20 March 2008, p. 19; Andrew Hill, 'HBOS tormentors are easy to spot but hard to catch', *Financial Times*, 20 March 2008, p. 18; Kate Burgess, Chris Giles and Brooke Masters, 'City probe into HBOS false rumours', *Financial Times*, 20 March 2008, p. 1. By the end of September 2008, HBOS had failed and been taken over by Lloyds TSB. Other banks had also failed, leading to a crisis of public confidence in banking and financial services.

lost 17 per cent of their value), a strong warning statement was issued by the Financial Services Authority.[3]

This story shows a meaning troublespot unfolding – a meaning troublespot whose full implications only later became apparent. The situation started with alleged communicative misbehaviour of a kind I described in Chapter 2: in this case, spreading of commercially sensitive rumours. Diffusion of those rumours was amplified beyond face-to-face communication by a network of media technologies, in this case mobile phones, text messages and a flurry of online messaging. (It has been reported that the rumours appear to have originated in Asia rather than in London.) Communication technologies allowed the rumours to ricochet further, through blogs and chat rooms. This resulted in rapid and widespread impact on commercial behaviour. Both HBOS and the financial regulator recognised an urgent problem in continued circulation of the rumours. So the bank intervened to deny them as 'complete and utter nonsense' and 'unfounded and malicious'. The Bank of England also stepped in, calling the rumours 'absolute fantasy'.

With the immediate situation contained, the FSA faced the challenge of restoring trust in the market by curbing such scaremongering. If it tried (and was given sufficient powers) to achieve this by exemplary prosecution as well as by means of the inquiry that was quickly announced, a way would need to be found through all the complications to do with meaning outlined in earlier chapters. Evidence would be needed to establish that rumours were in fact communicated, as well as to identify by whom, when and what about. A causal link would need to be shown between calculated intentions behind those rumours and manipulation of the market in HBOS shares. In each respect, criminal standards of proof would have to be met. Even if prosecutors chose to fall back on the lesser, civil cause of action of 'market abuse', they would still need to establish these things, albeit to a lower standard of proof. Getting to the bottom of who said or wrote what and when, what was intended, what was implied, and whether (as any defendant would argue) the source of any partic- ular piece of information is now forgotten and/or the gossip in context allowed other legitimate interpretations, would be difficult at best. Commentators con- sider it unlikely that any legal action will follow.

Beyond the FSA's own deliberations, however, a wider problem looms: that of a related loss of public confidence, amply demonstrated in the financial turmoil subsequently. The HBOS episode began with communications that, if

---

[3] Sally Dewar, the FSA's managing director of wholesale and institutional markets, announced that, 'There has been a series of completely unfounded rumours about UK financial institutions in the London market over the last few days, sometimes accompanied by short-selling. We will not tolerate market participants taking advantage of the current market conditions to commit abuse by spreading false rumours and dealing on the back of them. We remind market participants of the need to take extra care, in this market climate, to adhere to the market code of conduct.' www.fsa.org.uk.

traced, might be made an object of dispute. At the same time, news coverage of the story exacerbated a wider climate of concern regarding the economic outlook.[4] How jittery and unstable must financial institutions be, if unsubstantiated rumour can wipe millions off share values so quickly? How credulous and vulnerable are consumers, if disinformation can be so exploitative and yet so credible? On the other hand, what is it, precisely, that makes speculators expressing commercial opinion (outside of a duty of confidentiality imposed by a specific professional relationship) a kind of communicative misbehaviour? After all, the free flow of opinion and speculation, as we saw in relation to advertising, is normally considered essential information for buyers and sellers and a valuable lubricant in maintaining and 'balancing' efficient markets.[5]

## 12.2.1   Electronic rumour mill

As some news story from most days' media coverage might do equally well, the HBOS episode outlined above highlights major challenges in understanding – and for a regulator, intervening in – contemporary media meaning. Two challenges that I have not explored so far stand out.

The first challenge consists of having at least some specific text or utterance to argue about. In earlier chapters, I suggested that meaning troublespots are distinctive because modern media allow a reproducible record of communications, including spoken communication, to be scrutinised. In this case, by contrast, there are no specific communications to be scrutinised at all, only unattributed rumours on the airwaves and online. To combat the difficulty this presents, the FSA has urged trading organisations to tape and store all conversations, not 'for training purposes' like a call centre but more like phone-in insurance claims, seeking to catch people out in any communicative wrongdoing.

The second challenge is that of isolating an appropriate moment or audit point at which responsibility for meaning can be judged in a case like this. A frame must be imposed on interpretation within a continuing flow or spread of messages that have cumulative effect. As I have suggested, courts and

---

[4] Concerns in relation to the financial outlook contemporaneous with this example centred on a liquidity crisis and credit crunch, with problems radiating from US sub-prime mortgages, Bear Stearns and Northern Rock. Widespread speculation increased subsequently during the lead-in to recession, with further mergers, bank collapses, house repossessions and company bankruptcies that continue as this book goes to press.

[5] See James Boyle, *Shamans, Software and Spleens: Law and the Construction of the Information Society* (Cambridge, Mass.: Harvard University Press, 1996), esp. chapter 8, 'Insider trading and the romantic entrepreneur', pp. 81–96. Boyle's more recent work, *The Public Domain: Enclosing the Commons of the Mind* (New Haven, Conn.: Yale University Press, 2008), argues vigorously for greater public awareness of intellectual property issues, and a need for more precise (and limited) targeting of restrictions on information and innovation.

regulatory authorities must set boundaries on interpretive trouble if they are to bring litigation to a close. Messages are not incriminating unless their significance, as well as the fact that they took place, is shown.

Why do these two aspects of the situation present special challenges in a case like that of the HBOS short-selling rumour? Contemporary electronic communication flows on mobile phones, in chat rooms and on blogs form cumulative series like a conversation, even where they are reproducible. They radiate outwards and bounce between participants in a global, online dialogue. As a result, they are resistant to reification in ways that could facilitate retrospective grasp of their meaning. This complication in online communication – exactly its 'network' or 'web' character – makes online scams, Internet libel, and other forms of electronic miscommunication and disinformation difficult to regulate in the way that legal procedures of the kind I have discussed above have traditionally attempted. Online and mobile communication call for a combination of interpretive reconstruction with something else: an effort to get inside an unfolding, often international electronic conversation between many participants, some of them using multiple, alternative IDs. This is a task that I argued in the Introduction requires a different interpretive strategy from mulling over a single contested discourse 'object'.

Put these two challenges – having an 'object' text to examine and fixing the interpretive moment – together. It may be that the HBOS rumours will be traced to specific trader messages. It is possible that those messages will be tracked through their spread and adaptation across different interest groups and audiences. More likely, though, is that tracking multiple sources and flows of communication will prove too difficult. At source, the messages may have seemed sufficiently hedged or innocent to allow different interpretations, as opinion or speculation. They may well have only taken on their questionable significance in subsequent diffusion, as 'rumours'. Retreat by regulators from the difficulty of proving meaning is all the more likely because each link in a complex causal chain of communication and interpretation would need to be analysed for what should reasonably have been inferred from it; what was believed, desired or feared by the interpreter at the time; and in what climate of assumptions and speculation the incrementally mutating, relevant meanings were derived.[6] Complications of the kind I am outlining here lend support to

---

[6] Questions about the diffusion and propagation of meanings can be asked in different ways. One argument is that, to trace a social circulation of meanings, we need to examine cumulative effects of individual cognitive events linked in causal chains of repetition and modification across a given society, rather than jumping straight to a macro-scale interface between text and collective public mind. As a model for analysis (with helpful contrast between how slightly varying representations can build up a 'tradition' or can alternatively spread like a rapid 'epidemic', then just as quickly disappear), Dan Sperber proposes the framework of an 'epidemiology of representations' in *Explaining Culture: A Naturalistic Approach* (Oxford: Blackwell, 1996), pp. 56–76.

arguments put forward in discussion of media regulation in favour of shifting the regulatory balance away from legal intervention towards a lighter-touch regime that pre-empts difficult situations. Such a regulatory regime would seek to establish a media climate in which communicative values are institutionalised, professional communicators behave responsibly, and audiences interpret appropriately.[7]

## 12.3    Risky information

How realistic is such a vision of how the circulation of *meaning* (as opposed to the many other tasks facing media regulation) can be dealt with?

In relation to what I called communicative 'use' or behaviour in Chapter 2, ensuring a responsible media environment is a matter of incentives and restrictions embodied in professional codes and reflected consistently in standards of ethical behaviour. As regards what I described as media discourse 'effects', ensuring a more harmonious media environment requires greater tolerance of the values, beliefs and sensitivities of others, coupled where necessary with willingness to curtail public communicative behaviour in order to avoid inflicting injury. But what about disputes over meaning?

As regards interpretation, lighter-touch regulation of media content inevitably relies on a level of critical awareness that goes well beyond not believing everything you read in the newspapers. What is needed is a more general disposition to cope with uncertainty in relation to meaning: some recognition that while interpretive risk is an opportunity for creativity and entertainment, it can also be harmful in its impact and consequences. Risk of misapprehension must be taken seriously if deception and insult are to be minimised. What currently protects media audiences from manipulation and hurt is not their faith in ascertainable correctness or accuracy of meaning of the kind I discussed in Chapter 4 – or even media content regulation; it is their alertness to oblique rhetorical strategies and interests which surround whatever meaning is encoded or implied.

Many people would say that a plea for interpretive caution and detachment is merely pushing at an open door. Beyond legal decision-makers and a few dictionary enthusiasts, there is little regard already for the idea of fixed meaning in public communication, especially among the rising dotcom generation. If so, however, what view of meaning in discourse will replace commitment to the

---

[7] Bronwen Morgan and Karen Yeung argue that it is necessary to view regulation as a variety of interlocking models. In their terms, my discussion here is about a shift from a 'command' framework towards a 'communication' framework. See *An Introduction to Law and Regulation: Text and Materials* (Cambridge: Cambridge University Press, 2008). For extracts and discussion on 'regulatory instrument choice', see esp. pp. 79–150.

idea of single or correct meaning, other than cynicism that all public figures are liars and all marketing is hype?

One complication with seeing the changes taking place on this issue – a complication that seems to push in the opposite direction from postmodern scepticism and cynicism – is a sense that discourse conveys 'information', or nuggets of pre-wrapped meaning that are available to be googled, downloaded and pasted. This view of discourse as information contrasts with viewing discourse as representations presented in different circumstances, each time for some specific purpose and slanted rhetorically towards a perceived advantage of the communicator.[8] The easy availability of online information makes electronic searching and pasting a highly attractive way of finding discourse to consult, borrow and use. But there can be a naivety inherent in over-enthusiasm towards online material, which frequently returns as an equivalent urgency in warnings to young people to stay safe online, as well as in the educational challenge of inculcating more questioning attitudes towards the presumed authenticity and authority of online sources. So it is an urgent task to achieve a better balance between recognising the usefulness and interest of media discourse, on the one hand, and sinking into cynicism about communicators' motives, on the other. This is a task made all the more difficult by the need to accomplish it without fuelling an appetite to contest *everything*.

### 12.3.1   Direction of fit between discourse and world

In this book I have encouraged an understanding of media content as something whose significance must be created, and which can therefore be created in different ways. In developing my argument, I have drawn, both explicitly and implicitly, on ideas about critical media literacy. The 'critical' perspective is needed because, where categories of neutral information and self-serving persuasion become confused with one another, the different relations between discourse and world that these two modes of discourse express can corrode trust in what has recently been evocatively called 'the information battlespace'.[9]

Why confusion should surround the functioning of apparently 'neutral' chunks of information is something that calls for clarification. To see how discourse can engage with the world in different ways, consider the general notion of 'direction of fit' (or orientation of the mind's contents towards the world). Although this idea has much earlier origins in philosophy, it is first

---

[8]  For a view from cultural studies of representation as circulation of meanings (rather than as neutral information), see Stuart Hall, *Representation: Cultural Representations and Signifying Practices* (London: Sage/The Open University, 1997). For detailed analysis of issues raised if you ask what is 'represented' in a representation, see Stephen Heath, 'Representation', *CQ*, 50 (1–2) (2008), 87–99.

[9]  Nick Davies takes the phrase 'to dominate the information battlespace' from Pentagon strategy but extends it to non-military contexts, *Flat Earth News*, p. 236.

formulated in relation to language by Austin.[10] Here, however, I refer to the most widely discussed illustration of the idea, taken from another philosopher, G.E. Anscombe.[11]

Anscombe invites us to consider a situation in which a woman gives her husband a shopping list on which are written the words 'beer', 'butter' and 'bacon'. The man uses the list as he walks round the supermarket, putting things into his shopping trolley; in doing so, he tries to make the contents of the trolley match the information on the list. 'The world', in the form of the contents of his shopping trolley, is made to fit *a desire* expressed linguistically in the form of the list. As the man shops, however, Anscombe wants us to suppose that he is followed round the shop by a store detective. As the detective observes the shopper, he [*sic*] writes down what the man buys and so ends up with precisely the same list: 'beer', 'butter', 'bacon'. The same 'information' is now expressed in the same form in both lists. For the store detective, however, the list doesn't function as an effort to make 'reality' fit the list. Rather, the list is intended to fit an independently existing 'reality': information on the list records the goods that have been put into the trolley by the shopper. If on returning home the shopper were to be told that he hasn't bought the correct items, he would have to return to the shop and buy different *things*, because his list was a way of imposing an intention on (and changing) reality. If the store detective were told his list is incorrect, on the other hand, he simply has to alter the list to make it match what was actually there.

Anscombe's simplified scenario illustrates Austin's idea that one stretch of discourse, in terms of form, can perform conventionally different functions (an idea central to my discussion of offensiveness in Chapter 11). This is not just a question of communicative 'use' being tied to the purposes of the people involved. If the two lists are removed or published separately from the situation which produced them, they are identical. But the relation between what each says and the world beyond would be obscured. Only one of the discourses seeks to report how the world is; and only that function can be true or false. The other calls something into being. It predicts, or imagines the world as it might be. Both lists involve *representation* of information. But they differ fundamentally in intention, function and consequences. The implications Anscombe draws

---

[10] In 'How to talk – some simple ways' (in J. L. Austin, *Philosophical Papers*, ed. J. O. Urmson and G. J. Warnock (Oxford: Oxford University Press, 1979), pp. 134–53), Austin proposes the concept of 'direction of fit' in his account of why names for speech acts are 'more numerous, more specialised, more ambiguous and more significant than is ordinarily allowed for'; and why 'the difference between one named speech-act and another often resides principally in a difference between the speech-situations envisaged for their respective performances' (pp. 150–1). As well as triggering subsequent elaboration by G. E. M. Anscombe, the concept was taken up as 'crucial for any theory of intentionality' in John Searle's *Mind, Language and Society* (London: Weidenfeld and Nicolson, 1999), pp. 100–3.

[11] G. E. M. Anscombe, *Intention* (Oxford: Blackwell, 1959).

from this point are wider than Austin's. She describes different, overall 'directions of fit' that exist between intentional states of mind and the world around us, especially between representations that strive to represent things as they are (beliefs, perceptions and, in some accounts, memories) and other representations that express desires, intentions or wishes regarding how the world *might* be or how we plan to make it or let it be.

Historically, the 'mind-to-world' fit (i.e. the asserting or reporting propositional attitude, in which 'discourse tells us how someone believes things are') has been dominant in accounts of public communication. This is in part an outcome of a centuries-long struggle between the respective fields of logic and rhetoric: a struggle over how far discourse should seek truth and how far it should conjure up situations, persuading and inspiring through its own rhetorical power, bending the world to the communicator's will.

Perhaps increasingly, however, tension between these contrasting values in communication is being expressed in a new form. While the 'reporting' view, on which we constantly rely in coordinating with others our understanding of the world around us, invites us to see information as 'statements of how things are', much in our media environment now steers in the opposite direction. It talks up situations and events, visualising things as people would like them to be in a brochure for what things might be turned into or how the speaker would like others to see them.[12] There is of course no problem in principle with discourse serving different functions, including simultaneously. But if the difference between the two 'directions of fit' is obscured or annulled, then pressure on what public discourse means will inevitably increase, including in cases where there may have been no wish to deceive but where an event or situation has been simply oversold to suit personal, corporate or political interests.

For someone engaged in interpreting, establishing 'direction of fit' for discourse that does not provide any sign-posts as to how it is functioning can be difficult. Many claims put forward in commercial and political discourse involve a rhetorical 'direction of fit' between discourse and world: 'discourse expresses desire or intention about how things might be or could be'. They convey 'good news' stories in which, at worst, the form is reporting but the content is a world of make-believe. Such promissory discourse can nevertheless invite interpretation *as if* its direction of fit were a 'reporting' direction of fit: 'discourse reports how things are believed to be'. The resulting hybrid forms of reporting-and-promotion are widely recognised as problematic in terms of their truth status. As I argued in Chapter 10, this is a particular problem in disentangling 'information' and 'persuasion' in openly commercial speech. As a more general kind of 'post-truth' discourse that may or may not be

---

[12] For discussion across a number of fields, see A. Wernick, *Promotional Culture: Advertising, Ideology and Symbolic Expression* (London: Sage, 1991).

believed, either by those who propagate it or by those who receive it, such hybrid reporting–promoting styles present a far wider problem. They contribute to a media environment in which 'reporting' discourse can come to seem measured and dull, with no competitive edge of news or entertainment value in a crowded information marketplace.[13]

## 12.4    Trust and suspicion

For sales promotion, political spin and related kinds of expression to succeed in their persuasive purpose, they need a trusting population. Willingness to draw appropriate inferences, on presumption that communication serves a socially coordinating, practical purpose, is essential. A sceptical, cynical or paranoid population may be better placed to resist deception or exploitation. But that population would be hampered by its cultivated disbelief, scorn or fear in participating in shared action that depends on communication, in finding channels for informed debate or authoritative opinion, or in enjoying the benefit of unprecedented amounts of material in broadcast media and available online.

If it goes unchecked, erosion of communicative trust has inevitably destabilising social effects. Because of our tendency to learn interpretive strategies from experience, it can become increasingly difficult to know which individuals or institutional communicators to trust and which should be treated with suspicion. In the popular imagination, such situations are mostly associated with totalitarian regimes and with centralised propaganda by church or state.[14] But corresponding difficulties cannot be ruled out as a by-product of an otherwise contrasting 'free expression' media environment, especially one that consists substantially of commercial discourse and PR, computer-mediated interaction

---

[13]  Such promotional-reporting discourse seems an increasingly pervasive communicative style. Steven Poole nevertheless points out, in his Epilogue to *Unspeak*[TM], that a similar warning about people becoming so enthusiastic about their own PR that they too easily believe it themselves was given over two centuries ago, in *The Art of Political Lying* (1746), attributed to John Arbuthnot: 'they perswade one another, that what they wish, and report to be true, is really so'. *Unspeak*[TM], p. 236.

[14]  Distinctions between propaganda, PR and related forms of persuasion must be drawn carefully. Edward Bernays's *Propaganda* [1928] (New York: Ig Publishing, 2005) still provides worthwhile definitions (and the Ig edition gives a useful historical account of changing meanings of 'propaganda'). On propaganda and more recent events, see writings by Noam Chomsky, including *Media Control: The Spectacular Achievement of Propaganda*, 2nd edition (New York: Open Media Books, 2002). A fascinating account of CIA influence on European Left intellectuals during the Cold War is Frances Stonor Saunders, *Who Paid the Piper?* (Cambridge: Granta, 2000). For context and the history of public relations in the USA, see S. Ewen, *PR! A Social History of Spin* (New York: Basic Books, 1996), and for a detailed history of public relations in Britain, see Jacquie L'Etang, *Public Relations in Britain: A History of Professional Practice in the 20th Century* (London: Lawrence Erlbaum, 2004). For a critical evaluation of differences between propaganda and public relations, see Kevin Moloney, *Rethinking Public Relations. PR, Propaganda and Democracy*, 2nd edition (London: Routledge, 2006), esp. pp. 41–72.

with many unknown others, and sometimes involving significant intercultural differences of style and expectation. In such a media environment, the build-up, testing and where necessary withdrawal of trust that may occur over time in less pluralistic, face-to-face societies may become strained, and personal trust increasingly transferred to proxy indicators (such as stereotyped beliefs about the communicator, or reported online reliability ratings as evidence of previous trust-by-others).

Challenges to trust in a contemporary media environment were influentially discussed by the philosopher Baroness Onora O'Neill in her 2002 BBC Reith lectures, later published as the book *A Question of Trust*.[15] In common with more technical discussion of trust,[16] Baroness O'Neill distinguishes between giving trust and the trustworthiness of people and organisations in whom trust is placed. In communication in particular, as we have seen, trust is typically placed by an interpreter in the integrity or honesty of intention of the speaker or author, who is considered trustworthy or unreliable in guiding the interpreter towards relevant interpretations. Inferences involved in arriving at such relevant interpretation form an intermediate level between understanding what an utterance or text *says* and more general appreciation of the situation or events to which it relates.

Onora O'Neill questions whether there is adequate evidence of a genuine contemporary crisis of public trust, as many sociologists and journalists have claimed, and as I have outlined as a possibility.[17] Instead she notes pervasive, practical acts of trusting that must be reconciled with any assumed climate of suspicion. But rather than presenting a 'bad apple' account of only local failures of trust in society, O'Neill uses her reaffirmation of widespread trusting behaviour, and her account of rising social expectations as to trustworthiness, as a springboard into examining areas in which she feels serious breaches of trust do occur. She condemns in particular what she sees as displacement of problems of trust onto bureaucratic procedures of audit and regulation that use mandatory disclosure, by means of online publication of large amounts of data, as their commitment to transparency and accountability. O'Neill's recommendation, by contrast, is that contemporary societies should cultivate informed public awareness and consent on the basis of an ability to *check* credentials and to assess, as well as simply have access to, relevant information.

Many of Baroness O'Neill's proposals are uncontroversial, if difficult to see practical ways of implementing. Two major dimensions of trust with particular impact on communication seem nevertheless to cut across the difficulties she

---

[15]  Baroness O'Neill's 2002 Reith lectures can be heard at www.bbc.co.uk/radio4/reith2002/ and were published as Onora O'Neill, *A Question of Trust* (Cambridge: Cambridge University Press, 2002).

[16]  See for example Russell Hardin, *Trust* (Cambridge: Polity, 2006).

[17]  As well as citing trends, Hardin points to the possible unreliability of public perceptions, with his reminder that 'in the past century, it seems likely that no polity trusted its government more than Soviet citizens did for the decades of Stalin's rule'. Hardin, *Trust*, p. 160.

acknowledges. The first, which she discusses briefly, is how to adapt ideas of 'freedom of expression' to a twenty-first-century media environment which is now very different from the circumstances surrounding earlier rationales. As is frequently pointed out, powerful media conglomerates, lobbyists and PR companies now enjoy protection as much as individual citizens, allowing freedom of expression measures to serve very different social and political interests from those historically envisaged.[18] The second problem area, which O'Neill hardly discusses, is whether a ratcheting up of competitiveness in liberal capitalist societies accentuates conflict of interest between communicator and addressee in public discourse in ways that may prove damaging. In commercial and political communication, the communicator's self-interest (and the frequently urged 'need to get out there and sell yourself') may stand directly in the way of any obligation to more self-effacing ethical standards. Such conflict of interest, where it exists, potentially distorts the relationship presupposed by any generalised account of communication as directed towards mutual understanding and/or coordination of shared social commitments.[19] On this second issue, it remains an open question how far pluralistic capitalist societies will prove able to reconcile the personal and public, human and commodified interests that are in competition in communication.

## 12.5    Pragmatic interpretation

How likely is it that measures to strengthen trust in media discourse will lighten the burden of continuous enforcement in media content regulation, in the face of what seems an explosion of dispute and controversy?

At localised meaning troublespots as elsewhere, an essential educational task must be to encourage interpreters to view meaning from more than a single point of view. But in doing this, interpreters should not flop into an imagined free-play of all meanings being equally possible.[20] Alternative explanations of the meanings of media discourse need to be compared and the likelihood evaluated of

---

[18] On the historical development of communication as part of a recognised public sphere, see Briggs and Burke, *A Social History of the Media*, esp. pp. 61–87. Perspicuous discussion of how communication institutions interact with successive restructurings of the public sphere can be found in Thompson, *The Media and Modernity*. A succinct account of different understandings of the 'public sphere' within wider notions of civil society can be found in Michael Edwards, *Civil Society* (Cambridge: Polity, 2004), esp. pp. 54–71.

[19] Habermas and others are often criticised for believing that there could ever be a time when 'all parties will lay down their forensic arms and join together in the effort to build a new and more rational community'. See Stanley Fish, *There's No Such Thing as Free Speech ... And It's a Good Thing Too* (Oxford: Oxford University Press, 1994), p. 174. For Habermas's arguments on 'universal pragmatics' as an attempt to achieve convergence on mutual understanding, see 'What Is Universal Pragmatics?', in *On the Pragmatics of Communication*, pp. 21–103.

[20] In the essay 'Unlimited semiosis and drift: pragmaticism vs. "pragmatism"', in *The Limits of Interpretation*, Eco describes two commonly expressed stark alternatives: a text has only the

any given meaning having been foreseen. Interpreters need also to look ahead to implications of inferring a particular meaning, as well as sideways at how discourse will have been calculated to play differently for, and have different effects on, other groups of people with differing viewpoints, interests or values. Having weighed up alternatives, however, unless social life and interaction are to grind to a halt, interpreters must settle on a provisional interpretation. They have to set less plausible alternatives to one side (except in cases such as jokes, fiction or banter, where playing with elusive possibilities of meaning is likely to be part of the point). Looking from multiple viewpoints is what justifies a *socially* pragmatic approach for courts and regulatory bodies.

The view of meaning I am outlining here leaves much unresolved at the interface between interpretation and social action. But even such a partial account is already different, in emphasis, from approaches to meaning mostly taught in schools or elevated into interpretive standards. It is worth considering, therefore, whether pragmatic interpretation – instant and automatic in practice, if tortuous and sometimes pedantic when explicated – has a better chance of forging 'qualified' belief and consent than either of the two main, clear-cut alternatives: relying on acts of trust and an assumed stability of meaning; or accepting an interpretive free-for-all which, as Stanley Fish and others have shown, is never really free for all.[21]

Emphasising a relational approach to meaning, rather than interpretation fixed by code or intention, may sound like encouraging distrust rather than trust as the way to reduce contestation. Insisting on weighing alternative meanings up, and applying an extended idea of 'caveat emptor' as a practical warning, may serve a similar purpose. Shifting the balance of assumed responsibility in the direction of the interpreter may serve to counter-balance emphasis on presentation skills in modern media literacy with an appreciation of 'meaning' consequences. Many people trust: they believe that nearly everyone speaks the truth nearly all of the time, with only lapses by aberrant bad apples. Many others distrust: they take it completely for granted that virtually everyone in any public or commercial position routinely lies through their teeth. What is surprising is how little shading there is in between – not only in people's reported experience but also in their reflections on that experience. Exploring the grey areas, not only in law and regulation but as part of educated citizenship, is something that future policy debates will increasingly need to do.

---

meaning that is 'intended by its original author' or given by 'its objective nature or essence'; and a text 'can be interpreted in infinite ways'. He dismisses both views as 'instances of epistemological fanaticism', p. 24.

[21] Throughout *There's No Such Thing as Free Speech*, Fish puts forward a sustained critique of what he calls a kind of 'moral algebra' based on interpretive 'algorithms' and abstracted from historically inherited and continuing cultural conflicts.

Those in favour of lighter regulation of communication often maintain that, in a well-functioning marketplace and civic society, apparently conflicting pressures on communicators and their addressees are reconcilable. Conflicts because of commercial, ideological and other interests are overridden by longer-term, higher values of trust, cooperation and professionalism, despite a countervailing pressure towards self-promotion and competitiveness. If we are to evaluate what is said on this topic, however, we must constantly question and monitor 'direction of fit' between intentionality and the world. Some siren voices in the debate, for instance, go further than saying that conflicting interests in communication will coincide in a hypothetical future. They report little difference between the ideal of mutually trusting and trustworthy communication and the media environment we already live in.

## 12.6    Summary

In this final chapter, I have widened my discussion of meaning in the media to engage with social debates about representation, misrepresentation and unresolved questions to do with flows of 'information'. Through an illustration of the massive commercial damage that can result from electronic rumours and mistrust, I explored new challenges presented by the circulation of meaning in the open-ended networks of online discourse. Drawing on the writings of Anscombe, Searle, O'Neill and others, I outlined the centrality of trust in communication, and closed by asking how much trust or suspicion we should feel towards contemporary media communicators.

# References

Aldridge, Alan, *The Market* (Cambridge: Polity, 2005).

Anderson, Digby C., *All Oiks Now: The Unnoticed Surrender of Middle England* (London: Social Affairs Unit, 2004).

Andersson, Lars-Gunnar and Peter Trudgill, *Bad Language* (Harmondsworth: Penguin, 1990).

Anscombe, G. E. M., *Intention* (Oxford: Blackwell, 1959).

Appignanesi, Lisa and Sara Maitland (eds.), *The Rushdie File* (New York: Syracuse University Press and Institute of Contemporary Arts, 1990).

Augustine, St, *The Confessions* (London: Hendrickson Christian Classics, 2004).

Austin, J. L., *How To Do Things with Words* (Oxford: Oxford University Press, 1962).
  *Philosophical Papers*, ed. J. O. Urmson and G. J. Warnock (Oxford: Oxford University Press, 1979).

Bader, Jenny Lyn and Bill Brazell, *He Meant, She Meant: The Definitive Male/Female Dictionary* (New York: Warner Books, 1997).

Barendt, Eric, *Freedom of Speech* (Oxford: Clarendon, 1985).
  'Defamation and fiction', in Michael Freeman and Andrew Lewis (eds.), *Law and Literature: Current Legal Issues 1999*, vol. 2 (Oxford: Oxford University Press, 1999), pp. 481–98.

Barendt, Eric and Linda Hitchens, *Media Law: Cases and Materials* (London: Longman, 2000).

Barendt, Eric, Laurence Lustgarten, Kenneth Nornie and Hugh Stephenson, *Libel and the Media: The Chilling Effect* (Oxford: Clarendon, 1997).

Barthes, Roland, *Mythologies*, trans. Annette Lavers (London: Paladin, 1973 [1957]).

Barton, David, *Literacy: An Introduction to the Ecology of the Written Language* (Oxford: Blackwell, 1994).

Beck, Andrew, Peter Bennett and Peter Wall, *Communication Studies: The Essential Introduction* (London: Routledge, 2002).

Bell, Allan, *The Language of News Media* (Oxford: Blackwell, 1991).

Bell, Allan and Theo van Leeuwen, *The Media Interview: Confession, Contest, Conversation* (Sydney: New South Wales University Press, 1994).

Berg, Donna Lee, *A Guide to the Oxford English Dictionary* (Oxford: Oxford University Press, 1993).

Bernays, Edward, *Propaganda* [1928] (New York: Ig Publishing, 2005).

Biber, Douglas, Susan Conrad and Randi Reppen, *Corpus Linguistics: Investigating Language Structure and Use* (Cambridge: Cambridge University Press, 1998).

Bix, Brian, *Law, Language and Legal Determinacy* (Oxford: Clarendon, 1993).

Blakemore, Diane, *Understanding Utterances: An Introduction to Pragmatics* (Oxford: Blackwell, 1992).

Bok, Sissela, *Lying: Moral Choice in Public and Private Life* (Brighton: Harvester Press, 1978).

Bordwell, David, *Making Meaning: Inference and Rhetoric in the Interpretation of Cinema* (Cambridge, Mass.: Harvard University Press, 1989).

Boyle, James, *Shamans, Software and Spleens: Law and the Construction of the Information Society* (Cambridge, Mass.: Harvard University Press, 1996).

  *The Public Domain: Enclosing the Commons of the Mind* (New Haven, Conn.: Yale University Press, 2008).

Briggs, Asa and Peter Burke, *A Social History of the Media: From Gutenberg to the Internet*, 2nd edition (Cambridge: Polity, 2005).

Brown, Gillian, *Speakers, Listeners, and Communication: Explorations in Discourse Analysis* (Cambridge: Cambridge University Press, 1995).

Brown, Gillian, Kirsten Malmkjaer, Alastair Pollitt and John Williams (eds.), *Language and Understanding* (Oxford: Oxford University Press, 1994).

Brown, Gillian and George Yule, *Discourse Analysis* (Cambridge: Cambridge University Press, 1983).

Burgess, Kate, Chris Giles and Brooke Masters, 'City probe into HBOS false rumours', *Financial Times*, 20 March 2008, p. 1.

Butler, Judith, *Excitable Speech: A Politics of the Performative* (London: Routledge, 1997).

Cameron, Deborah, *Verbal Hygiene* (London: Routledge, 1995).

Cann, Ronnie, *Formal Semantics: An Introduction* (Cambridge: Cambridge University Press, 1993).

Carroll, Lewis [1871], *Through the Looking-Glass and What Alice Found There*, Illustrated by Helen Oxenbury (London: Walker Books, 2005).

Castells, Manuel, *The Rise of the Network Society* (Oxford: Blackwell, 2000).

Chase, Stuart, *The Tyranny of Words* (New York: Harvest Books, 1938).

Chomsky, Noam, *Media Control: The Spectacular Achievement of Propaganda*, 2nd edition (New York: Open Media Books, 2002).

Clanchy, Michael, *From Memory to Written Record* (Oxford: Blackwell, 1993).

Clayman, Steven and John Heritage, *The News Interview* (Cambridge: Cambridge University Press, 2002).

Clark, Herb, *Using Language* (Cambridge: Cambridge University Press, 1996).

Clark, Michael, *Paradoxes from A to Z* (London: Routledge, 2002).

Coleman, L. and P. Kay, 'Prototype semantics: the English word "lie"', *Language*, 57 (1981), 26–44.

Commission for Racial Equality, *Law, Blasphemy and the Multi-Faith Society* (London: Commission for Racial Equality, 1990).

Cook, Guy, *The Discourse of Advertising*, 2nd edition (London: Routledge, 2001).

Cotterill, Janet (ed.), *Language in the Legal Process* (Basingstoke: Palgrave, 2002).

Coulthard, Malcolm and Alison Johnson, *An Introduction to Forensic Linguistics: Language in Evidence* (London: Routledge, 2007).

Croft, Jane, 'Funding jitters annoy HBOS', *Financial Times*, 20 March 2008, p. 19.

Croft, William and D. Alan Cruse, *Cognitive Linguistics* (Cambridge: Cambridge University Press, 2004).

Crystal, David, *The Stories of English* (Harmondsworth: Penguin, 2005).

Cummings, Louise, *Pragmatics: An Interdisciplinary Perspective* (Edinburgh: Edinburgh University Press, 2005).

Davies, Nick, *Flat Earth News* (London: Chatto and Windus, 2008).

Davis, Jennifer, 'Locating the average consumer: his judicial origins, intellectual influences and current role in European trade mark law', *Intellectual Property Quarterly*, 2 (2005), 183–203.

Dinwoodie, Graeme and Mark Janis, *Trademarks and Unfair Competition: Law and Policy* (Boulder, Colo.: Aspen Publishers, 2004).

Drew, Paul and John Heritage, *Talk at Work: Interaction in Institutional Settings* (Cambridge: Cambridge University Press, 1992).

Dummett, Michael, *The Seas of Language* (Oxford: Oxford University Press, 1993).

Durant, Alan, 'On the interpretation of allusions and other "innuendo" meanings in libel actions: the value of semantic and pragmatic evidence', *Forensic Linguistics*, 3 (2) (1996), 195–210.
    'Meaning and public deception: a tale of more than "very, very few people"', *CQ*, 48 (3) (2006), 88–93.

Durant, Alan and Marina Lambrou, *Language and Media* (London: Routledge, 2009).

Eagleton, Terry, *The Meaning of Life* (Oxford: Oxford University Press, 2007).

Eco, Umberto, *The Limits of Interpretation* (Bloomington: Indiana University Press, 1990).

Edwards, Michael, *Civil Society* (Cambridge: Polity, 2004).

Eisenstein, Elizabeth, *The Printing Press as an Agent of Social Change: Communications and Cultural Transformations in Early Modern Europe*, 2 vols. (Cambridge: Cambridge University Press, 1979).

Emerson, Thomas, *The System of Freedom of Expression* (New York: Vintage Books, 1970).

Empson, William, *Seven Types of Ambiguity* (London: Chatto and Windus, 1930).

Ewen, S., *PR! A Social History of Spin* (New York: Basic Books, 1996).

Fairclough, Norman, *Critical Discourse Analysis: The Critical Study of Language* (London: Longman, 1995).
    *Media Discourse* (London: Longman, 1995).

Fang, Irving, *A History of Mass Communication: Six Information Revolutions* (Burlington, Mass.: Elsevier Science, 1997).

Faulks, Sir Neville, *Legal Aspects of Reputation. Report of the Faulks Committee on Defamation*. Cmnd. 5909 (London: HMSO, 1975).

Fish, Stanley, *Is There a Text in This Class?* (Cambridge, Mass.: Harvard University Press, 1981).
    *There's No Such Thing as Free Speech… And It's a Good Thing Too* (Oxford: Oxford University Press, 1994).

Fodor, Jerry, 'Three reasons for not deriving kill from cause to die', *Linguistic Inquiry*, 1 (4) (1970), 429–38.
    *The Modularity of Mind* (Cambridge, Mass.: MIT Press, 1983).

Freeman, Michael and Andrew Lewis (eds.), *Law and Literature: Current Legal Issues 1999*, vol. 2 (Oxford: Oxford University Press, 1999).

Gadamer, Hans-Georg, *Truth and Method*, 2nd edition, trans. Joel Weinsheimer and Donald Marshall (London: Sheed and Ward, 1989).

Gardiner, Michael (ed.), *Mikhail Bakhtin*, 4 vols. (London: Sage, 2002).

Geertz, Clifford, *The Interpretation of Cultures* (New York: Basic Books, 1973).

Geis, Michael, *The Language of Television Advertising* (New York: Academic Press, 1982).

Gibbons, John (ed.), *Language and the Law* (London: Longman, 1994).

(ed.), *Forensic Linguistics: An Introduction to Language in the Justice System* (London: Wiley Blackwell, 2003).

Gibbons, John and M. Teresa Turell (eds.), *Dimensions of Forensic Linguistics* (Amsterdam: Benjamins, 2008).

Gibbs, Raymond W., *Intentions in the Experience of Meaning* (Cambridge: Cambridge University Press, 1999).

Goddard, Cliff, 'Can linguists help judges know what they mean? Linguistic semantics in the court-room', *Forensic Linguistics*, 3 (2) (1996), 250–72.

Goffman, Erving, *Forms of Talk* (Oxford: Oxford University Press, 1981).

Goody, Jack, *The Interface between the Written and the Oral* (Cambridge: Cambridge University Press, 1987).

Gordon, W. T., *A History of Semantics* (Amsterdam: Benjamins, 1982).

Graddol, David and Oliver Boyd-Barrett (eds.), *Media Texts: Authors and Readers* (Clevedon: Multilingual Matters/Open University, 1993).

Graesser, Arthur and Rolf Zwaan, 'Inference generation and the construction of situation models', in C. A. Weaver, Suzanne Mannes and Charles Fletcher (eds.), *Discourse Comprehension: Essays in Honor of Walter Kintsch* (Hillsdale, NJ: Lawrence Erlbaum Associates, 1995), pp.117–40.

Green, David, 'Inferring health claims: a case study', *Forensic Linguistics*, 3 (2) (1996), 299–321.

Greenawalt, Kent, *Speech, Crime and the Uses of Language* (Oxford: Oxford University Press, 1989).

*Fighting Words: Individuals, Communities, and Liberties of Speech* (Princeton: Princeton University Press, 1995).

Grice, H. P., *Studies in the Way of Words* (Cambridge, Mass.: Harvard University Press, 1989).

Gunter, Barrie, *Measuring Bias on Television* (Luton: University of Luton Press, 1997).

Habermas, Jürgen, *On the Pragmatics of Communication*, ed. Maeve Cooke (Cambridge: Polity, 1999).

Hall, Stuart, *Representation: Cultural Representations and Signifying Practices* (London: Sage/The Open University, 1997).

*Halsbury's Laws of England*, ed. James Bowman and Lord Hailsham of St Marylebone, 4th revised edition (London: Butterworth, 2005).

Hardin, Russell, *Trust* (Cambridge: Polity, 2006).

Harris, Roy and Christopher Hutton, *Definition in Theory and Practice: Language, Lexicography and the Law* (London: Continuum, 2007).

Harrison, Tony, *V*, 2nd edition (Newcastle upon Tyne: Bloodaxe Books, 1989).

Hart, H. L. A., *The Concept of Law* (Oxford: Oxford University Press, 1961).

Hay, James, Lawrence Grossberg and Ellen Wartella (eds.), *The Audience and Its Landscape* (Boulder, Colo.: Westview Press, 1996).

Hayakawa, S. I., *Language in Thought and Action* (New York: Harvest Books, 1939).

Heath, Stephen, 'Representation', *CQ*, 50 (1–2) (2008), 87–99.

Hill, Andrew, 'HBOS tormentors are easy to spot but hard to catch', *Financial Times*, 20 March 2008, p. 18.

Hill, Jane H., 'Crises of meaning: personalist language ideology in US media discourse', in Sally Johnson and A. Ensslin (eds.), *Language in the Media: Representations, Identities, Ideologies* (London: Continuum, 2007), pp. 70–88.

Hirsch, E. D., *Validity in Interpretation* (New Haven, Conn.: Yale University Press, 1967).

Hirst, Paul Q., *On Law and Ideology* (London: Macmillan, 1979).

Hughes, Geoffrey, *Swearing: A Social History of Foul Language, Oaths and Profanity in English*, 2nd edition (Harmondsworth: Penguin, 1998).

Hurford, James, Brendan Heasley and Michael B. Smith, *Semantics: A Coursebook* (Cambridge: Cambridge University Press, 2007).

Hutchby, Ian, *Confrontation Talk: Arguments, Asymmetries and Power on Talk Radio* (Hillsdale, NJ: Lawrence Erlbaum, 1996).

Hutchby, Ian and R. Wooffitt *Conversation Analysis* (Cambridge: Polity, 2008).

Hutton, Chris, *Language, Meaning and the Law* (Edinburgh: Edinburgh University Press, 2009).

Hymes, Dell, *Foundations in Sociolinguistics: An Ethnographic Approach* (Philadelphia: University of Pennsylvania Press, 1977).

Jackson, Howard, *Lexicography: An Introduction* (London: Routledge, 2002).

Jaworski, Adam and Nikolas Coupland (eds.), *The Discourse Reader* (London: Routledge, 1999).

Jones, Nicholas, *The Control Freaks: How New Labour Gets Its Own Way* (London: Politico's Publishing, 2002).

Kalven Jr., Harry, *A Worthy Tradition: Freedom of Speech in America* (New York: Harper and Row, 1988).

Kempson, Ruth, *Semantics* (Cambridge: Cambridge University Press, 1977).

Kintsch, Walter, *Comprehension: A Paradigm for Cognition* (Cambridge: Cambridge University Press, 1998).

Kollewe, Julia, 'How the HBOS attack unfolded', *Guardian*, 20 March 2008 online at www.guardian.co.uk.

Labov, William and D. Fanshel, *Therapeutic Discourse* (New York: Academic Press, 1977).

Lacey, Nicola, *A Life of H. L. A. Hart: The Nightmare and the Noble Dream* (Oxford: Oxford University Press, 2004).

Lakoff, George, *Don't Think of an Elephant: Know Your Values and Frame the Debate* (White River Junction, Vt.: Chelsea Green Publishers, 2004).

Lasswell, Harold, 'The structure and function of communication in society', in L. Bryson (ed.), *The Communication of Ideas* (Urbana: University of Illinois Press, 1948), pp. 117–30.

Lecercle, Jean-Jacques, *Interpretation as Pragmatics* (London: Macmillan, 1999).

Leech, Geoffrey, *English in Advertising: A Linguistic Study of Advertising in Great Britain* (London: Longman, 1966).

  *Semantics: The Study of Meaning*, 2nd edition (Harmondsworth: Penguin, 1974).

  *Principles of Pragmatics* (London: Longman, 1983).

L'Etang, Jacquie, *Public Relations in Britain: A History of Professional Practice in the 20th Century* (London: Lawrence Erlbaum, 2004).

Levi, Judith and Anne Graffam Walker (eds.), *Language in the Judicial Process* (New York: Springer, 1990).

Levine, Kenneth, *The Social Context of Literacy* (London: Routledge, 1986).

Levinson, Stephen, 'Activity types and language', *Linguistics*, 17 (1979), 365–99.

  *Pragmatics* (Cambridge: Cambridge University Press, 1983).

  'Putting linguistics on a proper footing: explorations in Goffman's concepts of participation', in Paul Drew and Anthony Wootton (eds.), *Erving Goffman: Exploring the Interaction Order* (Cambridge: Polity, 1988), pp. 161–227.

Liebes, T. and E. Katz, *The Export of Meaning: Cross-Cultural Readings of Dallas* (Oxford: Oxford University Press, 1991).

Lyons, John, *Semantics*, 2 vols. (Cambridge: Cambridge University Press, 1977).

Lyotard, Jean-François, *The Différend: Phrases in Dispute* (Minneapolis: University of Minnesota Press, 1988).

MacKinnon, Catharine, *Only Words* (Cambridge, Mass.: Harvard University Press, 1993).

McLuhan, Marshall, *Understanding Media: The Extensions of Man* (London: Ark, 1964).

McQuail, Denis and Sven Windahl, *Communication Models: For the Study of Mass Communication* (London: Pearson, 1993).

Marsh, Joss, *Word Crimes: Blasphemy, Culture and Literature in Nineteenth-Century England* (Chicago: University of Chicago Press, 1998).

Mattelart, Armand and Michèle Mattelart, *Theories of Communication: A Short Introduction* (London: Sage, 1998).

Mercer, Neil, *Words and Minds: How We Use Language To Think Together* (London: Routledge, 2000).

Messaris, Paul, *Visual Literacy: Image, Mind, & Reality* (Boulder, Colo.: Westview Press, 1994).

Millwood-Hargrave, Andrea, 'Delete expletives?', research conducted for the Advertising Standards Authority, British Broadcasting Corporation, Broadcasting Standards Commission and Independent Television Commission, www.ofcom.org.uk.

Moloney, Kevin, *Rethinking Public Relations: PR, Propaganda and Democracy*, 2nd edition (London: Routledge, 2006).

Morgan, Bronwen and Karen Yeung, *An Introduction to Law and Regulation: Text and Materials* (Cambridge: Cambridge University Press, 2008).

Morley, David, *Television, Audiences and Cultural Studies* (London: Routledge, 1992).

Mueller-Vollmer, Kurt (ed.), *The Hermeneutics Reader: Texts of the German Tradition from the Enlightenment to the Present* (London: Continuum, 1994).

Myers, Greg, *Words in Ads* (London: Edward Arnold, 1994).

*Ad Worlds* (London: Edward Arnold, 1998).

Neill, Sir Brian, Richard Rampton QC, Timothy Atkinson, Aidan Eardley and Heather Rogers QC, *Duncan and Neill on Defamation*, 3rd edition (London: LexisNexis, 2009).

Neu, Jerome, *Sticks and Stones: The Philosophy of Insults* (Oxford: Oxford University Press, 2008).

Oborne, Peter, *The Rise of Political Lying* (London: Free Press, 2005).

Ogden, C. K. and I. A. Richards, *The Meaning of Meaning*, 10th edition (London: Routledge and Kegan Paul, 1972).

O'Keeffe, Anne, *Investigating Media Discourse* (London: Routledge, 2006).

O'Neill, Onora, *A Question of Trust* (Cambridge: Cambridge University Press, 2002).

Ong, Walter, *Orality and Literacy: The Technologizing of the Word* (London: Routledge, 1982).

Orwell, George, *Animal Farm: A Fairy Story* [1945] (Harmondsworth: Penguin, 2000).

*Nineteen Eighty-Four* [1949] (Harmondsworth: Penguin, 1970).

Osgood, Charles, G. Suci and P. Tannenbaum, *The Measurement of Meaning* (Chicago: University of Illinois Press, 1957).

Parris, Matthew and Kevin Maguire, *Great Parliamentary Scandals: Five Centuries of Calumny, Smear and Innuendo* (London: Robson Books, 1995).

Pecheux, Michel, *Language, Semantics and Ideology: Stating the Obvious*, trans. Harbans Nagpal (London: Macmillan, 1982).

Pinker, Steven, *The Seven Words You Can't Say on Television* (Harmondsworth: Penguin, 2008).

Poole, Steven, *Unspeak$^{TM}$* (London: Little, Brown, 2006).

Preston, Ivan, *The Great America Blow-up: Puffery in Advertising and Selling* (Madison: University of Wisconsin Press, 1975).

  *The Tangled Web They Weave: Truth, Falsity and Advertisers* (Madison: University of Wisconsin Press, 1994).

Putnam, Hilary, *Mind, Language and Reality: Philosophical Papers*, vol. 2 (Cambridge: Cambridge University Press, 1975).

Quinn, Frances, *Law for Journalists* (London: Pearson Education, 2007).

Rampton, Sheldon and John Stauber, *Weapons of Mass Deception: The Uses of Propaganda in Bush's War on Iraq* (London: Robinson, 2003).

Ramsay, Iain, *Advertising, Culture, and the Law* (London: Sweet and Maxwell, 1996).

  *Report of the Inquiry into the Export of Defence Equipment and Dual-Use Goods to Iraq and Related Prosecutions*, 6 vols. (London: HMSO, 1996).

Richards, I. A., *Practical Criticism* (London: Routledge and Kegan Paul, 1929).

  'Variant readings and misreading', in Thomas Sebeok (ed.), *Style in Language* (Boston, Mass.: MIT Press, 1960), pp. 241–52.

Rickey, Melanie, 'Vanity sizing', *The Times*, 22 September 2007, p. 27.

Robertson, Geoffrey, *Obscenity* (London: Weidenfeld and Nicolson, 1979).

Robertson, Geoffrey and Andrew Nicol, *Media Law*, 2nd, revised edition (Harmondsworth: Penguin, 1992).

Rushdie, Salman, 'Coming after us', in Lisa Appignanesi and Sara Maitland (eds.), *Free Expression Is No Offense* (Harmondsworth: Penguin, 2005), pp. 21–6.

Saeed, John, *Semantics* (Oxford: Blackwell, 1997).

Saunders, Frances, Stonor, *Who Paid the Piper?* (Cambridge: Granta, 2000).

Saussure, Ferdinand de, *Course in General Linguistics*, trans. and annotated Roy Harris (London: Duckworth, 1983).

Saville-Troike, Muriel, *The Ethnography of Communication: An Introduction*, 2nd edition (Oxford: Blackwell, 1989), pp.138–9.

Schauer, Frederick, *Free Speech: A Philosophical Enquiry* (Cambridge: Cambridge University Press, 1982).

Scannell, Paddy (ed.), *Broadcast Talk* (London: Sage, 1991).

Scollon, Ron, *Mediated Discourse and Social Interaction* (London: Routledge, 1999).

Scott-Bayfield, Julie, *Defamation: Law and Practice* (London: FT Law and Tax, 1996).

Searle, John, *Speech Acts: Essays in the Philosophy of Language* (Cambridge: Cambridge University Press, 1969).

  *Expression and Meaning: Studies in the Theory of Speech Acts* (Cambridge: Cambridge University Press, 1979).

  *The Construction of Social Reality* (Harmondsworth: Penguin, 1995).

  *Mind, Language and Society* (London: Weidenfeld and Nicolson, 1999).

Shuy, Roger, *Language Crimes: The Use and Abuse of Language Evidence in the Courtroom* (Oxford: Blackwell, 1993).

  *Fighting over Words: Language and Civil Law Cases* (Oxford: Oxford University Press, 2008).

Sinclair, John, *Reading Concordances: An Introduction* (London: Pearson, 2003).

Slessor, Tim, *Ministries of Deception: Cover-ups in Whitehall* (London: Aurum Press, 2002).

Solan, Lawrence, *The Language of Judges* (Chicago: University of Chicago Press, 1993).

'Linguistic experts as semantic tour guides', *Forensic Linguistics*, 5 (2) (1998), 87–105.

'The Clinton scandal: some lessons from linguistics', in Janet Cotterill (ed.), *Language in the Legal Process* (Basingstoke: Palgrave, 2002), pp.180–95.

Sperber, Dan, *Rethinking Symbolism* (Cambridge: Cambridge University Press, 1975).

*Explaining Culture: A Naturalistic Approach* (Oxford: Blackwell, 1996).

(ed.), *Metarepresentations: A Multidisciplinary Perspective* (Oxford: Oxford University Press, 2000).

Sperber, Dan and Deirdre Wilson, *Relevance: Communication and Cognition*, 2nd edition (Oxford: Blackwell, 1995).

Spilsbury, Sallie, *Media Law* (London: Cavendish, 2000).

Starkey, Guy, *Balance and Bias in Journalism: Representation, Regulation and Democracy* (Basingstoke: Palgrave, 2006).

Stubbs, Michael, *Words and Phrases: Corpus Studies of Lexical Semantics* (Oxford: Blackwell, 2002).

Sweetser, Eve, 'The definition of lie: an examination of the folk models underlying a prototype', in D. N. Holland and N. Quinn (eds.), *Cultural Models in Language and Thought* (Cambridge: Cambridge University Press, 1987), pp. 43–66.

Talbot, Mary, *Media Discourse: Representation and Interaction* (Edinburgh: Edinburgh University Press, 2007).

Tannen, Deborah, *The Argument Culture: Changing the Way We Argue* (New York: Virago, 1999).

Tarski, Alfred, 'The semantic conception of truth' [1944], in Leonard Linsky (ed.), *Semantics and the Philosophy of Language: A Collection of Readings* (Urbana: University of Illinois Press, 1972), pp.13–47.

Thomas, Jenny, *Meaning in Interaction: An Introduction to Pragmatics* (London: Longman, 1995).

Thompson, John B., *The Media and Modernity: A Social Theory of the Media* (Oxford: Blackwell, 1995).

*Political Scandal: Power and Visibility in the Media Age* (Cambridge: Polity, 2000).

Todorov, Tzvetan, *Mikhail Bakhtin: The Dialogical Principle* (Minneapolis: University of Minnesota Press, 1984).

Treanor, Jill, 'Authorities avert run on HBOS caused by false rumours', *Guardian*, 20 March 2008, p. 34.

Warburton, Nigel, *Free Speech: A Very Short Introduction* (Oxford: Oxford University Press, 2009).

Weaver, C. A., Suzanne Mannes and Charles Fletcher (eds.), *Discourse Comprehension: Essays in Honor of Walter Kintsch* (Hillsdale, NJ: Lawrence Erlbaum Associates, 1995).

Wernick, A., *Promotional Culture: Advertising, Ideology and Symbolic Expression* (London: Sage, 1991).

White, A. R., *Misleading Cases* (Oxford: Clarendon, 1991).

Wierzbicka, Anna, *English: Meaning and Culture* (Oxford: Oxford University Press, 2006).

Wilde, Oscar, *The Importance of Being Earnest* [1895] (Harmondsworth: Penguin, 2007).

Williams, Raymond, *Keywords: A Vocabulary of Culture and Society*, 2nd edition (London: Fontana, 1983).

Williams, Rowan, 'It is not a crime to hold traditional values', *The Higher*, 8 December 2006, p. 9.

Wilson, Deirdre and Dan Sperber, 'Linguistic form and relevance', *Lingua*, 90 (1993), 1–25.

Winston, Brian, *Media Technology and Society: A History from the Telegraph to the Internet* (London: Routledge, 1998).

   *Lies, Damn Lies and Documentaries* (London: British Film Institute, 2000).

Wittgenstein, Ludwig, *Philosophical Investigations*, trans. G. E. M. Anscombe (Oxford: Blackwell, 1953).

Wodak, Ruth, *Disorders of Discourse* (London: Longman, 1996).

Wolf, Maryanne, *Proust and the Squid: The Story and Science of the Reading Brain* (New York: HarperCollins, 2007).

LEGAL CASES REFERRED TO

Berkoff v. Burchill [1996] 4 All ER 1008

British Airways plc v. Ryanair Ltd [2001] ETMR 24; [2001] FSR 32

Campbell v. BBC [1990], unreported

Chaplinsky v. New Hampshire, 315 U.S. 568 (1942)

Charleston v. News Group Newspapers Ltd [1995] 2 AC 65

Director General of Fair Trading v. Tobyward Ltd and Another [1989] 2 All ER 266

DPP v. Whyte [1972] AC 849; [1972] 3 WLR 410; [1972] 3 All ER 12

Gelb et al. v. Federal Trade Commission 144 F.2d 580 [1944]

Grubb v. Bristol United Press [1963] 1 QB 309; 3 WLR 25; [1962] 2 All ER 380

Hulton v. Jones [1910] AC 20; [1909] 2 KB 444

Lewis v. Daily Telegraph [1964] AC 234

New York Times Co. v. Sullivan, 376 U.S. 254 (1964)

R. (on the application of Green) v. City of Westminster Magistrates' Court [2008] HRLR 12; (2007) EWHC 2785

R.A.V v. St Pauls (1992), 505 U.S. 377 (1992)

Reynolds v. Times Newspapers [2001] 2 AC 127; [1999], 3 WLR 1010

Roth v. United States 345 U.S. 476 (1957)

Schenck v. United States, 249 U.S. 47 (1919)

Slim v. Daily Telegraph [1968] 2 QB 157; [1968] 2 WLR 599; 112 SJ 97; [1968] 1 All ER 497, CA

Stern v. Piper [1997] QB 123; [1996] 3 All ER 385; [1996] 3 WLR 715

Youssoupoff v. Metro-Goldwyn-Mayer Pictures Ltd [1934] 50 TLR 581

WEBSITES REFERRED TO

Advertising Standards Authority, www.asa.org.uk

BSE inquiry, www.bseinquiry.gov.uk/report.htm

Committee for Advertising Practice, www.cap.org.uk

European Food Information Resource Consortium (EUROFIR), www.eurofir.net

Financial Services Authority, www.fsa.org.uk
'McLibel', www.mcspotlight.org/case/trial
MediaWise, www.mediawise.org.uk
Natural mineral water regulations 1999, www.uk-legislation.hmso.gov.uk
Ofcom, www.ofcom.org.uk
Presswise, www.presswise.org
Reith Lectures (Baroness O'Neill, 2002), www.bbc.co.uk/radio4/reith2002/
Rockridge Institute, www.rockridgeinstitute.org
SizeUK, www.sizeuk.org
Spinwatch, www.spinwatch.org.uk
Unspeak, www.unspeak.net

# Index

250